DUMBOCRACY:

Adventures with the Loony Left,
the Rabid Right and Other American Idiots

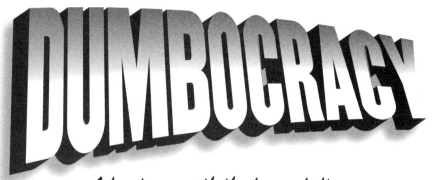

DUMBOCRACY

*Adventures with the Loony Left,
the Rabid Right, and Other American Idiots*

★ ★ ★

Marty Beckerman

disinformation®

© 2008 Marty Beckerman

Published by The Disinformation Company Ltd.
163 Third Avenue, Suite 108
New York, NY 10003
Tel: +1.212.691.1605
Fax: +1.212.691.1606
www.disinfo.com

Library of Congress Control Number: 2008934278

ISBN: 978-1934708-06-4

Design: Greg Stadnyk

Printed in the USA

10 9 8 7 6 5 4 3 2 1

Distributed in the USA and Canada by
Consortium Book Sales and Distribution
Toll Free: +1.800.283.3572
Local: +1.651.221.9035
Fax: +1.651.221.0124
www.cbsd.com

TABLE OF CONTENTS

III.
THE PROMISED LAND

POSTSCRIPT:

"Give us the Young. Give us the Young, and we will create a new mind and a new earth in a single generation."

—BENJAMIN KIDD

"Political tags—such as royalist, communist, democrat, populist, fascist, liberal, conservative, and so forth—are never basic criteria. The human race divides politically into those who want people to be controlled and those who have no such desire."

—ROBERT A. HEINLEIN

"I am afraid of you, little man, deadly afraid. For on you depends the fate of humanity."

—WILHELM REICH

★ ★ ★

Introduction:

DOUCHE BAG NATION

★ ★ ★

Opinions are like genitals: if you force others to swallow yours, something is seriously wrong with you.

Political ideologies are similarly like religions: the True Believer is always hungry for converts. Nothing reinforces your fucked-up worldview like unquestioning followers. And for True Believers, no method of outreach is too immoral: propagating untruths, brainwashing children or using the Constitution as a crusty old tampon.

Who *enjoys* politics anyway? What kind of sick, soul-dead wretch willingly—nay, *eagerly*—spends his free time debating the finer points of meaningless legislative bullshit? (You haven't *lived* until you've spent a night writhing on your bathroom floor—like a ravenous dope addict—muttering to yourself about the congressional filibuster.)

Why would anyone devote his or her time on earth—a cosmic millisecond, a miraculous godsend—to *whining?** What compels a man or woman to sacrifice any shred of individuality in order to join the Culture War, that eternal showdown of Left versus Right, Burger King versus McDonald's, Diet Fascism versus Communism Lite? What inspires these radical fringe activists who are incapable of *anything but bitching?*

I wanted answers to these horrible questions, so I dedicated four years of my life to interviewing hardcore extremists from both sides

---

* Unless they are getting *paid* for it like me.

of the spectrum, whether they resided on the Organic Commune or the Militarized Compound. I attended pro-choice and anti-abortion marches, pro-war and antiwar marches, pro-gay rights and anti-gay rights marches, and so forth. It was great physical exercise and horrendous mental torture.

I endured countless hours of awful sloganeering, awful weather, awful stampedes and awful people. And I learned something: I'm *proud* that I don't give a shit about politics, because people who *do* give a shit cause ninety-nine percent of the world's problems. What if the terrorists on 9/11 had thought to themselves, *"Eh, let's have a beer instead"*?

Those who *care* are responsible for America's disastrous foreign policy; for P.C. speech codes that punish the expression of unpopular opinions; for pregnant teenagers who never learned that they should use condoms (even if rubbers *do* make it feel like you're having sex with outer space); and for a nanny state that spends billions of dollars to discourage adults from enjoying pornography, marijuana, alcohol, cigarettes and unhealthy food. Worst of all, they are responsible for *never shutting the fuck up*. Left-wingers crave a future that will never exist and right-wingers crave a past that never existed. (To the extent that it *did* exist, it was alternately barbaric and boring; those who burned unmarried women at the stake with clear consciences would have never fucked one for fear of damnation. And genital warts.*)

Conventional wisdom says that apathy is a *bad* thing, but political passion inspires ultra-leftwing feminists to ban any book that offends a single woman,† and ultra-rightwing theocrats to criminalize any brand of non-marital sexuality, invade every nonwhite country, etc. If you've ever used the words "social justice" *or* "moral crisis" without irony, I probably fucking hate you.

---

* Witches—get it?

† This was an Indianapolis ordinance during the 1980s. See: "Prohibition Nation vs. Masturbation Nation."

Listen, I'm not an expert. At twenty-five I'm too young to have developed a consistent—let alone *coherent*—philosophy of the State. I'm not an economist or sociologist. I don't have the solutions to anything. But I do know this: *extremists are no fun.* Hardcore right-wingers wish to shove God down our throats, but hate the freedom of guys who shove things down one another's throats. (Hint: it's their cocks.) Meanwhile left-wingers wish to regulate our behavior with taxes on anything unhealthy/enjoyable, prohibitions on tactless speech, and regulations that determine how much time we spend in the shower. Unlike rancid hippies, the average person would rather have a pleasant scent than an environment. What's the point of a sustainable ecosystem that reeks like bongo-playing bohemians? Must we endure the B.O.-zone layer?

In the 1800s Friedrich Engels, coauthor of *The Communist Manifesto,* said that his ideology opposed "all the pleasures of life."[1] His descendents—Left *and* Right—are legion.

But some of us say "no" to this bullshit.

Some of us say "fuck you" to this bullshit.

Some of us say: prepare for an ass-kicking.

I.

ADVENTURES WITH ACTIVISTS

★ ★ ★

Castration Nation vs. Procreation Nation

(OR, "ABORTION: WHAT'S THE BIG FUCKING DEAL?")

★ ★ ★

Nothing drives people crazy like the legality—and increasing illegality—of vacuuming fetuses as if they were household dust bunnies. Extremists on both sides refuse to compromise: you either hate women or God depending on your stance. (Personally I feel that a baby loses its right to life when it disrupts my serenity by means of crying in a movie theater, airplane, restaurant, hospital delivery room, etc.)

However, the American people have a far more nuanced view than those activists who wage the battle. Whereas rightwing absolutists wish to ban abortion even in cases of sexual assault, incest and medical necessity, nearly ninety percent of Americans favor keeping the procedure legal at least sometimes, and sixty percent favor keeping it legal most of the time. Whereas radical feminists wish to keep abortion legal up to the moment before a baby is born, even if there is no medical necessity, seventy-three percent of Americans feel—*even if they are pro-choice*—that terminating a pregnancy is sometimes or always "morally wrong." More than two-thirds of Americans believe that the best policy is somewhere in the "middle ground."[1]

But why have democracy when we can have theocracy? So far in the twenty-first century the Religious Right has enjoyed many victories under King Retard, including the appointments of two anti-abortion justices to the Supreme Court, the limiting of funds for medical stem cell research—which eighty-six percent of Americans consider "vital"[2]—and the enactments of laws such as:

- The Global Gag Rule, which forbids U.S.-funded clinics to offer abortions to poor women overseas. (Abortion *and* welfare—it's enough to give any Republican a heart attack, especially since Republicans are usually so fucking overweight.)

- The Partial Birth Abortion Ban Act, which makes no exceptions for life-endangering pregnancies, according to the ACLU.[3] (If you want someone to pull your fetus halfway out of your body and then crack its skull with a pair of scissors, I can recommend some good fraternity parties.)

- The Interstate Abortion Bill, which criminalizes transportation of minors across state lines to receive abortions. (Driving and aborting: it's like drinking and driving, only you're *guaranteed* to kill a baby! *Wooooooooooooooooooooooo!*)

- Parental approval requirements for teenagers' abortions in nineteen states, even if their pregnancies are due to *incestuous rape*.[4] ("Hey, Daddy, can you sign this? But first can you take your dick out of me?")

However, Republican policies are often *responsible* for abortion: abstinence-only sex education guarantees higher teenage pregnancy rates in conservative states,[5] plus three-fourths of women who terminate their pregnancies "cite economic pressure as a reason."[6] If everyone were given condoms and money, right-wingers might finally shut the fuck up!

Trying to understand the motivations of pro-choice and anti-abortion radicals I attended the March for Women's Lives on the

National Mall in Washington, D.C., which attracted prominent leaders from both sides. It was one of the most agonizing days of my career. (Isn't there more to the breakfast of life than scrambled eggs?)

One last thought before we begin: American women received forty-five million abortions between 1973 and 2008, ending a fifth of all pregnancies.[7] (It's a *third* in Europe.[8]) The average birth weight is seven pounds, which means that the U.S. has produced up to three hundred and fifteen million pounds of Baby Goo since legalizing abortion.

Why *haven't* we cured World Hunger?

April 25, 2004

WASHINGTON, D.C. | *"Stop the Violence Against Abortion Clinics!" "Choice Equals Equality!" "Stop Capitalist Oppression!" "Keep Your Religion Off My Body!" "Anti-Capitalist Action Now!" "No More Coat Hangers!"*

Every man dreams of surrounding himself with a million screaming, passionate, manipulated young women—basically the average college experience—but the March for Women's Lives makes me want to crawl back into my mother's uterus and close the lid forever.[*]

According to the Associated Press, more than a million feminists have converged on the National Mall for this event, which is endorsed by the National Organization for Women, NARAL Pro-Choice America (formerly the National Association for the Repeal of Abortion Laws), the Feminist Majority, the American Civil Liberties Union and the Planned Parenthood Federation of America, which

---

[*] Sigmund Freud would suggest that I have *always* wanted this.

operates many abortion clinics and contends that life "starts when a baby takes its first breath."[9]

Slogans and smells bombard me from all directions as I follow the hideous herd of heterosexuality-hating heifers. They carry posters, pump their fists and condemn the Patriarchy with piercing shrieks, which is what my girlfriend sounds like when she wants me to take out the trash or put the toilet seat down.

"Keep Abortion Legal!" "Keep Your Bra, Burn Republicans Instead!" "Make Love, Not Laws!" "Stop the Pregnancy Police!" "My Body Is Not Public Property!"

Look at all these unshaven-legged, gap-toothed, ill-bathed, ratty-haired, rancid-smelling militant feminists! No guy in his right and/or sober mind would *touch* these nasty mastodons. Why do they *care* about the legality of abortion?

(George Carlin remarked that this holds true for the other side: "Why is it that most of the people who are against abortion are people you wouldn't want to fuck in the first place?")

A height-impaired, beauty-impaired feminist (let's call her "He-Man") distributes maps to the protesters. She is an abortion clinic "escort" from Pennsylvania, which means that she leads women into the Aborto-Chamber while pro-life demonstrators squeal outside.

"What do the Christians shout when you're escorting?" I ask.

"The usual terrifying things like 'murderers' and 'baby killers,'" says He-Man. "A woman has the right to choose. She has the right to choose to have a tonsillectomy. She has the right to choose to have back surgery. She has the right to choose to lift her chin. She certainly has the right to choose health care for herself." (Lifting your chin, terminating your pregnancy ... just a typical day in the suburbs.)

"Is there any merit to their argument that life starts in the womb, so it's wrong to—"

"None at *all*," He-Man scoffs. "And that's *not* their argument, which is that life begins at *conception*, and that's just incorrect."

"Should abortion up to the moment of birth be legal?"

"That's an *asinine* question. To have an *abortion* at the moment of *birth?* We're not talking about *fetuses*, okay? We're talking about *women*, and women get to *choose* if they want to become mothers. A lot of people have different ideas about the status of the fetus, but that's *not* the issue. The issue is *women*—women's *lives*, women's *health*—and to make it about anything else changes the subject in a way that's completely inappropriate and disrespectful."

Inappropriate? Disrespectful? *Moi?*

"The most merciful thing a large family does to one of its infant members is to kill it," wrote Planned Parenthood founder Margaret Sanger,[10] who proposed "sterilizing" up to "nearly half—47.3 per cent—of the [U.S.] population," and recommended "that parenthood is absolutely prohibited to the feeble-minded."[11]

Sanger believed that the government should "allow" only thirteen percent of the population "to reproduce," excluding "the blind, deaf and mute … and epileptic," who are "dead weight of human waste."[12] For these undesirables, "Segregation carried out for one or two generations" was "the immediate and peremptory duty of every State and of all communities."[13] She condemned "modern society, which has respected the personal liberty of the individual,"[14] and "welfare programs for their failure to weed out the feeble-minded and unfit."[15] (In 2008 Planned Parenthood apologized for accepting money from a bogus donor who told a fundraising employee that "the less black kids out there the better," to which the employee replied: "Understandable, understandable."[16])

In April 1933 the National Birth Control League, which would later become Planned Parenthood, published the Nazi Society for Racial Hygiene cofounder's article "Eugenic Sterilization: An

Urgent Need."[17] Sanger appointed Lothrop Stoddard, author of the 1920 screed *The Rising Tide of Color Against White World-Supremacy*, to her organization's Board of Directors. In 1940 Stoddard "met personally with Adolf Hitler" and SS Chief Heinrich Himmler, whom Stoddard praised for "weeding out the worst strains in the Germanic stock in a scientific and truly humanitarian way ... by the physical elimination of the Jews themselves from the Third Reich." He considered Nazi policy *"almost too conservative."*[18]

In Sanger's defense, she condemned the Holocaust and presented an award to Martin Luther King, Jr. She also helped overturn laws that forbade the sale of condoms. However, a "vigorous" 2004 Consumers Union study deemed Planned Parenthood's condoms the least effective of all brands.[19] (Which raises the question: where the *hell* do I apply to work at Consumers Union?!?)

Broken condoms mean higher revenues: Planned Parenthood clinics generate nearly $300 million per year, not including approximately $500 million in donations and taxpayer dollars.[20] The organization's president earns more than six times the average American's salary.[21] In 2005 a Planned Parenthood chapter created a cartoon in which a "Superhero for Choice" shoots, drowns and decapitates anti-abortion protesters—portrayed as monstrous, grunting zombies—and then says, *"That's more like it! Open for business!"*[22]

This is strange considering that Sanger wrote in 1920: "[T]he complete abolition of the abortion law will shortly do away with abortions, as nothing else will."[23] Whoops!

At least she wasn't as kooky as the doctor whom King Retard appointed to oversee the family planning division at the U.S. Department of Health and Human Services. This man's organization suggested that abortion causes breast cancer—which is ludicrous—and that condoms are "demeaning to women, degrading of human sexuality, and adverse to human health and happiness,"[24] which is *very* ludicrous. (Actually I have experienced *much* happiness thanks to rubbers. And I *was* demeaning women and degrading my sexuality at the time.)

"It's Your Choice, Not Theirs!" "If You Cut Off My Reproductive Rights, Can I Cut Off Your Penis?" "My Body, My Choice!" "Choice Today, Choice Tomorrow, Choice Forever!" "Euthanize Christians!"

On a stage between the Washington Monument and the Capitol building, several notables—and nobodies—address the million feminists who wear tank tops and militaristic camouflage. The notables include:

- *Ms.* magazine founder Gloria Steinem, herself an abortion recipient, who wrote in 1973: "By the year 2000 we will, I hope, raise our children to believe in human potential, not God."[25] In 2008 she proclaimed that "[g]ender is probably the most restricting force in American life,"[26] as if the last few decades had never happened: modern women earn more university diplomas and often higher salaries than men.[27] A woman received over 18 million votes in the 2008 presidential primaries, nearly gaining the Democratic presidential nomination. (Activists are often unable to recognize their own victories because they're too busy bitching.)

- Planned Parenthood president Gloria Feldt, NOW president Kim Gandy and former NOW president Patricia Ireland, whose belief that "the personal is political" is every activist's maxim.[28]

- NOW founder Betty Friedan, who attended Communist Front meetings[29] and compared American housewives to "the millions who walked to their own death in the concentration camps."[30]

- Actress Jane Fonda, who posed for photographs in 1972 with Communist North Vietnamese soldiers and accused captured American troops of lying about being systematically tortured.

- Untalented singer Ani DiFranco, who abhors ideological shades of gray: "Either you are a feminist or you are a sexist/misogynist. There is no box marked 'other.'"[31]

- Democratic Congresswomen Nancy Pelosi, Diane Feinstein, Barbara Boxer and the appropriately named Louise Slaughter.

- New York Senator Hillary Clinton, whose husband—President Blow Job—so respected her as an empowered, self-actualized woman that he ... well ... decided to become President Blow Job.

"Women will not bow down!" shrieks an activist on the stage. "We will be free! There are women in prison! Women who have disabilities will be free! All women with disabilities must have access to abortion!"

The enraptured marchers gaze forward and cheer every sentence.

"More women died from illegal abortions before 1973 than soldiers died in the Vietnam War," screams actress Cybill Shepherd after taking the stage. "We can't let it happen again! Women will rise again! We are marching not just for our lives but the lives of our daughters!"

Indeed, thousands of American women died from illegal abortions *before penicillin and antibiotics*, but according to the U.S. Centers for Disease Control and Prevention, only forty died from "back alley" procedures the year before *Roe v. Wade*.[32] Ten to two-dozen perish per year in the twenty-first century from *legal* abortions,[33] so the difference is less than thirty measly lives. As necessary as *Roe v. Wade* might have been, it hardly prevented the Back Alley Female Holocaust.

"Religion makes me *sick*," Shepherd says before quoting—in the very same breath—the *Reverend* Martin Luther King, Jr. (To be fair, this *is* more sophisticated than fellow celebrity Cameron Diaz's 2004 appeal to voters: "I mean, we could lose the right to our bodies … *if you think that rape should be legal, then don't vote.*"[34])

A "radical poet" takes the stage, dressed like a homeless woman, and speaks so forcefully that she hyperventilates.

"*I proclaim the emancipation of clitoris to shining clitoris!*" wails the Lady Shakespeare. "*Cunt revolution! Cunt revolution is here! We will fight our shackles and rise from our chains and say, 'Patriarchy, I survived!' We will be free! We will rise to freedom! We will rise from the giant cunt mold! They make it hard to have a cunt in this cunt-ry!*"

"Do you really think this lends credibility to your cause?" I ask the cheering feminist beside me. "Seems like if you're *born* with a cunt, it should be easy to *have* one."

I ask another attendee, twenty-year-old Sonya, for her opinion.

"I don't think, like, the babies are real, like, human *beings*, you know?" Sonya articulates. "It's … like … I want my right to *choice*—it's not a question of whether the baby is *alive* or not. That's not what I'm here to argue. I'm here to argue my choice to make … to make … to argue my *choice* to have an abortion, you know?"

Katrina and Maddie, a pair of teenage lesbians, distribute posters that proclaim: "QUEER RIGHTS <u>ARE</u> REPRODUCTIVE RIGHTS!"

"What does that *mean?*" I ask. "Gay people can't *reproduce*—at least not without scientists."

"Exactly," chirps one of the girls. "Gay people will *never* have abortions! So I think *everyone* should be gay! So nobody has to argue!"

This is the most brilliant notion that I've heard today.

Feminism has had many positive effects on society—equal pay for equal work, college educations for millions of young women, and the widespread curtailment of domestic violence—but its most passionate adherents are absolutely hysterical. A feminist organization creatively named the Feminists declared in 1969:

- "We must destroy love ... Love promotes vulnerability, dependence, possessiveness, susceptibility to pain, and prevents the full development of a woman's human potential by directing all her energies outward in the interest of others ... love is a delusion in the female."

- "[C]hildren are part of society but they should not be possessed by anyone."

- "We must destroy the institution of heterosexual sex ... the myth of the vaginal orgasm was created so that the female would remain sexually dependent on the male."[35] (Conspiracy theories are activists' explanations for everything, including their own frigidity.)

The 1971 "Declaration of Feminism" opined: "[I]t is important for us to encourage women to leave their husbands and not to live individually with men. ... All of history must be rewritten in terms of oppression of women. We must go back to ancient female religions like witchcraft."[36] According to Dr. Mary Jo Bane, the U.S. Assistant

Secretary for Children and Families in the 1990s: "[T]he fact that children are raised in families means there's no equality. It's a dilemma. In order to raise children with equality, we must take them away from families and communally raise them."[37] A NOW "Equality and Reference Specialist" defined pregnancy as "an absolute emblem that a woman has been invaded by a man and colonized."[38]

These radical feminists have *serious* psychodramas unfolding inside their craniums. Shulamith Firestone, author of the 1970 manifesto *The Dialectic of Sex: The Case for Feminist Revolution*, characterized human babies as "parasites," and pregnancy as "the temporary deformation of the body for the sake of the species."[39] She suggested: "[T]o eliminate the incest taboo we would have to eliminate the family, and sexuality as it is now structured. Not such a bad idea."[40] Naturally her work is required reading for gender studies courses at Harvard, Cornell, Brown, Stanford, Rutgers and many other universities.

Sally Miller Gearhart in her essay "The Future—If There Is One—Is Female," suggested: "To secure a world of female values and female freedom we must, I believe, add one more element to the structure of the future: *the ratio of men to women must be radically reduced so that men approximate only ten percent of the total population.* ... One option is of course male infanticide."[41] (Gearhart ultimately rejected this solution as unworkable.) In 2008 a Kansas abortion doctor, whom unchristian Christians had non-fatally shot and bombed on multiple occasions, received a standing ovation from members of the Feminist Majority Foundation after presenting a *slideshow* of aborted fetuses at the National Education Association's headquarters. (The doctor explained, "If the baby is born alive, that is sloppy medicine," because "you have to ... rush it directly to the hospital against the woman's wishes."[42]) A Princeton University professor, who believes that a dog "vigorously rubbing its penis" against you is "mutually satisfying,"[43] says: "I do not think it is always wrong to kill an innocent human being. Simply killing an infant is never equivalent to killing a person. ... All I am saying is, why limit the killing to the womb? Nothing magical happens at birth."[44]

These bizarre theories lead to equally bizarre policies:

- In July 2005 the ruling Socialist Party of Spain required men to perform fifty percent of housework, *even if only the husband has a job.* Spaniards "who refuse to do their part may be given less frequent contact with their children."[45] (Isn't this more of a *reward* for lazy men?)

- In 2004 the Swedish Left Party's Feminist Council proposed taxing all male citizens—but *not* females—to recoup the "economic costs of this aspect of socially destructive male behaviour," specifically domestic violence.[46] Never mind that women commit forty-one percent of spousal killings.[47] (Note to self: whomever I marry, *don't trust her.*)

- In 2004 the Harvard University Bisexual, Gay, Lesbian, Transgender and Supporters Alliance condemned "discrimination linked to gender-segregated bathrooms."[48] The Harvard *Crimson's* editorial board agreed because "there are some in the Harvard community that experience extreme discomfort and pressure when going to the bathroom."[49] (Quite possibly, truer words have never been spoken.)

- A U.S. Department of Education kindergarten lesson plan titled *Gender Violence / Gender Justice* instructs students to "[i]magine that the woman you care about the most is being raped, battered or sexually abused" for at least thirty seconds.[50] (What *else* would you teach five-year-olds? The *alphabet?*)

- In 2007 the New York City Council proposed symbolically banning the words "bitch" and "ho," which are "hateful and deeply sexist," from common speech.[51] That same year Australian men who dressed as Santa Claus for Christmas were "warned" to avoid the phrase "ho ho ho" because "it may be offensive to women."[52] ("Ho" is popular slang for "whore." Example of usage: "Oh my God, hos are such motherfuckin' *bitches.*")

If radical feminists are "pro-choice," they have a funny way of showing it. In February 2005 an Idaho feminist bound and *scalped* a sixteen-year-old girl with a knife for "acting in a way that the adult perceived as being offensive to women as a gender," according to police. "The top of her head ... was completely cut off."[53]

Simone de Beauvoir, author of *The Second Sex*, proclaimed: "Women should not have that choice [to raise their children at home], precisely because if there is such a choice, too many women will make that one. ... In my opinion, as long as the family and the myth of the family and the myth of maternity and the maternal instinct are not destroyed, women will still be oppressed."

Ms. de Beauvoir also explained: "[T]he abortion campaigns as such are nothing except that they are useful in destroying the idea of woman as a reproductive machine. ... Something along these lines is being tried in China."[54] *Time* magazine reported in 2005 that Chinese women who are impregnated for the second time—and fail to pay the Communist government four years' worth of income—are kidnapped, taken to sterilization clinics, and physically restrained while doctors eradicate their wombs. Authorities kill anyone who tries to interfere;[55] China incidentally has the world's highest execution rate.[56]

"I consider the Chinese government's policy among the most intelligent in the world," said acting NOW president Molly Yard. "[I]t is an attempt to feed the people of China. I find it very intelligent."[57]

Speaking of feeding people, Kansas City police investigated an abortion doctor in 2003 who would allegedly "microwave ... the aborted fetuses and stir it into his lunch."[58] You know how veal makes you feel guilty because it's from cute baby cows, but then you eat it anyway because it's so fucking delicious?

"Vegetarians for Choice!" "Women Must Choose Their Destiny!" "Feminism Is the Radical Idea That Women Are People!" "Keep Your Laws Out Of My Womb!" "Pro-Choice, Pro-Environment!" "Women United Will Never Be Defeated!" "Pro-Lifers Are Liars—They Don't Care If Women Die!"

A feminist named "Maze" screams down oppression while distributing a newsletter titled the *Revolutionary Worker,* which the Revolutionary Communist Party publishes. Maze never learned the colloquialism "Say It, Don't Spray It," and thanks to the saliva projected into my eyeballs I want to get tested ASAP for tuberculosis, syphilis, HIV, Black Death, etc. (Just like when I lost my virginity!)

"We have to fight this whole Christian fascist anti-women *offensive* coming from the highest levels of government," Maze rants. "It comes from the whole nature of this capitalist imperialist *system.* We can't let our struggle get derailed by falling for this 'lesser evil' thing and supporting the Democrats. We have to oppose this whole *system* if we want to fight for a day when the oppression of women no longer *exists.* And it's *righteous* that so many people are out here fighting this struggle—we stand shoulder to shoulder with everyone here—fighting against the oppression of women, against *patriarchy,* against the Christian *fascists!"*

"What *is* patriarchy?" I ask.

"Patriarchy is the whole way women are indoctrinated every day, told that they're less than human, told that their only role is to be mothers and breeders, told to shut up and what they have to say doesn't matter. We're out here standing up *against* all that. And we're saying it comes from the capitalist *system* we live under. And to truly have women's liberation, we have to have *revolution* to get *rid* of that system."

"So women have it better in communist societies?"

"Well, actually, if you look at China during the Cultural Revolution, they had a slogan: 'women are the path to the sky.' Yes, there were unprecedented advantages made for women. There's a picture from China of a woman working on a telephone poll during a lightning storm in 1971. So yes, in 1971 women in China were much more liberated than women in the U.S."

Electrocution in a rainstorm is *liberation?* From *existence?*

"Abortion was legal there in 1971 and it wasn't legal here except for a few states at the time," Maze says. "There were efforts to communize child care—communal kitchens and things like that—to free women from being trapped in the home. This was absolutely going on during the Mao period in China. Now *we* must have the *same* kind of revolution against patriarchy!" (Chairman Mao wrote that pro-democracy "reactionaries must be deprived of the right to voice their opinions ... we simply deprive them of their freedom of speech."[59] Sounds *awesome*, Maze!)

A middle-aged Maryland woman named Linda marches beside her teenage daughter. She holds a poster: "SURVIVOR: 1972 ABORTION." Was Linda the mother or the *fetus?*

"What brings you out here today?" I ask. "You wanted to see the Lincoln Memorial and accidentally found yourself in the March for Women's Lives, right?"

"I want to keep abortion free—I mean, legal—for my daughter and all the other young women," Linda says. "We fought hard for this right and we want to keep it."

"So you've had an abortion?"

"Yes, before it was legalized."

"And was that at a clinic or—"

"You could say it was a backstreet deal. I've never had a moment's remorse." This is atypical: women are two to three times more likely to commit suicide after receiving abortions.[60] "Now I have two healthy teenagers and I was ready for them when I had them."

"And if your daughter ever asked for an abortion?"

"Oh ..." Linda smiles at her daughter, who smiles in return, probably entertaining naughty forbidden thoughts of my musculature and a pair of chilled handcuffs. "Absolutely."

Not everyone at the March for Women's Lives is a supporter. A man named Chuck carries a colossal photograph of an aborted fetus, the bloody head of which has rolled off its splayed body.

"Baby-murdering and sodomy!" Chuck shouts into a megaphone. "Heed the word of God! This sick display here today epitomizes this so-called Christian nation. If this is Christian, then we don't need the Devil and the Muslims are right: America is the scourge of the Earth—the Great Satan—engaging in the politics of sodomy!"

I introduce myself to Chuck as a member of the Godless Liberal Media and ask what it is—in his opinion—that drives the demonstrators.

"Obviously they want to keep the right to kill babies," Chuck says. "This isn't a Christian nation. We don't believe in Jesus. If we did, we wouldn't be killing babies and promoting sodomy. ... They don't love Christ—they want to get God out of the public schools in America—and so they band together here for a good showing."

"So I take it you believe in Jesus?" I ask. "Ha! Ha!"

"Oh yeah, I got converted to Christ in '79. I used to be a wicked man. He died for my sins and I love him for it. ... For a good man, a Christian man, to stand by while four thousand babies a day are murdered with the blessings of the government, it's very vexing. Jim Kopp killed a mass murderer (abortionist Dr. Barnett Slepian in October 1998) and he got put in jail, but Jim Kopp is a hero of mine. When the government punishes a brave man for stopping the murder of thirty babies who would be killed the next day, it's sick."

Fun Factoid: in the last three decades Christian fundamentalists have committed "seven murders, 17 attempted murders, three kidnappings, 152 assaults, 305 completed or attempted bombings and arsons, 375 invasions, 482 stalking incidents, 380 death threats, 618 bomb threats, 100 acid attacks, and 1,254 acts of vandalism" in their war against abortion, according to *Newsday*.[61]

"So it's a Holy War?" I ask Chuck. "Book of Revelation? God versus Lucifer?"

"It is." Chuck nods ominously. "The lines are being drawn. Look here. You can *see* it."

Operation Rescue founder Randall Terry, who has organized hundreds of anti-abortion protests over the years—and tried to deliver an aborted fetus to President Blow Job in 1992—is also present at the March for Women's Lives. Terry does not endorse violence but *has* made such level-headed, gentlemanly statements as: "We don't want pluralism. We want theocracy. Theocracy means God rules ... I want you to let a wave of hatred wash over you. Yes, hate is good ..."[62]

Terry stands behind a police barricade as thousands of feminists march down Pennsylvania Avenue.

"Murder is *never* an act of love!" Terry shouts into his megaphone. "This is a *death march*—it's a *holocaust*. You will look back with embarrassment and *disgrace* at this day. You will look back and say, 'My God, what was I *doing?*' You would *murder* your sons and daughters! You would *murder* generations to come! *Shame* on you! This moral wrong should *never* have become a constitutional right!"

When it comes to "moral wrongs," Terry has faced many embarrassments:

- He divorced his wife of two decades and married his twenty-two-year-old secretary. Four years previously Terry had written: "Families are destroyed as a father vents his mid-life crisis by abandoning his wife for a 'younger, prettier model.'"[63]

- His two daughters were impregnated on three occasions before they turned seventeen years old.[64] His twenty-four-year-old son detailed numerous homosexual experiences in *Out* magazine.

- The Supreme Court ordered Terry to pay $600,000 after physically blocking access to abortion clinics. He begged supporters for financial donations and then reportedly purchased a luxurious house.[65]

"Shame on *you*," a feminist screams at Terry. "It's my *choice!*"

"Shame on *you*," Terry replies. "Adolf Hitler was very popular in 1945. ... And soon everyone *knew* he was a murderer—a murderer of *children*. ... Have you lost your way to *think*? Have you lost your *minds*?"

"*Freedom*," the feminist yells. "I believe in *freedom!*"

"The freedom to *kill*. Your freedom is *death*."

"*Choice! Choice! Choice!*"

"*Life! Life! Life! Life!*"

Like a superhero I leap over the police barrier and stick a microphone in Terry's face.

"Your thoughts?" I ask over the howls of thousands.

"These people cannot be *reasoned* with," Terry says. "Not only are they blind, they are *willfully* blind. Think about it. All the facts say this is a human being ... That's the exact same argument the slaveholders used. 'We don't know if they're human beings, but they're *our* human beings and we'll do with them what we want.' It's the exact same logic and the exact same rhetoric. ... These people are in a death march."

"Now for a question about your gay son—"

"*No.*" Terry scowls and turns away from me.

He most likely does not hear me ask: "What if scientists discovered a cure for homosexuality, *only it came from the remains of aborted fetuses?*"

Life under Republican rule sucks a massive load of elephant jizzum, but what would society look like under radical feminist rule?

For the answer let's turn to my *favorite* feminist, Valerine Solanas, author of *The SCUM (Society for Cutting Up Men) Manifesto*, who planned "to overthrow the government, eliminate the money system ... and destroy the male sex." She also promised:

> "*SCUM will kill all men who are not in the Men's Auxiliary of SCUM. Men in the Men's Auxiliary are those men who are working diligently to eliminate themselves ... A few examples of the men in the Men's Auxiliary are: men who kill men ... faggots who, by their shimmering, flaming example, encourage other men to de-man themselves ... To aid men in this endeavor SCUM will conduct Turd Sessions, at which every male present will give a speech beginning with the sentence: 'I am a turd, a lowly abject turd,' then proceed to list all the ways in which he is.*"

Women *have* experienced unjustified discrimination. Abortion *is* a necessary evil—hardly comparable to a tonsillectomy, however—that reduces poverty and drastically lowers crime,[66] plus it keeps my weekends exciting. Women receive the exact same number of abortions in countries where it is illegal,[67] so they might as well have safe ones.* But just because radical feminists have some valid

---

* Clarification: safe for women, not quite safe for fetuses. You can stop crying, honey, Mommy's here ... and she brought her favorite wire hanger. Do you have an itch? Mommy can *scratch* it.

points doesn't change the fact that these bitches are *completely fucking psychotic.*

It's obvious that they are filled with rage because they've never encountered a Man with the endurance, technique and flesh-span to stimulate their Siberia-like innards. Similarly right-wingers' loathing of abortion is directly linked to their fear of non-reproductive sexuality. *But there is a solution to this quagmire of a clusterfuck:* I shall dedicate my life to seducing ("terminating") every feminist and fundamentalist on Planet Earth in order to rid the world of bothersome complaining. I'll have no way of knowing *who* is a feminist or fundamentalist, of course, so I'll need to penetrate every single woman—every single *person*—on the planet regardless of Race, Faith, Class, Limbs, etc.

Say *yes,* my precious whores, for a woman's only right is to suckle upon my Glorious Jewish Cock! Christians, my Hebrew Phallus gives purpose to your existence! My Manhood Is Your *Lifeblood!* Guzzle! Guzzle! *Guzzzzzzzzle!*

"*Stop the War on Choice!*" "*All Abortions Would Be Legal If Men Had Wombs!*" "*Keep Your Hands Out of My Uterus!*" "*Against Abortion? Have a Vasectomy!*" "*Pro-lifers are the Real Killers!*" "*Stop the War on Women!*" "*My Body, My Baby, My Life, My Choice!*"

Stupid Hippy: "*It's our bodies!*"

Jesus Freak: "*Baby killers!*"

Stupid Hippy: "*Woman killers!*"

Jesus Freak: "*You're all sick!*"

Good Lord, I can't *take* this bickering anymore. No self-respecting journalist would force himself to listen to this godforsaken bullshit. There is no safe ground: you are either against Choice, Life, Freedom, Equality, Babies, God or *something* holy to *someone.* Never mind that both sides are pro-life *and* pro-choice: Christians cherish the lives of babies; feminists cherish the lives of women. Christians believe people should make better choices in bed; feminists believe that women should choose whether they're ready for motherhood. They might actually find some common ground if everyone were to *shut the fuck up* for five seconds.

Listen, pro-lifers: abortion is a *necessary* evil.

Listen, feminists: abortion is a necessary *evil*.

As I walk toward the subway to leave this wretched abomination known as the March for Women's Lives, I stop to interview a twelve-year-old named Michael who marches alongside the fetid feminist flock.

"Seriously, kid," I say, "what are you *doing* here?"

"Well, I think abortion should stay legal," Michael chirps. "At my age, I know kids wouldn't be ready for kids of their own."

"So if you knocked a bitch up, you'd take her to the clinic?"

"Oh … I think that I should be able to, yes." Michael smiles.

"Don't call chicks 'bitches,' dude," I admonish the boy. "They deserve *respect.*"

★ ★ ★

Sodomization Nation vs. Salvation Nation:

WHEN ONE MAN'S MORAL WRONG
MAKES ANOTHER MAN'S PENIS LONG

★ ★ ★

Author's Note: *This chapter will piss off conservative bigots* and *the Gay Tolerance Police. It's a good bet that somebody is going to lynch and/or rape the Author, quite possibly in that order.*

March 28, 2005

NEW YORK CITY | Rain crashes upon Times Square so hard that I struggle to keep my eyes opened. Speeding cars splash freezing water all over my clothes. Lightning bolts electrify the sky. The wind blows like the Gales of Hell. Apocalypse is in the air, and it's not simply the weather: the Phelps family of Topeka, Kansas—headed by Westboro Baptist Church pastor Fred Phelps—hoists posters that declare "GOD HATES FAGS" and "GOD HATES AMERICA."

The Phelps family is so infamous that even Congress has condemned its extremist actions. In 1998 Fred Phelps "prepared to dance on the grave at the funeral" of twenty-one-year-old Matthew Shepard, who was murdered for being gay,[68] and the Phelps family has picketed at thousands of other burials, landing them $3 million in punitive damages for "intent to inflict emotional stress."[69]

As a lawyer in the 1960s Phelps helped overturn racial segregation in Kansas—the pastor believes that it's wrong to discriminate against people for skin colors that they cannot choose—but he considers sexual orientation a choice and has zero sympathy for those "vain, proud, arrogant *beasts*" who "anally copulate":

- "Don't tell me God only hates the sin and not the sinner! There's not one iota of scripture for that. ... This maudlin kissy-poo stuff that you call the love of God is nothing but a Satanic lie ..."[70]

- "This very night you fags that are here are going to be rolling around, having sex with each other's feces, and drinking each other's semen and calling that an innocent, alternate lifestyle."[71]

- "Homosexuals now pervade and control American government at every level and branch."[72]

- "God laughs when homosexuals die."[73]

"What do you think the government should do?" I ask Margie Phelps, Fred's daughter. "Are you for punishing sodomy with *death?*"

"I'm going to give you a real simple proposition," Margie says. "There's a standard in the Bible and it's shown in the laws of God. The standard in the Bible ... is that they who do such things are worthy of death. Now that's God's standard. You take it from *there.*"

"What reactions do you usually provoke with these pickets?"

"A lot of vulgar nonsense. A lot of 'I don't believe God is real,' 'I don't believe God hates,' 'burn in hell,' 'fuck you.' This is like a lightning rod. ... That's why the Bible says His word is sharper than any two-edged sword. It pierces the heart of darkness—it separates the joint from the marrow. That's how powerful it is."

"What exactly *is* the 'fag agenda' you're protesting against?"

Sodomization Nation vs. Salvation Nation:

"It includes being able to marry each other, it includes lowering the age of consent for sex as low as they can get it. Above all they have one burning lust—besides their sexual lust—and that's the lust to be called holy. They are not going to stop until it's against the law to call it a sin. They *burn* to be treated as respectable and they will not stop until they force that—by force of arms—on the American people. They want every institution in this country to respect them and call them holy. … They've made 'judge' and 'hate' dirty words in our culture."

"To what extent—if any—do you feel the Devil is working through these gay activists?"

"Most of the humans ever *born* were Satan's children. Most of mankind ends up in hell. That's the default. Only an elect remnant doesn't end up in hell. Only an elect remnant goes to heaven. Now that's the language of the Scriptures. Most people go to hell. It so happens that when a society gets to such a state of baseness and disobedience to God, the fags take over. And that's the condition of things. Christ said, 'As it was in the days of Lott and the days of Noah, so it shall be when the Son of Man comes.'"

"Son of Man?" I ask. "That's Satan?"

"No, that's *Christ* coming back."

I've revealed my Jewish ignorance. *Oy vey!*

"Do you believe these are the end times?" I ask.

"I believe it's not long," Margie says. "No one knows the day but God, but He gave us some things to watch for."

"Like the fags?"

"They're *part* of it."

"Your group has strongly implied that AIDS is God's cure for homosexuality."

"It's not *implied*, it's *said*. There are a lot of passages in the Scriptures talking about God picking the calamity of the unrighteous and sending it. There's a lot of good Bible about that proposition.

There's no question that all the statistics—no matter how cooked—show that AIDS predominates among homosexuals. ... They also infected the blood supply."

"What about *heterosexual* sodomy?" I ask.*

"Any kind of sex between a man and wife is fine. That's all you need to know. We don't need to discuss the particulars. One man, one woman, one lifetime. These churches are filled with divorced and remarried people who are no different than the fags. That's why they can't tell them *not* to be fags. And the fags *know* that."

Children picket alongside Margie. I ask her if the kids enjoy bashing queers.

"They've been to these all their lives." She smiles. "They look forward to the picketing trips—it's just part of their lives."

New Yorkers pass the Phelps family on the sidewalk, either staring in disgust or screaming with outrage.

"This country is so degenerate," says Sam Phelps-Roper, another family member at the curbside protest. "When the moral standard erodes, every kind of filth is accepted."

"What about gay men who don't hurt anyone, don't steal anything, and live an otherwise moral existence?" I ask. "Do they *still* go to hell?"

"First of all, I see sodomy as the lowest rung on the ladder of depravity. How many societies has the Lord Almighty destroyed with fire and brimstone for the sin of sodomy?" (Uh ... isn't Greece still a country?)

"To what extent do you feel that Satan is working to promote the 'fag agenda'?" I ask.

"He is like a roaring lion seeking whom he may devour. He's

---

* According to the National Center for Health Statistics, forty percent of American adults have had anal sex, but only six percent have had homosexual experiences. It's unclear whether "homosexual experience" includes watching the Academy Award-winning gay cowboy drama *Brokeback Mountain*, but it definitely includes watching the entire *Lord of the Rings* trilogy more than once.

very active in the affairs of this earth—certainly he is. That's a pretty simple question."

"So the Devil likes sodomy?"

"He likes anything that God has called an abomination. He is an idolatrous, murderous liar."

"So every time one fag sodomizes another, Satan smiles?"

"Sure," Sam says with a smile of his own. "He sure does."

Soaked and shivering, I leave the protest to meet a gay friend at a nearby Taco Bell. Our conversation quickly sinks into the gutter.

"How could you *ever* perform oral sex on a woman?" asks my gay friend. "*Yuck.*"

"It's not the most pleasant taste," I say, "but then they'll do the same for you."

"So it's like *rimming.*"

"Uh …" I say. "What?"

"You know, *ass*-licking."

"No, it is *not* like *rimming* because *straight* people have assholes *too.*" The other diners stare at us. "You never see *us* licking each other's rear ends like *dogs*," I say in my best Phelps voice. "You *degenerates*, you idolatrous *sodomites* who occupy the lowest rung on the ladder of depravity, just enjoy the taste of *shit* more."

"Actually," my gay friend smirks, "if the guy showers first, it's *really* not that bad."

When it comes to homosexuality, Americans are more divided and torn than the average homosexual's asshole. For activists of the Left and Right there is no middle ground: you are either an anti-gay bigot or a faggot-loving enabler. Either a furious God forbids you to enter His paradise or cute lefty college chicks forbid you to enter theirs.

Right-wingers believe that homosexuality is responsible for the destruction of our society. (And Republican males would know—they are nearly all self-loathing closet cases.˙) The American people are far more tolerant:

- Although fifty-three percent of Americans want to amend the Constitution to ban same-sex marriage,[74] fifty-five percent support "civil unions" that would provide the same benefits.[75] Three-fourths of American college students support civil unions.[76]

- Eighty-five percent of Americans believe that gay people deserve equal job rights, and more than half consider gay people qualified to work as schoolteachers.[77]

- In 2002 the American Academy of Pediatrics endorsed gay adoption.[78]

- Fifty-two percent of Americans consider homosexuality an acceptable lifestyle.[79]

- In 2004 Massachusetts legalized same-sex marriage. (In 2008 California did the same.) Only a third of its gay couples bother to wed, however,[80] probably because lesbian partners—two *women*—take a *lifetime* to plan the ceremony.

---

* Recent cases of supposedly antigay conservatives caught in the act: U.S. Senator Larry Craig (tried to seduce an undercover cop in a public bathroom); Florida Representative Bob Allen (agreed to pay an undercover cop $20 for a bathroom blow job); the Reverend Ted Haggard, chief of the National Association of Evangelicals and spiritual advisor to King Retard (enjoyed methamphetamine-fueled sex marathons with a gay prostitute); Spokane, Washington Mayor Jim West (seduced young males online); Pennsylvania County Commissioner Bruce Barclay (secretly videotaped hundreds of sexual encounters, many with male escorts, according to police); and U.S. Representative Mark Foley (flirted with underage male pages for a decade, asked them to measure their penises, naturally served as chairman of the House Caucus on Missing and Exploited Children).

Sodomization Nation vs. Salvation Nation:

It wasn't always this way: in 1776 all thirteen American colonies punished sodomy with the death penalty.[81] By 1968 only Illinois had decriminalized gay intercourse,[82] which Nevada punished with lifelong jail terms.[83] In the 1970s seventy percent of Americans considered homosexuality "always wrong," sixty-seven percent believed that gay people should not work as doctors and teachers, seventy-four percent believed that they "are dangerous and try to become sexually involved with children," half believed that "homosexuality can cause the downfall of civilization," and the vast majority tried to never associate with gay people.[84] (Were there no *gyms* in the 1970s? Salons? Theaters? Antique stores? Republican National Conventions?)

Conservatives don't simply hate gay people for violating biblical sexual restrictions; they also hate gay people for wanting families. In 2006 congressional Republicans pushed for a gay marriage ban with the following rhetoric: "I think God has spoken very clearly on this issue," "I refer [opponents] to the Holy Scriptures," "Marriage is not about love—it's about a love that can bear children,"* "The world did not start with Adam and Steve," and *"This is probably the best message we can give to the Middle East …"*[85] (And right-wingers accuse *liberals* of appeasing Islamist terrorists and tyrants?)

Voters in eleven states banned gay marriage in 2004 after a Republican campaign pamphlet suggested that if the Democrats won the White House, gay marriage would be "ALLOWED" and the Bible "BANNED."[86] The man who orchestrated the 2004 GOP campaign, presidential advisor Karl Rove, "was raised by a homosexual father who abandoned his family to lead an openly gay life in Palm Springs," according to *Radar* magazine.[87] Bitter much?

In 2005 Texas and Florida legislators voted to bar homosexuals from adopting children,[88] supposedly because kids need a traditional

---

* A February 2007 UNICEF report found that American children are significantly more deprived of parental attention and general welfare than those in gay-friendly nations such as Sweden, Denmark and Finland. The study did not mention whether "attention" included anal fisting.

family, but the latter state allows unmarried *hetero*sexuals to adopt its five thousand orphans.[89] Utah places orphans with strangers instead of gay relatives.[90] But if the recent accrual of civil rights for gay people jeopardizes the traditional family structure, as Republicans warn, why is the U.S. divorce rate at its lowest in forty years?[91]

According to Brown University researchers, homosexuals are responsible for less than one percent of reported child abuse.[92] Children are seventy-five percent *more* likely to experience abuse if "scolded and punished ... for asking sex questions, for masturbating, and for looking at sexual pictures," and nearly forty percent more likely if raised with "conservative family values."[93] (No wonder the Pope considers gay marriage an "ideology of evil" and "obstacle to world peace."[94] The Vatican knows a few things about molesting young boys!)

But perhaps the redefinition of marriage *would* have unforeseen consequences:

- The organization CUDDLE (Cousins United to Defeat Discriminating Laws through Education) lobbies for the legalization of incestuous marriages, and accuses traditionalists of "genetic discrimination."[95]

- In 2005 the Netherlands, the first nation to legalize gay marriage, recognized the wedding of three partners.[96]

- The North American Man-Boy Love Association lobbies for the relaxation of child molestation laws. A NAMBLA spokesman says, "Right now the situation of man/boy love in America is quite analogous to the situation of Jews in Nazi Germany ..."[97] (Some of us might argue that it's not analogous *enough*.)

- In 1944 Sweden decriminalized homosexuality *and* bestiality. The latter is only punishable if "prosecutors can prove that the animal suffered physical or psychological injury."[98] If Rover fails to develop Post-Traumatic Stress Disorder, you're in the clear.*

Former Education Secretary William Bennett writes that if leftwing activists manage to legalize gay marriage, "What arguments would they invoke [against polygamy, bestiality and pedophilia]? Tradition? Religion? The time-honored definition of the family? These are the very pillars they have already destroyed."[99]

But "family values" activists invoked the specters of legalized polygamy, incest, bestiality and pedophilia in order to keep *interracial* marriage off the books. Thirty states prohibited unions between whites and blacks before World War II. In 1967 the Supreme Court overturned these laws, which were still on the books in sixteen states.[100] (This is a prime example of the "judicial activism" that narrow-minded Republicans loathe.) In 1871 the Indiana Supreme Court ruled that citizens must "follow the law of races established by the Creator himself, and not ... intermix contrary to their instincts."[101] In 1958 a Virginia judge declared: "Almighty God created the races white, black, yellow ... and red, and he placed them on separate continents. ... The fact that he separated the races shows that he did not intend for the races to mix."[102]

Why *should* the U.S. base its policies on the Book of Leviticus? Perhaps we need constitutional amendments to stipulate:

- "Everyone who curses his father or his mother shall surely be put to death." (Leviticus 20:9)

---

* Marty Beckerman's Rules of Thumb for Consensual Man/Beast Action: "No Buck, Okay to Fuck!" "No Bray, Hump Away!" "No Bark, What a Lark!" "If It Doesn't Claw, Bone It Raw!" "Suck a Duck!"

- "Your male and female slaves are to come from the nations around you." (Leviticus 25:44)

- "Do not cut the hair at the sides of your head or clip off the edges of your beard." (Leviticus 19:27)

- "Anything in the seas or in the streams that has no fins and scales … are an abomination for you, and an abomination for you they shall remain: you shall not eat of their flesh and you shall abominate their carcasses." (Leviticus 11:10–11)

- "He that blasphemes the name of the Lord … shall surely be put to death." (Leviticus 24:16)

Is homosexuality even a "choice," as Bible-thumpers claim? Is *hetero*sexuality? (My gay friends claim that "everyone is a little bit queer," but I've only found this accurate *after* ten shots of vodka.)

Identical twins are forty percent more likely than adopted siblings to share homosexual preferences.[103] In 2006 Canadian researchers suggested that "sexual orientation may be determined by conditions in the womb …"[104] In 2007 University of Utah biologists who studied worms concluded that "sexual orientation is wired in the creatures' brains."[105]

Oregon researchers had "considerable success" altering the sexual orientation of gay sheep through hormone replacement technology.[106] The president of the Southern Baptist Theological Seminary commented: "If a biological basis is found, and if a prenatal test is then developed, and if a successful treatment … is ever developed, we would support its use as we should unapologetically support the use of any appropriate means to avoid sexual temptation and the inevitable effects of sin."[107] So it's okay to play God if the Almighty doesn't get it *right?*

Christian conversion camps, which rake in major bucks, seek to "cure" gay youths. In 2007 King Retard nominated the founder of one such "recovery ministry" for Surgeon General.[108] However, Tennessee police investigated an Exodus International affiliate ministry—one of a hundred and twenty—for "psychologically abusing" homosexual teenagers and "minor children."[109] In 2007 three former Exodus International leaders admitted that the organization's techniques cause "isolation, shame, fear and loss of faith ..."[110] Those who undergo "aversion therapy" often suffer "severe emotional ... consequences" and "continuing predominance of homoerotic fantasy," according to researchers.[111]*

We are simply born with certain inflexible qualities. Two-thirds of male children who express "gentleness" and "sensitivity," as opposed to competitiveness and aggression, discover their same-sex attraction between the ages of eleven and fourteen.[112] But don't question their manhood: a European study of twenty thousand men, and an American study of five thousand, "fully confirmed the larger-than-average genital size of homosexuals,"[113] which shatters the myth that gays are lesser men. (And it shatters rectums.)

Activists on the radical Left, however, wish to brainwash children in the same way with Tolerance Training. A lesbian author explained in the *Advocate*, the longest-circulating American gay magazine, "It is the first fact of civilization: Whoever captures the kids owns the future."[114] The 1999 anthology *Queering Elementary Education* suggested:

- Schools should forbid the words "family" and "parents," because "the predominant assumption is that *family* means

---

* Freud could have told you this in 1935: "[T]o convert a fully developed homosexual into a heterosexual does not offer much more prospect of success than the reverse, except that for good practical purposes the latter is never attempted." Question for Sigmund: do gay dudes subconsciously want to kill their *mothers* and fuck their *fathers?*

nuclear family and *parents* mean a mom and a dad."[115] Schools should replace holiday songs with "music to teach against homophobia," such as "Mama, What's a Dyke?" This song ends with children declaring, "And sometimes I wish that *I* had two mommies."[116]

- "Acknowledging children as sexual beings ... in elementary grades dislodges the classroom from the 'safe haven' of heteronormativity. ... The gravest threat that the recognition and acceptance of lesbian/gay families in elementary schools pose is the removal of the family as instrument of heterosexual socialization."[117]

- Boys should no longer pee standing up: "The ways boys and girls urinate is different [and] heteronormativity manifest[ing] itself."[118]

- "Science is socially constructed, value laden and context bound ... challenge the notion that science is the same everywhere, that it is 'universal' and that it is a direct reflection of 'truths' in the natural world ... Like homosexuality and bisexuality, heterosexuality is socially constructed."[119] (Aren't *right*-wingers the ones who hate science?)

In 2001 California required its schools to adopt sexual orientation sensitivity training for kindergarteners. One California school instructed students to participate in role-playing such as claiming that they were "born" gay.[120] (This should be easy: when I was in kindergarten I thought that girls were grosser than snot.) The Children of the Rainbow curriculum, nearly implemented in New York City, would have explored homosexuality with "actual experiences via creative play ..."[121] In 2006 a teacher-approved survey asked Wisconsin students, "If you have never slept with someone of your same gender, then how do you know you wouldn't prefer it?"[122]

A textbook used in Massachusetts schools, which students were allegedly not allowed to take home for their parents' perusal, suggested: "Testing your ability to function sexually and give pleasure to another person may be less threatening in the early teens with people of your own sex ..."[123] Personally I found that it was less threatening with my mattress, pillows, socks, shampoo bottles, etc.

An official from the National Education Association boasted at a Gay, Lesbian and Straight Education Network conference: "The fear of the religious right is that the schools of today are the governments of tomorrow. And you know what? They're right."[124] GLSEN distributes educational material to public schools condemning "the belief that *hetero*sexuality is 'normal,'"[125] which—considering that ninety-six percent of the population is heterosexual—seems like a closed debate. When a parent secretly recorded a taxpayer-funded GLSEN presentation for students on "fisting," which described it as "an experience of letting somebody into your body that you want to be that close and intimate with," the organization asked a judge to issue a "national gag order."[126]*

This power-crazed, anti-First Amendment mentality is typical of activists on the Left *and* Right. Neither side is innocent when it comes to the curtailment of civil liberties, which we will discuss next.

But first: Marty Visits a Gay Bar!

---

* Gagged *and* fisted? Kinky!

March 29, 2005

ARLINGTON, VIRGINIA | I return from the NYC Phelps protest after midnight and scour my neighborhood for food. The only restaurant still open is Freddie's Beach Bar. This is *clearly* a gay establishment: rainbow flags, neon décor and karaoke. But I am starving so I order a burger and beer from the blonde waitress, who most likely doesn't receive many come-ons from her clientele. (The irony of patronizing a gay bar after interviewing the Phelps family somehow doesn't strike me.)

"Excuse me," says a well-groomed gentleman named Ken. "You're *straight*, aren't you?"

"How did you guess?" I ask.

"I can *tell*." Ken extends his arm for a handshake. When I stand he squeezes my posterior as if it's a lemon and he wants lemonade.

"Whoa!" I say. "Back off, buddy!"

"You're so *cute* for a straight boy. All the straight ones are."

"Flattery will get you nowhere." I retrieve the voice recorder from my backpack. "Unless you give me an interview."

Ken consents with a smile. (Not the first time.)

"Why do you think America is so anti-gay?" I ask.

"All established religions—Catholicism, Islam—say homosexuality is wrong and sinful, just because of one line. I used to be Catholic. *Nothing* turns people gay like the Catholic Church."

"How would you compare sex with a woman's vagina to sex with a man's anus?"

"Ass is *tighter*." Ken grins. "When I would have sex with women before I came out, it felt like I was performing a chore. But my first experience with a man, there was no need to perform a chore. It was the best turn-on sex—it was so tight I *cried*."

A forty-year-old named Mike buys me another beer. (Holy shit, I should come to gay bars more often! Usually *I'm* splurging to get laid!)

"I contemplated suicide as a teenager because I didn't *want* to be gay," Mike confesses. "My Catholic upbringing and my desire to have a family, to have children, to have a traditional lifestyle … it was what I really wanted. It was very painful to want something but to know internally that I was gay. I didn't *want* to be. I absolutely positively did not *want* to be. … I don't think America understands that we don't have an option—if we *had* an option, we would be something else. If there were any possible pill to make me a heterosexual so I could have a wife and child and live the normal way, I would do it in a heartbeat. But I am what I am, so I can't change that."

Wow, Mike, *you're* a happy fucking drunk.

Next I speak with an Iraq war veteran from Kansas named Tom, who claims that Fred Phelps picketed at one of his friend's funerals. I ask how it felt to grow up as a homosexual in the ultra-conservative state.

"It was bad," Tom says. "It was *hell*. I wanted to get out of Kansas so bad, and then I went into the Army."

"Where they *love* gay people," I jest.

"When I was in Iraq, I kept telling myself, 'If I get back alive, I'm going *straight* to a gay porno store.'"

"Do you want to marry a guy someday?"

"There are people in the gay movement who spend so much money and time on that issue, but I don't think most homosexual men really pay attention to it. I don't think too many gay men *are* monogamous."

"Yeah, isn't gay marriage like going to Disneyland and only getting to enjoy *one* of the … uh … rides?"*

Next I approach Miguel, a trans-gendered wo/man creature. S/he has long black hair, a falsetto voice and the face of a professional boxer.

"When did you realize that you weren't like the other children?" I ask.

---

* I made this argument to my girlfriend. "Are you gay?" she replied. "Seriously, I want to know right now instead of ten years from now. Why else would you compare sex with men to *Disneyland*?"

"Probably in kindergarten," Miguel says. "When all the boys went out to play ball, I would play with Barbie dolls ... I kept it very secret."

"What's your opinion of sex-change operations?"

"If it makes a person happy, that's the important thing. If a person is depressed or living an unhappy life because society says they have to be someone they're not, I feel that's bad. If they want to be a woman, basically go ahead."

"Just chop it off?" I wince. "Welcome to womanhood!"

"That's right. Exactly. You just have to live your life."

"What percentage of the straight community do you think is closeted homosexual?"

"Probably fifty-fifty," Miguel guesstimates.

"You think *half* of straight guys are secretly—?"

"When I go to straight bars I get my drinks paid for me."

"So what do you think of these right-wingers who say that all gay people go to hell?"

"My religious beliefs are between God and myself. Everyone else can kiss my *bee*-hind and I could care less."

"You consider yourself religious?"

"Yes, I am religious—I'm Catholic."

"Every gay person here is *Catholic*," I observe. "Why *is* that? All those S&M crucifixes?"

"I don't know what to say; I have a brother who's gay and a cousin who's gay."

"Do all these Jesus freaks who hate gay people just need a really hard ass-fucking? Would that set them 'straight'?"

"*That* wouldn't even do it," Miguel sighs.

Satisfied with my interviews—and dangerously intoxicated—I decide to leave Freddie's Beach Bar and Restaurant. But first I enter the restroom to urinate. As I relieve myself the unlocked stall door opens.

"Mmmmm ... you have *such* a cute *ass* for a *straight* boy."

Call me a homophobe; I zip my pants before I've finished pissing.

(Yes, this actually happened. And yes, I *do* have such a cute ass for a straight boy.)

The GOP is obsessed with depriving gay Americans of any and all freedoms. Meanwhile radical leftists are eager to silence their critics through draconian P.C. legislation. Whenever either side scores a victory, the American people get collectively fucked in the ass.

In 2003 the Supreme Court ruled that sodomy laws—which criminalize private bedroom behavior between two consenting adults—violate the Constitution. In order to prevent the horny homos from humping, Republican Senator Rick Santorum apparently suggested that the U.S. government designate *all* sexual intercourse illegal: "If the Supreme Court says that you have the right to consensual sex within your home, then you have the right to bigamy, you have the right to polygamy, you have the right to incest, you have the right to adultery ... homosexuality ... man on child, man on dog, or whatever the case may be. ... It all comes from, I would argue, this right to privacy that doesn't exist in my opinion in the United States Constitution, this right that was created." [127*] Since Santorum is a hardcore Catholic—and therefore opposes *in vitro* fertilization—the only natural conclusion is that he desires the extinction of humanity. (Hey, if *everyone's* dead, there won't be any *cocksuckers!*)

---

* Yes, Santorum, it *was* created—by the *Founders*. Fourth Amendment to the U.S. Constitution: "The right of the people to be secure in their persons, houses, papers, and effects, against unreasonable searches and seizures, shall not be violated, and no Warrants shall issue, but upon probable cause ..."

The televangelist Pat Robertson promised to "do everything I can to restrict the freedom of these [gay] people …"[128] Robertson and his friend the Reverend Jerry Falwell, two of the biggest names in rightwing politics until the latter graciously died of a heart attack in 2007, blamed homosexuals for provoking God's wrath on 9/11. The bloated Falwell reportedly said that homosexuals would "just as soon kill you as look at you,"[129] and Robertson—who met with King Retard on a half-dozen occasions—believes that Satanism and homosexuality "seem to go together."[130]

Robertson is hardly the only traditionalist who wishes to bind, gag, tease and spank gay people. A Republican candidate for the Hawaiian senate argued for the execution of homosexuals in 2004.[131]

"Dig a hole," says Republican Alabama representative Gerald Allen, "and dump them in it."[132] Allen was referring to *books* written by gay authors or featuring gay characters, but it's worth noting that Adolf Hitler dumped thousands of gay people into the ground. As of 2004 Allen had met with King Retard on five occasions. According to CBS News, "Allen originally wanted to ban even some Shakespeare."[133]* He told reporters that "I don't look at it as censorship," but "as protecting the hearts and souls and minds of our children."[134]

In 2007 University of Washington researchers found that gay youths are six times more likely to attempt suicide,[135] but Republicans reportedly tried to suppress a similar federal study.[136] Iowa Republicans refused to sign legislation that would punish students for bullying gay classmates.[137] Gay Americans are not allowed to donate blood despite a nationwide shortage,[138] and under King Retard the U.S. Food and Drug Administration ordered sperm banks to reject their semen."[139] (This raises two questions: Are Republicans afraid that homosexual sperm breeds homosexual offspring? And why does the federal *food* agency regulate *ejaculations?*)

---

* "Were kisses all the joys in bed, one woman would another wed"?

The U.S. military officially defines homosexuality as a mental disorder,[140] and discharged ten thousand gay soldiers—including three hundred and fifty doctors and medics—between 1994 and 2005,[141] wasting $364 million worth of recruitment and training funds.[142] The Army discharged sixty Arabic-speaking linguists, *essential* to the War on Terror, between 9/11 and May 2007.[143]

A spokesman for the Department of Homeland Security suggested that same-sex couples "move to another country,"[144] but homosexuality *is* useful to our national defense: Fox News Channel reported that Pentagon "scientists considered developing a chemical weapon with aphrodisiac qualities that would make enemy soldiers hopelessly, physically attractive to one another so as to paralyze their ranks and destroy morale."[145] (This gives new meaning to "fire in the hole.")

No wonder Republicans consider the Iraq war a success: in 2006 Shiite militias—unchecked by Saddam Hussein's *secular* despotism—burned to death anyone suspected of homosexual leanings.[146] That same year the Retard Administration joined forces with its arch-nemesis Iran—which systematically *executes* gay people—to ban a gay rights organization from addressing the United Nations.[147] What a heartwarming display of Christian-Muslim ecumenical outreach!

Radical American conservatives, like those Shiite terrorists, occasionally take the law—*God's* law—into their own hands, forgoing the minor stipulation "thou shall not murder." Beltway Republicans might deprive gay people of liberty and the pursuit of happiness, but some nuts deprive them of *life*. In the 1990s extremists killed more than thirty gay people because of their orientation.[148] One convict said, "I'm not guilty of murder, I'm guilty of obeying the laws of the Creator."[149] In 2007 a Texas man killed a gay male flight attendant—is there any other kind?—and claimed that he was "called by God … to carry out a code of retribution" after studying the Bible for "thousands and thousands and thousands of hours."[150] A devout Florida man killed his three-year-old son because he "was concerned that the child might be gay."[151]

The Federal Bureau of Investigation estimates that one thousand five hundred antigay hate crimes are committed per year,[152] and announced in 2007 that hate crimes had risen by eight percent nationwide.[153] Gay students are four times more likely to receive threats with deadly weapons than their straight counterparts.[154] In 2002 fifteen New Jersey teenagers kicked a fourteen-year-old classmate while chanting, "Kill the faggot! Kill the faggot!"[155] Students at a California high school knocked a gay student unconscious and carved the word "FAG" into his abdomen.[156] In 2006 four heterosexual New York youths allegedly lured a gay man to a "remote location" with promises of group sex and beat him within an inch of his life.[157] (It would be *really* ironic if they raped him afterward.)

Just as religious fundamentalists want to force their morality on others, whether through legislation or violence, a radical fringe of the Left feels the same desire to enforce its values. In 2004 Canada officially banned criticism of homosexuality, which now carries a maximum penalty of *five years* in prison. A Canadian human rights tribunal subsequently fined two men thousands of dollars for placing Bible references in advertisements and refusing to conduct business with a homosexual organization. A member of the Canadian Parliament explained: "Anybody who has views on homosexuality that differ ... will be exposed rather dramatically to the joys of the Criminal Code."[158] But Canada also investigates criticism of Islam,[159] which in turn criticizes homosexuality, so why not jail anyone who dares to hold an opinion?

A 2007 British anti-homophobia law carries a sentence of *seven* years in jail,[160] which reflects the attitude of gay British rock star Elton John, who said in 2006: "I would ban religion completely. ... It turns people into really hateful lemmings and it's not really compassionate."[161] In 2004 France outlawed sexist and anti-gay comments and jokes. A sense of humor means a year in jail and a $45,000 fine. According to the French National Commission on Human Rights, the legislation bans "certain films, books and even the Bible ..." Merely referring to homosexuality as "abnormal" is grounds for punishment.[162]

In 2005 a Massachusetts elementary school principal asked police to jail a father who objected to sensitivity training for his five-year-old.[163] A Minnesota high school principal disciplined a sixteen-year-old student for wearing a "Straight Pride" sweatshirt, which the administrator considered "offensive" despite the fact that it didn't express anything negative about homosexuality.[164] In 2008 a Florida high school banned "all expression of opinion—negative or positive—about homosexuality."[165] Who needs free speech when *no* speech is far more orderly?

The ivory tower is hardly immune to this totalitarian temptation:

- Carnegie Mellon University fired a staff advisor for refusing to wear a gay pride symbol during mandatory "gay and lesbian sensitivity training."[166]

- Texas A&M University requires all faculty members to "celebrate and promote" homosexuality.[167]

- During its "Feel What It's Like to Be Gay Day," Williams College in Massachusetts requires *hetero*sexual students to wear the sticker, "Hello, my name is _____, and I'm Gay!"[168]

- At the University of Pennsylvania religious students with gay roommates are reportedly forced to say: "In my community we regard this behavior as wrong, but those are just our values. ... I am becoming tolerant and setting aside the dogmatic intolerant view with which I arrived here in Philadelphia."[169]

- According to *U.S. News & World Report*, in the 1990s George Mason University punished heterosexual students for "keeping physical distance from a known gay or lesbian or staring at two homosexuals holding hands."[170] (So it's wrong to pay too little *and* too much attention—exactly like dating a woman!)

A judge in Colorado ruled that parents who teach "homophobic" ideas should lose custody of their children.[171] Ironically two Virginia judges have ruled that a gay man and a lesbian cannot have access to their biological children because "the child will grow up confused about gender differences ..."[172] So queers *and* queer-bashers lose their kids. Do we really want a society that restricts the breeding privileges of anyone who has *viewpoints?*

In 2004 Pennsylvania added antigay speech to its hate crimes list,[173] and police subsequently arrested four Christians for reading the Bible aloud at a gay pride rally and failing to disperse. A state prosecutor charged the Christians with "possession of instruments of crime," and attempted to jail each for half a century.[174] In early 2005 a Philadelphia judge dismissed the case with this statement:

> *"We are one of the very few countries that protect unpopular speech. And that means that Nazis can march ... That means the Ku Klux Klan can march where they wish to. We cannot stifle speech because we don't want to hear it ..."*[175]

It *also* means that citizens have the right to pursue their own happiness—as long as they don't harm anyone else—even when popular notions of faith condemn their lifestyles. Listen, Republicans: the propagation of your archaic bullshit is directly

Sodomization Nation vs. Salvation Nation:

responsible for creating a culture in which sexual minorities are physically and *psy*chically tormented. Listen, gay activists: no matter how worthy your goals, you are no more justified in criminalizing your opponents' beliefs than they are justified in criminalizing your families and sexuality.

Finally, it would be majestic if radical leftists *and* religious rightists learned how to stifle their *own* speech. Nothing like a mouthful of throbbing, meaty, veiny cock to make people *shut the fuck up.*

March 11, 2005

WASHINGTON, D.C. | "—radical evangelical Christian activists along with other radical evangelical Christian bigots—"

"The Right is using people as *pawns.*"

"*Slavery* was defended using the *same* Bible."

"You have to *at least* be for civil unions or else you're a bigot."

"I hope this rally brings us closer to peace, equality and love."

Welcome to the Marriage Equality Rally in Dupont Circle, the capital's most gay-friendly neighborhood.

"I'm an Old Left activist," says Katrina, an African-American draped in a flowing multicolored garment. "We know how to use propaganda too." (According to the official rally flyer, she created a "Wiccan-based public ritual group seeking to heal the city.")

Katrina compares today's homophobia to the racial injustices of Southern racial segregation: "They said it wasn't a big deal to eat outside. They said it wasn't a big deal to sit at the back of the bus. But when Rosa Parks took a stand, it *electrified* people and made them realize that it's all connected. There is no separation between the right to vote, the right to eat, to go to school, to work, to buy a home; it's all connected. We need to continue their fight."

Earth to Katrina: American homosexuals *can* vote, eat, go to school, work and buy homes. All they *can't* do (yet) is claim tax deductions for fucking one another.

"We're all in this human family *together*," says a female pastor from a local leftwing church. She likens conservatives to children: "We must get over our *selfishness*. Two-year-olds cry 'Mine! Mine!'"

An *enormous* woman, who wears an *enormous* muumuu and sports *enormous* frizzy hair, addresses the Marriage Equality Rally.

"Everybody here seems to define marriage in terms of only *two persons*," says the Hippy Hippo. "I am all for equality of marriage. I think it is a human right. And I think it is a vital human right that all of us engaged in loving human relationships not be legally restricted in marriage to *two* partners."

"Uh …" The leftwing pastor is dumbfounded. "Until we can get the rights for two people … uh … um … we need to start someplace … um … and so let's see what we can do with *gay* marriage—the right of *two* of us to get married—then we can take a look at potential *possibilities* to expand a little bit more. But you need to start someplace and … um … this is where we've chosen to start. And that would be a more … uh … *difficult* matter of course down the road, but politically I think if we get this one first, then we open up the opportunity for … for … more … uh … *special* cases and possibilities."

"Absolutely," says the Hippy Hippo. "Just as long as we get to the beginning."

"I don't know much about … uh … multiple-*partner* relationships," says a homosexual D.C. councilman. "But one of the standards we have for marriage is that it promotes *stability* in society. And you're talking about saying … um … that … that … uh … it's fairly *untraditional*. I don't really hear much about what … uh … that would do for *society*. And also it just seems … I'd like to hear more about it ... but I ... I ... I don't think it's fair to say that all of us think it's the 'beginning.' " It's unclear if the gay councilman realizes that he sounds *exactly like a Republican.*

"What about democracy?" I ask the activists. "People in a dozen states just voted to outlaw gay marriage. What's the point of changing laws if you can't change people's beliefs?"

I receive the same reaction as a black man—or a smartass pipsqueak Jew, which I am—at a KKK convention.

"Putting people's RIGHTS up for a popular VOTE? Those rights are HUMAN rights!"

"Why settle for gay marriage ONLY in Massachusetts?"

"This is a NATIONAL issue! People need PROTECTION!"

"The PROBLEM with giving people the right to vote is that it's going to push the country to not HAVE gay marriage. It doesn't make SENSE."

"It doesn't WORK that way. It NEVER worked."

Afterward I approach one of the activists, a young woman named Jennifer, who belongs to Queers for Racial and Economic Justice.

"Hey, I've figured out the solution to this whole gay marriage debacle that will make *everyone* happy," I explain. "Want to hear it?"

"Um ..." Jennifer says. "Okay ..."

"All right, the U.S. should invade Cuba and turn it into Gay Island,* right? This will make *queers*—am I allowed to say that?— *queers* happy because you'll have your own Tropical Gay Israel where same-sex marriage is celebrated and you can frolic like woodland creatures. It will make *Republicans* happy because America will topple a communist dictatorship and kill a lot of brown people. And it will make *Cubans* happy because homosexuals have more disposable income to spend than heterosexuals—no children to support, right?—and this influx of cash will revive Cuba's wrecked economy. *Everybody* wins with Gay Island!"

---

* "Guantanamo Gay"?

"Oh …" Jennifer looks horrified. "I'm *guessing* that the Cubans don't want to be a colony of the United States. And I don't think we need another imperialistic war. And why would we send all the gay people to *Cuba* again?"

★ ★ ★

Invasion Nation vs. Negotiation Nation:

MAKING THE WORLD SAFE FOR DUMBOCRACY

★ ★ ★

Author's Note: *There are many brave men and women in the U.S. Armed Forces whom I would never disparage, but they are at the mercy of imbecilic politicians who recklessly send them to their dooms and then revoke the very freedoms for which they fight. (The troops know this: they donated three times more money to antiwar candidates than pro-war candidates in the 2008 presidential primaries.[176]) As Senator Barack Obama said in 2002, "I'm not against all wars, just stupid wars." I share this sentiment with one variant: I'm not against all people, just* stupid *people.*

August 30, 2004

NEW YORK CITY | *"FULFILLING AMERICA'S PROMISE,"* proclaims the banner strung across Madison Square Garden. *"A SAFER WORLD, A MORE HOPEFUL AMERICA!"*

This is ironic considering that everyone in New York City expects Madison Square Garden to explode in the next few days, but Truth is the first casualty of war at the Republican National Convention. Security is unprecedented. Thousands of Secret Service agents and police officers stand throughout the complex. Department of Homeland Security agents, armed with M-16s and flanked by bomb-sniffing dogs, confiscate cameras, cosmetics, soda cans, hairspray, cologne, umbrellas, miniature American flags and *apples*, which terrorists can supposedly utilize as "lethal aerial weapons," according to the *New York Daily News*.[177]

Threats of foreign jihadists and homegrown anarchists has resulted in widespread panic, hysteria, and—yes—*terror*. The New York tabloids forewarn: "Anarchy Threat to City: Cops fear hard-core lunatics plotting convention chaos." These delinquents are "hard-core extremists with histories of violent and disruptive tactics," who have been "trained in kidnapping techniques, bomb making, and building improvised munitions."[178]

But there is another threat besides American anarchists: leaked intelligence reports indicate that al-Qaeda, the international terrorist network that took credit for killing three thousand Americans on September 11, 2001, plans to strike again in three days. The Department of Homeland Security raised its color-coded Terror Alert Level from yellow ("Significant Risk of Terrorist Attacks") to orange ("High Risk of Terrorist Attacks"). Our underpants have changed colors to brown.

The New York Police Department has forty thousand officers on duty.[179] Cops in full riot gear—shields, helmets, guns, mace and clubs—stand on every street corner in Manhattan. It is like something out of a post-apocalyptic science-fiction movie. I am cautious to wear respectable clothes so the NYPD storm troopers don't mistake me for another young protester. They are in Full Brutality Mode. They have no interest in discussing the First Amendment. To keep your skull intact, you had better look like someone who can afford a lawyer. Or better yet look like someone who *is* a lawyer.

Despite the ubiquitous threat of death, fifty-five thousand Republicans have "ventured behind enemy lines" to leftwing stronghold New York City.[180] One of these true believers is fifty-eight-year-old Jeremiah, a preacher from North Carolina, who confronts antiwar protesters outside. He wears a "JESUS" t-shirt and carries a poster: "IN GOD AND [KING RETARD] WE TRUST!"

The protesters scream at Jeremiah: *"I thought children of God don't judge others!"* and *"Who would Jesus bomb?"*

"Do they have a point?" I ask. "Wasn't Jesus a pacifist, unshaven hippy like these people?"

"Jesus was a pacifist in his *first* life," Jeremiah explains. "But listen to me: *God is a killer.* Jesus will return as a *warrior.* Look at the Book of Revelation … Jesus is going to come back as a *killer.* Don't you *forget.* God will kill two-thirds of the population, two-thirds of the *earth.*"

Jeremiah slaps my back—a friendly gesture, not a hostile one—so hard that I lose feeling in my entire body. Unfortunately I don't lose my hearing and must listen to five hundred thousand protesters scream: *"War off! Peace on!" "No police state!" "This is what fascism looks like!"*

Inside Madison Square Garden the Republicans carry posters: *"We Support Our Troops!" "A Nation of Courage!" "No Peace Before Victory!" "[Retard] IS Freedom!" "God Speaks Through ANOTHER [Retard]!"*

Footage from World War II, Vietnam and Korea—interspersed with images of modern fighter jets—plays on an enormous video screen. A tiny old lady in a wheelchair applauds the Technicolor war footage. Veterans of WWII take the stage and denounce the Democratic challenger, Senator John Kerry—a decorated Vietnam veteran—as a weak-kneed, lily-livered, yellowbellied coward. Never mind that isolationist Republicans opposed American intervention in "Europe's war" during the 1940s, and King Retard spent the Vietnam years snorting coke out of strippers' assholes.

Country musician Darryl Worley, whose pro-war anthem "Have You Forgotten?" reached the top of the post-9/11 charts, plays a god-awful song and says, "God bless the men and women in uniform."

Lest anyone accuse the GOP of exploiting 9/11 for political gain, three 9/11 widows take the stage and ask for a moment of prayer.

Speaking of prayer, do Republicans love God or *what?* They can't go three *seconds* without mentioning the Invisible Dude:

- Former New York City Mayor Rudy Giuliani, who made millions of dollars from shameless post-9/11 speeches (and is on his third marriage because of his saintly philandering): "Thank God [King Retard] is our president. ... Either you are with us or with the terrorists. ... God bless all those defending our freedom; God bless America."*

- A Georgian alternate delegate: "[King Retard] supports God, and God supports [King Retard], absolutely." [181]

- Congressman Duncan Hunter, who launched a short-lived presidential campaign for the 2008 election: "God wants a Republican to be president." [182]

- The Republican governor of Texas: "If you don't confess your sins to God almighty through the authority of Christ and his blood ... you're going straight to hell with a nonstop ticket." [183]

- The Iowa Republican chairman: "This is the GOP, God's Official Party." [184] When antiwar demonstrators scream at the Iowa delegation, the chairman says: "You got to understand something about the Devil ... The Devil will try to throw you off. The Devil will try to keep you busy." [185] A reverend with the Iowa delegation says: "We pray for these demonstrators who seem so confused ... They are putting so much energy into, just, *hatred* and we pray,

---

* Another Giuliani classic: "Freedom is about authority. Freedom is about the willingness of every single human being to cede to lawful authority a great deal of discretion about what you do." Yet another: the definition of torture "depends on who does it."

Lord, that they could … support the country the way the rest of us want to do." [186]

Presently Senator John McCain says, "We're Americans and we'll never surrender—*they* will." The right-wingers shriek, "*USA! USA! USA!*"

Formerly known as the most moderate Republican in the Senate, McCain would later sell his soul for the '08 GOP nomination, saying that it "would be fine with me" if the U.S. military stayed in Iraq for "a hundred years," "a thousand years" or "a million years." [187] In 2000 McCain rebuked the Reverend Jerry Falwell as an "agent of intolerance," but in 2007 praised the theocratic hatemonger as "a man of distinguished accomplishment who devoted his life to serving his faith and country." [188] Similarly out of character, McCain referred to gay soldiers as an "intolerable risk to morale, cohesion and discipline," [189] declared that "the Constitution established the United States of America as a Christian nation" although the document makes no reference to God, and explained that he "doesn't want a Muslim in the Oval Office," according to the *New York Daily News*. [190] He was "very honored" to receive the endorsement of the Reverend John Hagee, who said that "God caused Hurricane Katrina to wipe out New Orleans because it had a gay pride parade the week before … Hurricane Katrina was, in fact, the judgment of God against the city of New Orleans." McCain even insinuated that al-Qaeda would prefer a Democratic victory. [191] For longtime McCain admirers who cherished his maverick centrism, this shameless pandering and demagoguery was a more painful torture than any technique that the Vietcong utilized on the senator's fingernails.

A Republican attorney takes the stage and defends the PATRIOT Act, which allows the U.S. government to indefinitely detain U.S. citizens without access to the legal system. The lawyer sneers at the notion "that the PATRIOT Act is a threat to our liberties."

Tell this to the Oregon man whom federal agents seized for weeks, and threatened with death, after mistaking his fingerprints for someone else's.[192]

As I leave Madison Square Garden for the night I bump into Jerry Falwell, founder of the Moral Majority,* who believes that "God is pro-war." I've dreamed of interviewing Falwell for *years* so I could ask about his many insights:

- "The Bible ... is absolutely infallible, without error in all matters pertaining to faith and practice, as well as in areas such as geography, science, history, etc."

- "The idea that religion and politics don't mix was invented by the Devil to keep Christians from running their own country."

- "It is a tragic commentary on our world today that impressionable young people are taught at most public schools ... that the theory of evolution is fact, while the Bible is but a storybook filled with ridiculous miracles. ... No evolutionist can be truly happy."

- "I hope to see the day when, as in the early days of our country, we don't have public schools. The churches will have taken them over again and Christians will be running them. ... Christians, like slaves and soldiers, ask no questions."

- "If you are not a Christian, it is truly a sad thing. It is sad because one day you will meet God, unprepared, and spend eternity in hell."

---

* Major Amorality: in 1987 and 1993 the Federal Election Commission and Internal Revenue Service reprimanded Falwell for channeling followers' charitable contributions to rightwing political organizations.

Invasion Nation vs. Negotiation Nation:

- "God has raised up America in these last days for the cause of world evangelism and ... I don't think America has any other right or reason for existence ..."

- Referring to the Antichrist: "of course he'll be Jewish." (It ain't *me*, babe!)

- "It is the responsibility of ... every evangelical Christian ... to get serious about re-electing [King Retard]."[193]

I shake hands with Falwell—who has a grip like a fucking grizzly bear—and mentally prepare my burning journalistic questions.

"Holy shit," I say. "You're ... like ... Jerry *Falwell*."

"How do you do, sir?" Falwell asks and walks away.

Welcome to the End of Days, bitches. According to *Time* magazine, fifty-three percent of American adults "expect the imminent return of Jesus Christ, accompanied by the fulfillment of biblical prophecies concerning the cataclysmic destruction of all that is wicked."[194]

It's not just the yokels who have caught Apocalypse Fever: a month before the 2003 U.S. invasion of Iraq, Pentagon officials met with the cryptographer author of *The Bible Code*, who claimed that the Old Testament juxtaposed the phrase "Who is destroyed?" with "Hussein" and "5763," the Jewish calendar year analogous to 2003. The author described the experience thus: "I had told [the Pentagon officials] that we faced a danger so great it was captured only by the words of Biblical prophecy ... And they had believed me."[195] He also predicted that "Atomic Holocaust" was assigned to 2006. (Not so much, considering the 2008 publication of this book.)

Many Christian fundamentalists believe that the Bible predicts our rapidly approaching doomsday: a final war between Jews and Persians (the leader of Iran—who refuses to abandon nuclear power—has called for Israel "to be wiped off the map"), a single European currency, and an island metropolis—fallen to atheism—mourning "demolish[ed] towers."[196] In 2006 the congressional secretary of the House Republican Conference said: "As for Armageddon, I just note with interest that's what the Bible says. That it's on the Plains of Megiddo. Right there in Israel. And it makes you wonder where this conflict's all going to ultimately lead. And I happen to believe it will ultimately lead to what the Bible says."[197]

But historian Jonathan Kirsch warns that the Book of Revelation was used to justify "[t]he conquest of Jerusalem by medieval crusaders, the Bonfire of the Vanities ... and the thousand-year *Reich* promised by Adolf Hitler ..." Even President Ronald Reagan was "eager to win over the American military establishment ... on the divine implications of nuclear combat with the Soviet Union."[198] In 1984 Reagan speculated: "We may be the generation that sees Armageddon."[199] King Retard, Sr., told troops during the first Gulf War that they were "doing God's work," and denied that "atheists should be considered as citizens, nor should they be considered patriots; this is one nation under God."[200]

At the February 6, 2003 National Prayer Breakfast, the director of the Central Intelligence Agency told federal lawmakers, three thousand military personnel and the Commander-in-Chief: "Put on the full armor of God so that you can take your stance against the Devil's schemes. Our struggle is not against flesh and blood but ... against the powers of this dark world, and against the spiritual forces of evil in the heavenly realms. Therefore, put on the whole armor of God, so that when the day of evil comes, you may be able to stand your ground ... with the belt of truth buckled around your waist, with the breastplate of justice in place and with your feet fitted with the readiness that comes with the gospel of peace. Take up the shield of faith, the helmet of salvation, and the sword of the spirit, which is the word of God, and pray at all times."[201]

This was hardly an isolated incident. In 2003 Lieutenant General William G. Boykin, a top military advisor, proclaimed: "We in the army of God, in the house of God, kingdom of God have been raised for such a time as this. ... [King Retard] is in the White House because God put him there ... and the enemy is a guy named Satan."[202]

In 2004 the U.S. Air Force Academy removed a controversial banner: "I am a Christian first and last ... I AM A MEMBER OF TEAM JESUS CHRIST."[203] In 2007 the Pentagon canceled its plans to distribute packages to troops that contained Bibles and a "computer game ... in which 'soldiers for Christ' hunt down enemies who look suspiciously like U.N. peacekeepers."[204] Seven thousand soldiers testified in 2008 that they felt pressured to "accept a fundamentalist evangelical interpretation of Christianity," and many were disciplined for resisting.[205] (Fun Factoid: in 2007 University of Michigan researchers found that people are far more aggressive after "exposure to a biblical description of violence."[206])

While weighing the decision to invade Iraq, King Retard asked for advice from Texas televangelist James Robison,[207] a personal friend, who claims that Retard confided to him in 2000, "I feel like God wants me to run for president."[208] The preacher's answer was hardly a surprise. In 1980 Robison said: "There'll be no peace until Jesus comes. That's what the Anti-Christ promises. Any teaching of peace prior to His return is heresy. It's against the word of God! It's anti-Christ!"[209]

August 31, 2004

On Tuesday morning terrorists strike everywhere *except* for New York City. Palestinian suicide bombers kill fifteen Israeli civilians and injure a hundred more. Iraqi insurgents kill twelve hostages and upload photographs—slit throats, bullets in the backs of skulls—to the Internet. Female bombers kill nine Russian civilians and injure fifty-one at a Moscow subway station. Muslim Chechen rebels massacre four hundred Russian schoolchildren and take eight hundred others hostage.

Antiwar activists in New York are prone to lesser acts of violence. A nineteen-year-old protester allegedly stomps a policeman bloody, but is arrested the next day when found *wearing the exact same clothes.*[210] The vast majority of protesters are peaceful but this makes no difference: police lock nearly two thousand nonviolent citizens in holding pens at the Pier 57 warehouse, fenced with razor wire and lacking any comforts, only concrete floors.[211] The antiwar protesters are held for up to seventy-two hours with no formal charges or access to lawyers, *exactly how the U.S. government treats suspected terrorists.*

Fun Factoid: the chairman of the Hudson River Part Trust, which operates Pier 57, is "a well-connected Republican fundraiser,"[212] who said in a 2003 press release: "I am very excited to see what development lies in store for Pier 57. This is an awesome opportunity for cultural development ... and, when completed, is sure to be an asset for both the Park and for all of New York."[213] Who *wouldn't* view a private prison that interns the Republican Party's opponents as an "asset"?

In Union Square a public high school teacher bickers with an eighteen-year-old soldier who supports the war.

"You know better than the 9/11 Commission?" the teacher yells. "You know better than the United Nations? You know better than *everybody?* Where did you find the weapons of mass destruction? Where were they? They're a bunch of *lies!*"

"They're in Syria right now," says the teenage soldier.

"What? Who told *you?* You got the word from *God?* Give me the *evidence.* Give me one *piece* of evidence. You don't even *know* the evidence. You don't *have* it. Everybody in the *world* knows Saddam didn't have weapons of mass destruction. The 9/11 Commission—"

"One of my *friends* died over there!"

"And he died for nothing. He died for oil. I had four students who died over there for nothing. And I told them, 'Don't you go over there for oil.' And one of them came back to me and said, 'You were right, I should've *never* gone over there—if I would've died, I would've died like a dog for nothing, and that's what's going to happen to *you.* You don't have to die for money, oil and *lies.* We're *supporting* you."

"You *don't* support the War on Terror."

"That is a *myth.* That is a *lie.* This whole thing was a total *diversion* to *scare* us so we vote for this guy. You *know* it."

"Aren't they *free* now? Aren't fifty million people *free?*"

"*Free?*" the teacher scoffs. "How many people are being *murdered?* How can you believe these *myths?* You might be a brave person—you *are* a brave man—but you're being brainwashed and suckered by the corporate structure of this country. You better wise up."

"*You're brainwashed by the Jew-run media!*" a protester screams, prompting confused expressions from the teacher *and* soldier.

This guy is far from the only paranoid in this crowd. Protesters distribute hundreds of pamphlets that describe Byzantine conspiracy theories. They condemn "this war driven by greed for oil and lust for power and fueled by lie after lie," accuse White House officials of concealing chemical attacks against the American public, and blame the U.S. for "piles and piles of rotting, stinking corpses all over the planet," in the words of ultra-leftwing author Ward Churchill, a

University of Colorado professor, who considered the 9/11 attacks "Justice."[214] A woman from a 9/11 "truth" group informs me that she is a "Trotskyite."

"So you're a communist?" I ask.

"There's no such *thing* as communists." She snickers. "We all *know* that. They're just like *terrorists*—there's no such *thing*."

"Then who flew the planes into the World Trade Center?"

"Probably CIA operatives. Anyone who was Jewish knew 9/11 was coming."

"What?" I shriek. "Why didn't *I* know?" (This conspiracy theory is ridiculous, of course, because terrorism requires manual labor.* You think we nebbishes know how to use box cutters? We might hurt ourselves! And then we'd have to *sue* ourselves!)

"Roosevelt knew of Peal Harbor beforehand," the woman rambles. "Get under your school desk and you won't be nuked. *Ha!*"

Back at Madison Square Garden the evening's proceedings commence with a prayer: "Jesus, may you continue to look over our courageous troops. ... May God continue to bless our commander-in-chief, who fights for liberty in a world of tyranny ... We need Jesus. We need [King Retard]."

Senator Elizabeth Dole takes the stage in a hideous yellow suit. "In Afghanistan and Iraq, the dark clouds of oppression have parted for fifty million people," Dole says.

Fun Factoid: two-thirds of Iraqis wish that the U.S. had never invaded their country,[215] and Afghanistan threatened a Christian with the death penalty in 2006 for rejecting Islam, still a capital crime.[216]

"Two thousand years ago a man spoke about the dignity of life, and in America I call that man Lord," Dole continues. "In America we are free to worship without activist judges. The

---

* Full disclosure: I cribbed this joke from P. J. O'Rourke, whose name is slightly less Yid-sounding than Muqtada al-Sadr's.

Invasion Nation vs. Negotiation Nation:

Constitution says freedom *of* religion, not freedom *from* religion. The divinity of God isn't something Republicans invented but it *is* something Republicans will defend."

A video on the monitor glorifies "faith-based initiatives," which funnel millions of taxpayer dollars to "programs that save Americans one soul at a time."[217] The video features Senator Rick Santorum, who says that "individual freedom ... destroys the basic unit of our society because it condones behavior that's antithetical to strong, healthy families."

A New York Giants football player and his wife take the stage. "Help me reelect a leader who doesn't just *wish* breast cancer away," the wife says. "He *wills* it away." (No, honey, King Retard *believes* in Jesus; he's not *actually* Jesus.)

California Governor Arnold Schwarzenegger receives a standing ovation. "The world no longer fears the Soviet Union," says the star of *Last Action Hero*. "And it is because of the USA." Thousands of Republicans howl: "*USA! USA! USA! USA!*"

As I leave the RNC for the night, a man hands me a pamphlet titled "Does God Love You?" that explains:

> *"By God's standard of righteousness even the most moral person is looked upon by God as a desperate sinner on his way to Hell. The Bible teaches that no one is good enough in himself to go to Heaven. ... Hell is very real, and things are that bad for the individual who does not know the Lord Jesus Christ as Savior. ... Q. Are you saying that there is no way to escape Hell except through Jesus? What about other religions? Will their followers go to Hell? A. Yes, indeed. They cannot escape the fact that God holds us accountable for our sins."*

And *just* when I was going to convert to Sikhism ... those turbans are sexxxy!

By the end of the day the NYPD has arrested more than a thousand protesters at Central Park and Ground Zero.

"The NYPD needs to learn the First Amendment," screamed a twenty-six-year-old peacenik.

"Shut up!" a policeman replied, shoving the traitor to the ground.[218]

Like every other Republican belief, the notion that patriots must support the war is absolute bullshit.

"No nation could preserve its freedom in the midst of continual warfare," wrote James Madison, the architect of the U.S. Constitution. "If Tyranny and Oppression come to this land, it will be in the guise of fighting a foreign enemy."

In the early twentieth century U.S. Army propagandist George Creel convinced Congress to ban any newspaper that resisted military censorship. He warned Hollywood executives in 1917: "There is no time now to discuss a producer's abstract right to make and market any kind of picture he pleases. Probably he possesses that right. But public right takes precedence over any private right, especially in time of war."[219] He even jailed the producers of a film about the American Revolution because it "question[ed] the good faith of our ally, Great Britain."[220]

Creel urged young Americans to enter the "War to End War," which would "Make the World Safe for Democracy."[221] But democracy is not necessarily the same as freedom: the U.S. government prosecuted more than two thousand Americans under the 1917 Espionage Act for opposing World War I, including many Christians who followed Jesus' pacifism. These "subversives" earned twenty-year prison sentences for their dissent, all of which the Supreme Court upheld.[222] "What we had to have was no mere surface unity, but a passionate … white-hot mass instinct," wrote Creel, who was "fighting for the mind of mankind."[223]

During World War II the U.S. government jailed six thousand pacifists—mostly Christian ministers—and sentenced seventeen to death for their treasonous nonviolence.[224] According to the book *Conscientious Objectors and the Second World War*, antiwar Americans "had their eyes gouged to the point of severe injury; they were stripped and scrubbed with brooms [and] exhausted from forced useless labor; they were prodded with bayonets; they were dragged through latrines; they were chained, in solitary confinement, to the doors of their cells for nine hours a day; they were subjected to a stream of water from a fire hose held directly against their faces for two hours at a time."[225]

In the wake of 9/11 America followed this precedent. Authorities have arrested hundreds of liberal Christians for peacefully protesting outside the White House,[226] detained citizens—at the White House's behest—simply for wearing antiwar t-shirts,[227] spied on thousands of antiwar protesters,[228] threatened to revoke a church's tax-exempt status after a reverend said that Jesus opposed violence,[229] and banned critics of Republican policies—including Democratic Senator Ted Kennedy and Nobel Peace Prize winner Nelson Mandela—from traveling onboard commercial aircraft.[230] (They should have banned the boozehound Kennedy from getting behind the wheel of a car.)

In 2003 the California Anti-Terrorism Task Force blasted nonviolent protesters with rubber bullets and tear gas canisters. An official defended the tactics thusly: "If you have a protest group protesting a war where the cause that's being fought against is international terrorism, you might have terrorism at that protest. *You can almost argue that a protest against that is a terrorist act.*"[231] Not quite Thomas Jefferson's "dissent is the highest form of patriotism."

The Pentagon has developed a microwave gun that causes "intolerable pain in less than five seconds" and possibly skin cancer.[232] In 2006 the secretary of the Air Force recommended testing such a microwave weapon "on American citizens in crowd-control situations before being used on the battlefield."[233] King Retard proposed "for the good of the people" overturning an 1878 law that forbids the U.S. military to act as a domestic police force.[234] In 2006 the director of the CIA denied that the phrase "probable cause" appears in the Fourth Amendment,[235] and former Speaker of the House Newt Gingrich called for Congress "to limit freedom of speech to combat terrorism."[236] The following year Arizona, Oklahoma and Louisiana banned antiwar t-shirts.[237]

In 2004 Republican Senator Orrin Hatch claimed that terrorists "are going to throw everything they can between now and the election to try and elect Kerry,"[238] implying that half of American voters—and a long-serving American senator—were on the evildoers' side, just as a previous generation of Republicans accused all Democrats of harboring communist sympathies. (Which is unfair; only *half* of Democrats harbor communist sympathies.) Republican Senator Trent Lott, who lost his position as Senate Majority Leader after appearing to defend racial segregation, said that no citizen should "criticize [King Retard] while we are fighting our war on terrorism, especially when we have troops in the field."[239] In 2006 King Retard said that Democrats provide "comfort to our adversaries."[240]

Many Americans internalized this shameless fear-mongering and served as surrogate enforcers for the Republican Party:

- In 2004 Florida police arrested an eighteen-year-old Army enlistee who allegedly threatened to kill his girlfriend after she expressed support for the Democratic nominee. He allegedly held her at knifepoint, spat on her, and said, "You'll never live to see the election" as she screamed "no no no."[241]

Invasion Nation vs. Negotiation Nation:

- In 2004 Minnesota police arrested three high school students for allegedly brutalizing a seventeen-year-old with a baseball bat after he questioned their dedication to the Republican Party.[242]

- In 2005 a sixty-five-year-old Kentucky Republican killed his best friend for opposing the Iraq war. The man's daughter said, "It was just a political disagreement, like a whole lot of people have."[243] (The political disagreements that I have with my friends end with us forgetting about it over beers, not *murdering* each other.)

The executive branch has seized the power to search our mail and monitor our phone calls, but these invasions of privacy have failed to catch a single terrorist, according to the *New York Times*.[244] In 2005 Congress discovered that a Homeland Security division had violated federal privacy laws a quarter of a million times, and the FBI has—with the Attorney General's knowledge—committed many other violations.[245] In 2007 the Justice Department admitted conducting more than a hundred and forty thousand searches without securing warrants.[246] New airport X-ray machines reveal travelers' *genitals* to security screeners.[247] (Fun factoid: when *I* fly, the screeners need to use *extra*-large monitors.)

Who do we have to blame for this creepy voyeuristic techno-totalitarianism? *Nobody but ourselves.* More than a third of Americans, including half of Republicans, believe that the government should have the power to "randomly" search citizens' mail.[248] Thirty percent of Americans believe that "the U.S. government [should] have the authority to detain American citizens suspected of terror links without giving them access to the legal system."[249] A Republican congressman said that citizens who criticize this policy "hate America,"* and "I

---

* "I consider [trial by jury] the only anchor ever yet imagined by man, by which a government can be held to the principles of its constitution"—Thomas Jefferson, America Hater.

hope it's your families that suffer the consequences" of a terrorist attack.[250]

In 2006 a right-wing radio host suggested that "all Muslims in the United States should be identified with a crescent-shape tattoo or a distinctive arm band." One of his listeners countered: "What good is *identifying* them? You have to set up encampments like during World War Two with the Japanese and Germans."[251]

Thirty-five percent of Americans, including fifty-five percent of Republicans, condone torture of prisoners,[252] despite reports that our interrogators have tortured dozens of detainees to death,[253] forced them to dig their own graves,[254] kidnapped their wives,[255] and threatened to have their mothers raped.[256] An Army translator who witnessed two nights of interrogations committed suicide as a "protest."[257] (In 2008 ABC News reported that the White House had secretly approved the abuses for which officials had previously blamed "bad apple" soldiers.[258])

When *noble* soldiers exposed the abuses, Pentagon brass forced them to undergo psychiatric counseling, charged them with treason and publicly released their names for retribution.[259] Never mind that torture nearly always leads to false confessions, which causes the U.S. to waste money and manpower on foiling plots that never existed.[260]

However, King Retard insisted that "as long as the War Crimes Act hangs over [interrogators'] heads, they will not take the steps necessary."[261] Acting Attorney General Alberto Gonzales described the Geneva Convention as "quaint,"[262] proving that he is too fucking crazy to run a Taco Bell. How did this *pequeño loco* get the *Justice Department?*

September 1, 2004

"*This is what a police state looks like!*" the protesters chant as they march through Union Square Park. "*Show us what democracy looks like!*"

"You are committing disorderly conduct," a policeman says, readying his nightstick and riot shield.

"*What about free SPEECH?*" "*Go arrest [KING RETARD]!*" "*Go arrest [KING RETARD] for WAR crimes!*"

"You have to *remove* yourselves." The policeman slams hippies to the concrete with his shield. "Get the fuck out of the *way*, punks! *Move!*"

"*America is FALLING now!*" "*It's falling to the FASCISTS!*"

"If you use that microphone again, you'll be arrested for noise pollution."

"*The First Amendment!*" "*The FUCKING First Amendment!*" "*If you love killing people, you're a Republican!*" "*If you love SLAVERY, you're a Republican!*"

"What's *wrong* with you?" a protester shouts at an African-American policewoman. "How can you *wear* that uniform? What about Rosa *Parks?*" (The female officer appears befuddled.)

Many of the left-wingers are just as unhinged as the bloodthirsty apocalypse nuts at the Republican National Convention.

"*We can't build our society on Iraqi oil!*" a protester screams. "*No more BLOOD for oil and no more OIL in the FIRST place!*"

"What if we design cars powered by Iraqi *blood?*" I ask the protester—who has *no* sense of humor.

"*[King Retard] should've captured Osama bin Laden in 1998!*" another protester proclaims. "*He had the CHANCE in 1998 but he WAITED!*"

"Wasn't *Clinton* the president at that point?" I ask.

"Well ... yeah ... but it's still the *government*, man."

A twenty-three-year-old from New Jersey named Harry—who has ingested many, *many* intoxicants—wears a "FUCK [RETARD]" button.

"He might *not* be a liar but *all* politicians are liars," Harry articulates. "So we should go to war with the whole country—let's just fuck up the whole country. We're killin' innocent people. We're killin' children. We're killin' … killin' *everyone*. And people here were like, 'We're bombin' children, it's so much *fun*, we're bombin' *kids*, we're bombin' people who don't have *shit* to do with *anything*, it's so much *fun*.' What the *fuck*, man? We're … we're … we're *united*, and we fucking stand for *freedom*, but what the fuck are we *doing*? All the countries ahead of us are *against* us now! [King Retard], you're a *liar!* You're a *politician* and you *lie!*"

"Would you sleep with either of his daughters though?" I ask.

"*Hell* yeah," Harry grins. "The blonde one's fuckin' hot as hell. *That's* a question I can answer. Yes, I would fuck either of his daughters. What the *fuck*, man?"

Sixty-year-old Bill, a self-described "professional revolutionary for thirty years," claims to have protested every war since Vietnam in Union Square.

"What *is* a professional revolutionary?" I ask.

"Someone dedicated to basically achieving a new system based on human need, not private property," Bill explains. "While you were still in elementary school in August of '86,* under direct order of the Attorney General of the United States, I was forced to flee to the Soviet Union. … The U.S. government is waging economic war against its own citizens. *Why* are they doing this? To reduce the *population*—it's called Social Darwinism. Covert mass murder."

"Why would anyone *want* that?"

"The ruling class. All of history has been exploitation of one class over another: feudalism, slavery, capitalism. We need a socialist

---

* Actually I was in preschool. At least I look mature for my age.

revolution here in the United States. I'm a Leninist. All the social programs here in the United States owe their existence to the Soviet Union. ... I personally had previous knowledge of the Kennedy assassination by three months ... it was all *Nixon*, all the *capitalists*. After Watergate, all election decisions are decided in advance to prevent a workers' state—to prevent an *uprising*."

For someone who cares passionately about a workers' state, Bill looks suspiciously like he doesn't have a job.

A twenty-three-year-old protester named Travis wears a USSR t-shirt and covers the lower half of his face with a black mask.

"I love Russia," Travis informs me.

"New Russia or *old* Russia?" I ask.

"Both. Capitalism promotes war—it's *crap*italism."

Far more entertaining is a bearded giant of a man named Lawrence, who has a twinkle in his eyes and very few teeth.

"They know more than they're telling the public!" Lawrence bellows. "And NASA proves they cannot safely run the space system, and *they're* from Texas. ... The supernatural vibration of infinity is around us."

"Are you talking about God or—?" I try to ask.

"*No*, infinity *vibrates* causing energy, *creative* energy, the *Creator*, endless *thought* process. That vibration of *infinity* is all *around* us."

"You did a lot of acid in the Seventies, didn't you?"

"Oh yeah, I smoke marijuana two or three times a day. Marijuana allows your brain to better see the present moment beyond yourself. Oh, I've tried them *all.*"

"Did you check with your psychiatrist before you stopped taking the drugs that *he* gave you?"

"They put drugs in *your* brain—before they put the drugs in *my* brain, they set out to put the drugs in *their* brains. Radios, televisions, horns, bells, sirens—artificial *noises* put an artificial *vibration* into the present *moment*, denying people present access to supernatural *infinity* and also the vibrations of people *around* them."

Slightly more coherent, or so I believe at first, is a former U.S. soldier who says: "When I came home, I found out that two and a half million Iraqis died because of sanctions I enforced. This is a burden on my soul. … When we talk about nonviolence, we don't call it 'non-dark.' This stuff we're talking about is the *source*, and we need to rethink what it *means*. The term non-violence is a translation from *ahimsa*, another term for that is *satyagraha; satyagraha* is also translated as *soul force*. Now this idea of *force* is what I'm *talking* about." (What the fuck *are* you talking about?)

Another protester's poster explains: "ANARCHISTS WILL DESTROY ALL PRESIDENTS, PAST PRESENT AND FUTURE: MILLION WORKER MARCH—DEMAND $1,000/HOUR LIVING MINIMUM WAGE!"

A Pennsylvanian protester named Randy stands with a poster that proclaims "9/11 WAS AN INSIDE JOB," a belief that more than a third of Americans share.[263] "I think [King Retard] is the real terrorist actually," Randy says. "He's creating a lot of hysteria and paranoia." Yes, Randy, you should look into a mirror.

A vastly more articulate protester—perhaps the *only* articulate protester here—is Vietnam veteran Elliot Adams. "Emotionally the cost of war is immeasurable," Adams says. "More Vietnam vets have committed suicide since Vietnam than *died* in Vietnam. The number of Vietnam veteran suicides skyrocketed after the invasion of Iraq."

"Were you drafted back then?" I ask.

"I volunteered for the service, I volunteered to be a paratrooper, I *volunteered* to go to Vietnam. I was told my country needed me to save it from communism. … My country didn't need me to save it. … Vietnam is a hell of a way from the U.S. coast. Let's look at terrorism. Is terrorism a threat to the U.S., do you think?"

"According to the guy over there who says 9/11 was an inside job, it's not."

"Well, I don't buy that. You think terrorism's going to bring America down? Did 9/11 have any potential to bring America down? Not a chance in hell. Not a chance in *hell*. When we talk about people dying, twenty thousand people die every year in the United States from the flu. ... We had three thousand people die in the terrorist attacks. If you're talking about the threat of death, thirty thousand die a year in car accidents. Two hundred thousand die from smoking cigarettes. ... There's a huge parallel between Iraq and Vietnam in the sense that it has *nothing* to do with national security. ... Our militarism and our continued discretionary wars—it's a symptom of a much larger disease."

I've had enough of politics for the day—and for the rest of my life—so I spend the evening at a filthy dive bar instead of the RNC. On the bar's television, however, the vice president—who said in 1994 that invading Iraq would not be "worth ... very many" American lives, but changed his mind after gaining power—explains in his trademark Angry White Man growl: "Senator Kerry doesn't appear to understand how the world has changed. He talks about leading a 'more sensitive war on terror,' as though al-Qaeda will be impressed with our softer side."

Drunk from Jack Daniel's and depressed from this horrible crypto-Nazi bullshit, I force myself to read the 2004 Republican Party Platform, distributed to journalists at the RNC: "The freedom we enjoy also makes us vulnerable to attack ... Defense spending has only been higher twice since World War II ... These long-overdue budget increases help fulfill the President's commitments."

Before I lose consciousness in a pool of my own puke—which I attribute to reading the jingoistic RNC Platform, not pounding the whiskey—I scribble a few notes unworthy of publication: "... raped Iraq ... pregnant w/ terrorist babies ... bloody fucking miscarriage ..."

In the words of Ernest Hemingway: "I don't like to write like God. It is only because you *never* do it, though, that critics think you *can't* do it."

As the U.S. has degenerated from a democracy to a Dumbocracy, we have trained *eleven-year-olds* in soldiery through a program called the Junior Cadet Corps. These children "wear uniforms," learn the specifics of "rank, armed forces, leadership, drill presentation, flag etiquette,"[264] and overwhelmingly "hope to go into the military."[265] They "are promised a spot in JROTC," the Junior Reserve Officers' Training Corps—which claims more than tree hundred thousand cadets nationwide—as soon as they hit puberty. Parents love the program for teaching "discipline." One cadet's mother, when asked if she was concerned that her son might die in combat someday, replied: "No, I'm a big believer in God."[266]*

The Army receives $2 billion per year for recruiting,[267] and $95 million for advertising, ultimately spending $11,000 per recruit *before* Basic Training.[268] The Pentagon-developed online video game *America's Army*, "the Official U.S. Army Game," claimed more than four million registered players in 2004. A hundred thousand new users join per month. The Army spends $4.5 million per year to operate the game,[269] which American youths collectively play for a hundred and fifty thousand hours per day. These "kids" are "virtually *inside* the Army," says the project director. "Today's soldiers are gamers; it's a generational thing. … You could get a message that says guys that perform like you do in the game do really well in the Army."[270]

But the game contains little bloodshed and no dismemberment. A journalist who traveled with U.S. soldiers in Iraq wrote: "When

---

* An Arizona woman died from heart failure in 2004 after seeing her twenty-five-year-old son's corpse, freshly shipped home from Iraq. She obviously did not believe in God strongly enough.

Invasion Nation vs. Negotiation Nation:

they actually shot people, especially innocent people, and were confronted with this, I saw guys break down. The violence in games hadn't prepared them for this."[271] In 2006 a U.S. soldier described killing Iraqi insurgents: "I felt like I was in a big video game. It didn't even faze me, shooting back. It was just natural instinct. Boom! Boom! Boom! Boom! ... It didn't even seem real, but it *was* real."[272]

A lieutenant colonel gushed over the game: "This is a fantastic recruiting opportunity. We would like to sign up as many as possible."[273] A former official at the Marine Corps Warfighting Lab says: "Remember the days of the old Sparta, when everything they did was towards war? In many ways, the soldiers of this video game generation have replicated that ..."[274] A former West Point professor referred to games such as *America's Army* as "murder simulators which over time, teach a person how to look another person in the eye and snuff their life out."[275]

The official U.S. Marines website once proclaimed: "One must first be stripped clean. Freed of all the notions of self. It is the Marine Corps that will strip away the façade so easily confused with the self. It is the Corps that will offer the pain needed to buy the truth. And at last each will own the privilege of looking inside himself to discover what truly resides there. ... We came as orphans, we depart as family."[276]

What they *don't* tell you is that you might lose your fucking mind. Soldiers in combat situations are twice as likely to break down mentally as get killed.[277] An estimated one and a half million Vietnam vets suffer from Post-Traumatic Stress Disorder,[278] and thirty percent of U.S. troops returning from Iraq and Afghanistan likewise suffer from "anxiety, depression, nightmares, anger and an inability to concentrate."[279]

In 2007 the "overwhelmed" Army spent $33 million to increase its psychiatric staff by twenty-five percent,[280] but a third of troops believe that "seeking treatment would hurt their careers," according to the Associated Press.[281] The suicide rate for U.S. soldiers in Iraq is higher than the Vietnam figure,[282] and hit new records in 2007 and 2008.[283] A religious military officer allegedly remarked that those suicidal soldiers are "burning in hell."[284] Considering that U.S. soldiers are forbidden to drink, gamble, look at pornography, fuck anyone other than their spouses,[285] and have oral sex with anyone *including* their spouses,[286] it's easy to understand their motivations for self-destruction.

The average age of soldiers who are psychologically traumatized from warfare is nineteen.[287] Many veterans of the War on Terror are joining three hundred thousand other veterans in America's homeless shelters.[288] Thousands of young veterans must return their signing bonuses of up to $30,000 because they cannot mentally fulfill their commitments.[289] Many more troops are denied their subsidized college tuition because their deployments are "deliberately" a single day short of the two-year minimum.[290]

Veterans receive long-term federal health benefits only if they are declared more than thirty percent psychologically incapacitated,[291] a nebulous measurement, but sometimes the symptoms are rather obvious: killing strangers after firing randomly out the window;[292] raping a fourteen-year-old girl, killing her entire family and then burning the bodies;[293] abducting and killing a female college student;[294] and slashing a child "with a Samurai sword in front of neighbors."[295] In 2006 a nineteen-year-old Iraq veteran allegedly stabbed his wife "seventy-one times with knives and a meat cleaver" and then performed "indecent acts related to the mutilation of his wife's remains."[296] Perhaps he simply could not get used to lowering the toilet seat after returning from duty?

To reduce this kind of psychosis, Pentagon researchers are working on a pill that would create "Guilt-Free Soldiers." According to Dr. Leon Kass, chairman of the White House Council on Bioethics, "It's the morning-after pill for just about anything that produces regret, remorse, pain, or guilt."[297] A representative for Vietnam Veterans Against the War objects: "That's the devil pill. That's the monster pill, the anti-morality pill. That's the pill that can make men and women do anything and think they can get away with it."[298]

For a minority of soldiers, however, the Devil Pill is unnecessary. "In all my years in the army I was never taught that communists were human beings," said Army Lieutenant William Calley, convicted in 1971 for ordering his division to kill five hundred men, women and children in the Vietnamese village of My Lai. "We were there to kill ideology carried by—I don't know—pawns, blobs, pieces of flesh. ... We never conceived of old people, men, women, children, babies."[299]

In 2005 an estimated thirty thousand U.S. soldiers uploaded photographs of Iraqis' corpses and dismembered body parts to the Internet in exchange for free access to pornography.[300] The federal government charged none of the soldiers with violating the Geneva Convention, but instead arrested the website owner for distributing obscene materials. (*Not* the corpse photos—the *porno*.[301])

We need to capture or kill the terrorists who plot to kill us. No acoustic rendition of "Give Peace A Chance" will convince the theocratic butchers to leave us alone. But in defending ourselves, we must not become everything that we oppose. "The earlier [military] preparation begins, the better," said that wacky guy Adolf Hitler. "This is the expression of an authoritarian state—not of a weak, babbling democracy—of an authoritarian state where everyone is proud to obey."[302]

September 2, 2004

"Warmongers Go Home!" "Rednecks Not Welcome in NYC!" "How Do You Ask a Soldier to Be the Last One to Die for a Lie?" "We Support the Troops—When They Shoot Their Officers!"

A Republican activist confronts the antiwar protesters, who are lucky that the NYPD hasn't arrested them along with two thousand other peaceniks for the audacious crime of petitioning their government for a redress of grievances.[303] He stands beside a giant mound of sand and holds a poster that clarifies: "290,000 GRAINS OF SAND FOR 290,000 IRAQIS WHO DISAPPEARED UNDER SADDAM."

"This is *ignorance,*" shouts a young protester. "*Ignorance!*"

"I don't get it," says another leftist. "Like ... what's wrong with *peace,* you know?"

"*Lies!*" screams yet another, as if it were up for debate that Saddam Hussein was a monster.

Inside Madison Square Garden a bishop leads the opening prayer on the evening of King Retard's speech: "Blessed Father, in the name of Jesus, we come thanking you for the many blessings we have here in America. ... We pray today for the safety of the men and women in our armed forces who are protecting our freedoms and providing freedoms for others. ... We ask that you continue to provide strength to [King Retard] and the First Family. God, protect and grant wisdom to him as he leads America and the world against the Forces of Evil. And Father, your will be accomplished through this convention ... Amen."

Grammy-winning gospel singer Donnie McClurkin entertains the GOP faithful, which makes sense: McClurkin has reportedly referred to homosexuality as a "curse" and claimed that gay people are "trying to kill our children."[304]

General Tommy Franks, who orchestrated the Iraq war, receives a five-minute standing ovation. "Freedom is never free," Franks proclaims as Stars, Stripes and Fighter Jets flash across the video screen.

New York Governor George Pataki takes the stage. "I thank God that on September Eleventh, we had a president who didn't wring his hands and wonder what America had done wrong to deserve this attack,"

Pataki says. "He didn't run from history. He *faced* it. ... Some people have called this an abuse of power; I call it progress. ... He is one of those men God and fate somehow lead to the fore in times of challenge."

Madison Square Garden explodes with earsplitting, heart-stopping, reality-warping applause as King Retard approaches the podium, which is *a wooden cross adorned with the Presidential Seal.* Fifty thousand true believers lunge forward—crying, gasping, *enraptured*—and they are filled with the same fanaticism as the protesters outside: the same blind faith in their own righteousness, the same savage thirst for victory. Not against terrorism, not against tyranny, but against the *Other Side.*

To activists of the Left and Right, the War on Terror is only one tiny facet of the larger Culture War. The venomous polarization over our foreign policy is simply another excuse for their never-ending *game*, only this time our *lives* and our *world* are at stake. Anyone who truly cares for freedom *or* peace must either accept this manufactured mirage—our national scripted soap opera, our security projected through the lens of sensational entertainment, our democracy reduced to the intellectual vacuity of World Wrestling Entertainment—as an adequate substitute for reality, or keep his silence for fear of atrocious demagoguery from both camps. *You are either with the Islamo-fascists or the Amerikkka-fascists, but you cannot be with your conscience.* There is no "I" in U.S.A.

"Here buildings fell," King Retard says. "And here a nation rose."

No, the nation fell too, and for one horrible reason: the terrorists gave us an excuse to tear it down ourselves.

★ ★ ★

Terrorization Nation vs. Zionization Nation:

HIPPIES FOR HAMAS

★ ★ ★

Author's Note: The Israeli-Palestinian conflict drives people psychotic. It's an incomprehensibly complicated issue with no easy solutions, but activists on both sides view the situation in black and white—and blood red—instead of nuanced grayscale. For obvious reasons I have removed many identifying details from those interviewed hereafter. Call me a coward; you would too.

T hat's strange," I say to another Jewish reporter as I walk through a metal detector to enter the Palestinian conference. "The Arabs are screening *us* for bombs!"

Strange is the only word for this gathering of college-aged atheists who defend theocratic terrorists and demand "equality," but refuse to condemn Islamist death sentences for homosexuals because this qualifies as judgmental ethnocentric neo-colonialism. Or something.

It would take a million pages to explain the history of this region. A brief *summary* would take a thousand. Not many historical sources are unbiased anyway, so let's skip the past and assess the present: everyone seems to agree that peace in the Holy Land will majestically lead to peace on earth. The consensus is that a two-state solution is the best option, but extremists on both sides complicate the situation:

ultra-Orthodox Jews, who are powerful in Israeli politics, believe that modern Israel has a divine right to the land of *biblical* Israel—much of which Palestinians call home—and some are willing to assassinate liberal Israeli politicians who negotiate treaties with the opposition. Meanwhile the Islamist terrorist organization Hamas, the de facto ruling party in the Palestinian territories, slaughters Jewish civilians *and* members of the more moderate Fatah party, which was *formerly* a terrorist organization, but which now seeks a two-state solution, although it can't agree with Israel over possession of East Jerusalem, which both sides claim as their God-given capital, but which the international community doesn't recognize as belonging to either. Got that? Are the painkillers working yet? Is the noose snugly wrapped around your throat?

Neither the Israelis nor the Palestinians are going anywhere despite the blood-soaked fantasies of extremists from each populace, so the chaos continues. Numerous outside groups fan the flames in order to further their own agendas: right-wing American Christians who believe that violence in the region will hasten Jesus' return; Islamists from al-Qaeda to Iranian leaders who score propaganda points by bashing the Jewish State; a minority of American Jewish lobbyists and magazine editors who place Israel above all other issues and accuse even its mildest critics of anti-Semitism (contrary to conventional wisdom, only six percent of American Jews identify Israel as their number one priority; the vast majority focus on the economy, health care and U.S. national security, according to the *Nation*[305]); and unhinged left-wing loudmouths who blindly support guerilla warfare because it shocks their square bourgeois parents.

Case in point: an organizer of the Palestinian conference presently compares Zionism to Apartheid and decries "Israel's illegal occupation of Palestinian land." For someone with such fiery rhetoric, he is shockingly hesitant to talk specifics. I ask which *parts* of Israel he considers "occupied," since there is a huge difference between the West Bank and the entire *country*. The organizer coyly replies: "We have no official statement because that would be a political platform."

The conference has unofficial ties to an organization that sends American college students to disrupt Israeli military operations, and sometimes live with the families of Palestinian "freedom fighters," according to its travel coordinator. It denies having links to terrorist groups, but members *have* met with future suicide bombers responsible for killing and wounding numerous Israeli civilians. The leaders of this left-wing organization have defended Palestinian violence and compared Palestinian terrorists to America's Founding Fathers. How many children did George Washington randomly dismember?

Another conference organizer accuses Israel of "racist policies," but condemns pro-Israel students for criticizing Palestinian executions of homosexuals. Apparently it's none of their business.

Hundreds of college students, many of them non-Arab, wear checkered *kaffiyehs*—the headdresses that Palestinian leader Yassir Arafat popularized—and "FREE PALESTINE" t-shirts. A Muslim student tells me that many American college students wear the *kaffiyeh* as "a fashion statement," but have no idea "what it represents," which is "the struggle [and] resistance ... of the fighters or the kids throwing rocks," including all Palestinians from "bombers to young kids."

I ask the Muslim student if any tension exists between religious Arabs and atheistic socialists fighting for the Palestinian cause.

"No, I don't think there's any conflict at all," he says. "I'm religious myself, so there is this difference between myself and your average leftist, but that's never really conflicted. You meet at a common goal."

A non-Muslim conference attendee, who spent two weeks in the Palestinian territories over his summer vacation, shares this view. His interest in the Middle East grew after "reading Noam Chomsky," the famous leftist professor and best-selling author who believes that "the U.S is one of the leading terrorist states." Chomsky met with the "reasonable" terrorist organization Hezbollah in 2006,[306] and Osama bin Laden has praised him as "among one of the most capable of those from your own side,"[307] further explaining: "The interests of Muslims coincide with the interests of the socialists in the war against the crusaders."[308]

I ask the leftist student if it's strange taking the side of people who recently elected the murderous theocratic fanatics of Hamas.

"I don't really think there is a conflict there," the student says. "Amongst the Left, in a lot of the socialist groups in Palestine fighting for justice, underlying everything is fighting for Palestine. How you feel the best way to do that ... can be different, but underlying everything, everyone is united. ... Everyone is committed to peace and justice."

Not so much. This kid belongs to a college club whose president in turn belonged to a student organization whose chaplain "prepared" two of the 9/11 hijackers for "martyrdom," and has since fled the country.[309]

Orthodox Jews interrupt the conference and shout down the speakers. Security guards drag two of the protesters outside kicking and screaming. The audience applauds. "Your dissent has been noted," says a spokesman to much laughter.

A speaker claims to quote Gandhi: "If all the choices we had were between violence on the one hand and submission on the other hand, we would choose violence a thousand times over rather than submission." An Internet search for this quote yields no results, which isn't a surprise considering that Gandhi responded to occupation with *fucking pacifism.*

Another speaker, a university professor and self-described "socialist" who defends the use of "violence" in achieving Palestinian goals, receives applause for condemning "the terrorism of" the U.S.

and Israel. The professor then scoffs at the notion of creationism, which provokes no reactions from the young Muslims in religious garb.

I interview a middle-aged anti-Israel organizer who helps dozens of activists "in their twenties" travel to the Palestinian territories.

"We have stayed in homes that are targeted for demolition due to being families related to suicide bombers," the woman admits. "And they do not support non-violence … they supported their loved ones in the suicide bombing, but the Israelis do not have the right to come in the middle of the night and bulldoze their houses down."

In 2003 twenty-three-year-old activist Rachel Corrie died while trying to stop an Israeli bulldozer from demolishing a Palestinian home, which the Israeli army suspected concealed an underground bunker. She has become a hero for many passionate college-aged leftists. A Palestinian Hamas supporter believes that Corrie's "death serves me more than it served her," because she "will bring more attention than [Palestinian] martyrs."[310]

One of Corrie's admirers at the conference, a female college student who wears a "Living Wage" button on her jacket, says that even though "obviously I don't support terrorism," and "leaving aside their violence," Hamas has "done a lot for the Palestinian people," such as building "schools and hospitals" and "educating kids."* She rolls her eyes when I mention that the U.S. government designates Hamas as a terrorist organization. She says that Hamas is "a social-based organization." What kind of social life do *you* have, baby?

It's not only students who are unable to criticize bloodthirsty religious thugs from the undeveloped world; professors and administrators are just as obsequious to relativistic faddishness:

---

* In 2007 children's television in Hamas-controlled Gaza featured a version of Mickey Mouse that glorified violent jihad against Zionists for the impressionable little tykes. Educational!

- A director at UCLA said: "We're in no position to condemn a suicide bombing because none of us has experienced what they've been through under fifty-three years of oppression."[311]

- Norman Finkelstein, an academic who has held faculty positions at numerous prestigious universities, expresses "solidarity" with Hezbollah thusly: "People have the right to defend their country from foreign occupiers, and people have the right to defend their country from invaders who are destroying their country. That to me is a very basic, elementary and uncomplicated question."[312]

- Officials at San Francisco State University reportedly investigated and harassed conservative students for criticizing Hamas and Hezbollah.[313]

- An administrator at Florida Gulf Coast University forbade members of the academic community to display "Proud to be an American" stickers after 9/11 because these "could offend international students."[314]

- In 2006 administrators at a Colorado middle school forbade students to wear clothing with the U.S. flag or "anything that's patriotic,"[315] because this could "intimidate or offend others."[316] In 2007 a North Carolina high school implemented a similar policy.[317] An astute student asked, "If this country means freedom, then why can't we fly our own flag?"[318]

What does the future hold for this strange marriage of secular activists and Islamist militants?

Perhaps nothing: in 2005 an Israeli news service reported that Palestinians asked Israel to banish young left-wingers who had introduced "drug use and sexual promiscuity" to the local youth.

An Arab man said: "These anarchists come here and undermine the education we give our children. At first we took them in with hospitality—after all, they claimed they wanted to help us, so why kick them out? But very quickly they infuriated me with their lewd behavior."[319]

Of course, there is crazy bullshit on the other side: "One million Arabs are not worth a Jewish fingernail," said an ultra-Zionist rabbi in 1994.[320] Peace will never come to the Holy Land unless A) one side is dead, or B) both sides extinguish the flames of fundamentalism.

The Palestinians are in a shitty situation—much of which is their leaders' faults, much of which is not—but killing innocent civilians is never a justifiable reaction to objectionable circumstances; it's ludicrous that college-educated people are unable to perceive this. Yes, it's disgusting that right-wingers accuse all liberals of supporting terrorists, but *extreme* leftists who romanticize the most violent factions of Islamic society *are* traitors—if not to their country, then to liberalism itself.

By the way, the restrooms in the Palestinian conference building utilize waterless urinals in order "to protect and preserve the environment." The stink is unfathomable.

★ ★ ★

Moralization Nation vs. Intellectualization Nation:

THE DECLINE AND FALL
OF AMERICAN CIVILIZATION

★ ★ ★

"For the slave ... understands nothing but the tyrannous, even in morals. He loves as he hates, without nuance, to the very depths, to the point of pain, to the point of sickness ..." [321]

—FRIEDRICH NIETZSCHE

February 7, 2008

WASHINGTON, D.C. | It's unnecessary to ask for directions; the poster-sized photographs of splayed, blood-soaked aborted fetuses are a decent tip-off that I have arrived at the Conservative Political Action Conference. By the end of the day, after subjecting myself to hours of hysteria, I wish that my mother had vacuumed *me* out of the womb.

In 2005 I covered CPAC, the largest annual gathering of right-wing activists, politicians and college students, for *Playboy* magazine:

"The less virtue we have in our society, the more the need for government to control our lives," Republican Senator Rick Santorum tells hundreds of young conservatives. Hours later I'm hanging out with two CPAC attendees, Steve and Doug, at the debauched bar Coyote Ugly.

"If you want to fuck a girl in the ass, you can't *ask* for it," Doug explains. "You have to do it *subtle*. Get some saliva on your finger when you're fucking her in the pussy and slide it up her asshole, then press gently. She'll love it and after that she's open to *anything*."

"*Fuck* Rick Santorum—I'm getting laid tonight!" Steve yells, seemingly keeping this promise in the early morning after he climbs into a taxi with three brunettes from the George Washington University College Democrats. He can't remember the name of his hotel, so the three coeds— who describe themselves as "huge sluts" who "would totally get an abortion"—direct the cabbie to their dorm instead.

"So what if I'm a Republican?" Doug says. "I love sex and I hate family values. I'm never falling in love. ... You can get into Republican girls' pants but it's a challenge. You have to lay on the 'how are you doing?' and 'you're so beautiful' shit. Liberal girls are much easier."

Steve and Doug are two of many CPAC attendees who identify themselves as "party hard Republicans." But not every young Republican greeted me with open arms. A few luminaries, including Santorum, refused to speak with a reporter from *Playboy*. A student scolded me for representing a "smutty porno mag that should be banned." Another told me: "I believe in the Bible, not having fun."

The 2008 conference opens with a 1974 video clip of Ronald Reagan. This is definitely *not* the only invocation of the Gipper:

- The chairman of the American Conservative Union, which sponsors CPAC, proclaims that the GOP must return to Reagan's principles.

- Five old white men praise Reagan to the skies during a panel discussion. Every other word is "Reagan."

- Columnist Robert Novak explains that "Reagan is everybody's favorite president," and has "faded into the mists of myth instead of reality." Yes, Bob, this is called *idolatry.*

Republicans get themselves so insanely hard for this guy; it's like witnessing a vicious act of necrophilia. Why flog the dead horse when you can *fuck* it instead?

More speakers praise Reagan for rejecting moderate compromises and embracing "bold colors," not weakling "pastels." One speaker says: "Show of hands—who here voted for Ronald Reagan?" But a huge number of attendees are under twenty-five; the right-wing geezers don't realize that Reagan is a *relic of the past.* Their repeated summoning reeks of desperate, nostalgic impotence. If only these antiquated culture warriors *themselves* developed Alzheimer's and *forgot* ... uh ... President ... uh ... what's his name again? Who are you? Who am *I?*

The men in attendance nearly all wear American flag pins on their lapels, most likely fearing that otherwise they might appear as if they support our foreign enemies. They are either young, handsome Alpha Males or middle-aged, craggy-faced, grotesquely bloated Old White Men whose decades of disgust and hatred seep from their pores and permeate the air. You can *breathe* their bitterness.

However, the females at CPAC are overwhelmingly brunette, twenty-something and *gorgeous.* Say what you will about right-wingers; their chicks are *hot.* I'd love to invade their underground bunkers with a shock and awe campaign, if only they would surgically strike those pesky terror-spreading embryos.

The vice president delivers the first major address of the day and receives a passionate standing ovation. He accuses Democrats of surrendering to terrorists, defends "tough" interrogation techniques, demands retroactive immunity for telecommunication companies that helped the government spy on American citizens, and deftly implies that Iraq had something to do with 9/11. A friend of mine wonders aloud if the building management has checked the lightning rods lately; there is no way that God can tolerate this magnitude of bullshit.

The first exhibitor downstairs is the National Black Republican Association, which proclaims on a t-shirt: "Martin Luther King Was A REPUBLICAN." A woman behind the table goes on a rant about how "it was Democrats who started the Ku Klux Klan" and "it was Democrats who Martin Luther King was fighting," as if the political realignments of the civil rights era—Democrats becoming liberals on desegregation; Southern conservatives becoming Republicans—had never happened. This is like accusing modern Republicans of Nazism because their predecessors opposed American entry into World War II. (Modern Republicans are Nazis for a million *other* reasons.)

Merchants sell dozens of bumper stickers: "I Don't Believe the LIBERAL MEDIA," "Evolution is SCIENCE FICTION,"* "U.S. Out of the U.N.," "The Democratic Party: The Choice of the Communist Chinese," "Poverty will be eliminated when the stupid and lazy are eliminated," and "GOP: God's Official Party." Shirts and hats imply that mainstream Democratic politicians are Commie Traitors.

A woman who hawks pro-war comic books gives me her best sales pitch and asks if I'm a conservative.

---

* Science was never my best subject—in fact it was my *worst* subject—but unlike the majority of Republicans, I'll assume that scientists know more than I do.

"I'm with the media," I say, indicating that I am an objective observer.

"Are you with the *conservative* media?" she asks. "Or are you another shill for the *liberals?*"

(Fun Factoid: the woman's comic books are printed in black and white, not shades of gray. Appropriate!)

William Bennett, who served as Reagan's Education Secretary and Drug Czar—and lost millions gambling in Vegas despite his ceaseless lectures on the moral benefits of self-restraint—informs a CPAC employee that he is rooting for the St. John's University basketball team.

"Want to *bet* on it?" I blurt. Bennett stamps away.

Former Massachusetts Governor Mitt Romney chides Democrats for their "surrender" to terror. A male GOP attendee behind me keeps muttering: "Handsome guy ... handsome guy ... *such* a handsome guy ..."

Speaking of closeted Republican homosexuals, the toilets in the men's restroom are divided by walls—not stall doors—which makes Republican Senator Larry Craig's favorite seduction technique impossible. (Fun Factoid: at one point I considered spending the entire convention in the bathroom asking right-wing guys if they want to suck me off, but then I realized that they all would have said yes. A homosexual is a man who wants to have sex with other men; a Republican is a man who wants to have sex with homosexuals.)

A few activists hoist gigantic anti-immigration posters, one of whom rants into my voice recorder for ten minutes about Mexican colonization. I conclude the interview thusly: "Yo, I'm heading out for lunch—you want me to bring back Chipotle or Taco Bell?" (My Solution to the U.S.-Mexican Border Crisis: let everyone in Mexico cross the goddamned border if they have a bucket of fresh guacamole. Crisis Averted.)

There is so much palpable *anger* on display. A man sneers: "Prisons should not be *resorts*." A woman explains that she is "very, *very* angry about open borders and amnesty." Another woman growls, "The militant gays are *their* base." Check out the conservatives' reading material, which is distributed throughout the conference halls:

- A pamphlet titled "10 Reasons Why Abortion Is Wrong" lists the number one reason as "Abortion Offends God," and paves the way for "same sex 'marriage' and euthanasia."[322] (Pregnant gay people will get married and then kill themselves?)

- The magazine *Whistleblower* examines "Why So Many Americans Are Embracing Witchcraft" and "sexing each other in the moonlight while summoning spirits and casting spells." The magazine's publisher concludes that Christians must never practice yoga, but instead "serve like an occupying army of love and peace until Jesus comes back to reign as king."[323] (After this happens, can we still sex each other in the moonlight?)

- The Ohio Christian Alliance boasts that it helped ban slot machines statewide and is lobbying for a ban on human cloning. (Bonus Question: if you fuck your own clone, does it count as incest or masturbation?)

Other pamphlets and publications demand anti-evolution curriculums in public schools, defend the imprisonment of American citizens without trial, deny the existence of global warming, declare "JOE McCARTHY VINDICATED,"[324] disparage literary sexual content, and decry the "relentless effort to remove God from the public schools." (If God is omnipresent, *can* He be moved? Let alone *re*moved?)

Moralization Nation vs. Intellectualization Nation:

An activist stands by a knight's helmet. He says that the Modern World lacks "the whole order of principles and values that were established during the Middle Ages." A return to medieval times? Republicans? *Naaaah*.

A middle-aged conservative screams at a group of college-aged CPAC attendees: "Drugs will *never* be legalized! The government has a responsibility to maximize the potential of every citizen, which is not *possible* if people are numbing their brains with *narcotics!*"

He notices me transcribing his rant onto paper.

"Are you a *reporter?*" the Old White Man shouts. "Are you writing this *down?* You *better* not quote me!"

"No, this is the number of a guy who deals weed. He can help you mellow out."

"I have *never* smoked marijuana!" the man shrieks as the young students laugh. *"I will never smoke marijuana!"*

At five o'clock the next morning the doors open for King Retard's speech. He defends his decision to invade Iraq, trashes the Democrats, and says, "My energy is up, my spirit is high, and I will finish strong," which is most likely what all of these Republicans told their anonymous bathroom lovers last night.

Later in the day the CEO of the National Rifle Association bashes the Supreme Court over gun control. Unfortunately for irony, the metal detectors from this morning have been taken away.

A Republican congressman proclaims that Democratic candidates "work every day to promote abortion at home and abroad." (Yes, they trek across the globe with vacuum cleaners, hunting for preggos.) He explains that conservatives stand for "liberty and limited government," and then—without any irony—calls for a constitutional amendment to ban same-sex marriage. Apparently liberty is expendable when it's not "ordained by God," or at least your proctologist.

A right-wing writer, who wins a special CPAC award, says: "When's Reagan coming [back]? He is unlikely to show up for a generation …" Is this guy suggesting that Reagan is the *messiah?* Or a *zombie?* Or *both?*

Notorious ultra-conservative author Ann Coulter, who caused a media firestorm at last year's CPAC when she referred to former Democratic Senator John Edwards as a "faggot," signs her books, which contain profound, nuanced thoughts such as:

- "We should invade [Muslim] countries, kill their leaders and convert them to Christianity. … We carpet-bombed German cities; we killed civilians. That's war. And this is war."[325]

- "There are no good Democrats. … There is no plausible explanation for the Democrats' behavior other than that they long to see U.S. troops shot … They fill the airwaves with treason … Even Islamic terrorists don't hate America like liberals do. They don't have the energy. … Liberals are driven by Satan and lie constantly."[326]

- "I would like evolution to join the roster of other discredited religions …"[327]

- "Frankly, I'm not a big fan of the First Amendment."[328]

- "It would be a much better country if women did not vote. That is simply a fact."[329]

- Agreeing with the statement that "we should just throw Judaism away": "We just want Jews to be perfected … You have to obey laws. … That is what Christians consider themselves: perfected Jews."[330]

I'd love to ask Coulter for specifics on how to "perfect" myself—while carving through her uterus with a chainsaw—but the line to meet her is a mile long; Lucifer brought a dozen first editions for her to sign.

Students for Academic Freedom founder David Horowitz, a radical left-wing activist turned radical right-wing activist, instructs the audience: "When you see an Islamic fascist, call him that." (Sticks and stones may break their bones, but rocket-propelled grenades are slightly more effective.) He demands that moderate College Democrats "repudiate Hamas and Hezbollah," because—as everyone knows—wanting your grandmother to receive Social Security benefits means that you loathe the Jewish people.

Conservatives like Horowitz are obsessed with liberal professors taking over academia. So is the Islamist president of Iran, who said: "Today, students should shout … and ask why liberal and secular lecturers are present at the universities."[331] Sound familiar?

Author Dinesh D'Souza, whose book *The Enemy At Home: The Cultural Left and Its Responsibility for 9/11* infamously rationalized al-Qaeda's core beliefs, criticizes our "faith-based" belief in evolution, downplays the significance of the Salem witch trials, and questions whether the Spanish Inquisition "counts as a great historical crime."

Activists distribute a pamphlet suggesting that terrorist "training facilities" are located "across America … with thousands of trained members, ready to strike us in our homes, churches, synagogues—wherever we are." Furthermore, "the threat of an organized Islamic attack upon our schoolchildren" is something that should keep us up at night.[332] Kind of like how our schoolchildren have the boogeyman to keep *them* up at night.

Why should adults be any different?

What would Zombie Messiah Reagan do?

II.

PROHIBITION NATION

★ ★ ★

Introduction:

A TIRADE AGAINST PURITANISM

★ ★ ★

We were once the Home of the Free and the Land of the Brave. Now we're the Home of the Frigid and the Land of the Slaves.

Activists of the Left and Right, whose only pleasure is derived from depriving *others* of pleasure, have erected a Nanny State that forbids the enjoyment of anything. Our government spends zillions of dollars, and passes zillions of laws, to protect you from pornography, marijuana, alcohol, cigarettes and unhealthy food. Not only is this knee-jerk moral totalitarianism unnecessary, it often *exacerbates* the vice in question; forbidden fruit is far sweeter than mundane bullshit.

Am I a porn freak? No.

Am I a McDonald's glutton? No.

Am I a stoner? Not since college.

Am I a cigarette smoker? Not since tomorrow.

Am I a drunk whose every morning is spent hunched over the toilet, ejecting brown chunky filth from my gullet? Fuck you for asking.

The point is this: America is fast becoming a nation of boring, prudish, zero-fun *bitches*. We are subjected to massive propaganda campaigns and senseless police crackdowns thanks to political activists who have no use for freedom *of*, only freedom *from*.

You have a right to party. And it's time to fight for it.

★ ★ ★

Prohibition Nation vs. Masturbation Nation

★ ★ ★

"One of my objections to the Bible is that it contains hundreds of grossly obscene passages not fit to be read by any decent man."[1]

—BERTRAND RUSSELL

"The only thing pornography is known to cause is the solitary act of masturbation."[2]

—GORE VIDAL

Americans love pornography. We collectively spend $10 billion per year to watch naked adults in action, the same amount that we spend on wholesome family entertainment.[3] More than a third of American males and a fifth of American females are porn viewers, including seventy percent of teenagers.[4*]

This worries the self-appointed, self-righteous guardians of public morality. In 2004 the Republican-led Congress held hearings on "porn addiction," in which Christian "experts" compared naughty movies to heroin and demanded a multimillion-dollar public health campaign that would have alerted citizens to the "dangers" of whacking off.[5]

The past few years have seen a huge spike in anti-pornography fervor. Of course, anyone who exploits children deserves nothing less than castration by wolverines, but Republicans have prosecuted the distributors of mainstream pornography, which features consenting

---

* The Author does not need pornography; he has mirrors.

adults. Adult filmmakers, whom the U.S. government had left alone in the '90s, suddenly received $50,000 penalties and six-month jail sentences in the '00s.[6] Indecency fines rose from $48,000 to $8 million under GOP rule.[7] Congressional Republicans voted to increase obscenity penalties tenfold,[8] and snuck another increase into a *defense allocation bill* so that opponents would look like traitors.[9]

In 2004 a federal judge ruled that states can outlaw sex toys, and then scoffed at the notion of a "constitutional liberty interest in private sexual intimacy."[10] Attorney General John Ashcroft, who believes that Americans "have no king but Jesus," ordered Department of Justice staffers to cover nude statues with drapes.[11]

However, our elected leaders are not so innocent. When a high-class D.C. escort service threatened to reveal the names of its clients in 2007, federal authorities stepped in because the information—such as a Republican senator's phone number—was "sensitive."[12] Convicted of running a $2 million prostitution ring, the madam supposedly killed herself. (Fun Factoid: residents of Washington, D.C. "masturbate more than men anywhere else in the U.S."[13] Coincidence?)

Jesus Freaks would jeopardize our national security to rid America of smut. According to DOJ insiders, the "pursuit of smut-peddlers has supplanted other DOJ law enforcement activities—including anti-terrorism efforts—as the department's top priority."[14] A disgruntled FBI agent complained, "Honestly, most of the guys would have to [investigate] themselves."[15] In 2005 the Attorney General said that the War on Porn has "the same priority" as the War on Terror,[16] and fired U.S. attorneys who refused to prosecute obscenity cases.[17] Do the terrorists plan to crash giant *dildos* into our skyscrapers?!?*

The former chairman of the Federal Communications Commission, which rules on obscenity violations—and desperately wants to regulate cable television, satellite radio and Hollywood films

---

* Former New York Mayor Rudy Giuliani, who famously banned Manhattan's adult bookstores, boasted: "I took a city that was full of pornography and licked it to a large extent." Your prognosis, Dr. Freud?

in addition to broadcast channels[18]—described censorship as "fun."[19] His successor said, "You can always turn the television off and, of course, block the channels you don't want, *but why should you have to?*"[20] Never mind that ninety percent of American parents would rather set their own guidelines than have the federal government regulate TV programming.[21]

In 2007 the Public Broadcasting System censored a documentary on World War II because soldiers—gasp!—*cursed* in the midst of carnage. David Harsanyi, author of *Nanny State*, commented: "Does anyone else find it ironic that a film documenting the great sacrifices of freedom will have the words of the very men who fought for it edited out?"[22]

Our prudishness reaches comical heights. In late 2004 Washington legislators demanded that a barbeque restaurant remove a painting of pink cartoon pigs. According to the local Design Review Board, *"naked pigs might lead to paintings of naked people."* A BBQ-loving customer asked, "When was the last time you saw pigs with clothes on?"[23]

Censorial theocratic Puritanism is nothing new. In 1646 colonial Massachusetts forbade questioning the divinity of Jesus.[24] Even *after* the American Revolution many states imprisoned citizens who "maliciously reviled God or religion."[25]

Anthony Comstock, the U.S. Director of Censorship, burned twelve *tons* of "obscene books,"[26] including the works of Voltaire, Whitman, Hemingway, Remarque and Tolstoy.[27] Comstock, who believed that the Devil caused the "cancer" of pornography,[28] punished the distribution of obscene works with ten years of hard labor. "No sect nor class has ever publicly sided with the smut dealer," Comstock proclaimed, "except the infidels, the liberals, and the free-lovers."[29]

Propaganda claimed that masturbation caused "blindness, insanity, and other crippling conditions."[30] In the 1940s the U.S. Navy rejected enlistees who showed "evidence of masturbation," because this "would weaken the fighting spirit."[31] Half of medical school students in 1959 considered insanity a side effect of masturbation.[32] Psychotic parents forced their male children to wear "straps with sharp spikes that stabbed the penis if it began to become erect."[33] Doctors popularized circumcision to discourage masturbation, which is preposterous; I'm masturbating as I *type* this.

In the 1970s the Supreme Court ruled that individual communities can outlaw any speech, film or document that lacks "serious literary, artistic, political or scientific value."[34] A book offensive to Alabamans might *not* qualify as obscene in New York or Massachusetts. (Aren't *books* themselves offensive to Alabamans?)

President Richard Nixon, who believed that "pornography is to freedom of expression what anarchy is to liberty," created a task force to find links between XXX and crime. Two million dollars later the commission reported: "There is no warrant for continued government interference with the full freedom of adults to read, obtain or view whatever material they wish." The commission discovered that the majority of rapists viewed *less* pornography than the average American male and lived in *conservative Christian households*.[35]

Like every other Republican in history, Nixon preferred to live in his own reality, not the one that actually exists. He vowed to prosecute obscenity to the fullest extent of the law and condemned his own task force for its "public disservice," adding that "American morality is not to be trifled with."[36] His friend the Reverend Billy Graham condemned the commission's findings as "diabolical,"[37] blamed *Jews* for "all the pornography," claimed *Jews* held a "stranglehold" on America, and suggested that the White House "might be able to do something" about the *Jews*.[38] (Fun Factoid: Jewish people tend to read the *New York Times* weddings section for lurid voyeuristic pleasure, not *Hustler*.)

In the 1980s Ronald Reagan, the Republican Demigod, created *another* task force to find a link between pornography and crime.

The researchers failed to discover a connection, but the final report nevertheless urged the prohibition of pornography, sex toys and lovemaking guides for *married* couples.[39] A Catholic priest who advised the task force later used charitable funds to pay for young male prostitutes.[40] (Since when do priests *pay* to molest people? Not including out-of-court settlements.)

Leading anti-pornography crusader Tim LaHaye, author of the multimillion-selling *Left Behind* novels that modernize the Book of Revelation, proposes "an amendment to our federal Constitution" that would "protect us from this plague."[41]* LaHaye explains: "Boys particularly need to steer clear of anything visually inflammatory" because "they should be channeling their energies into academic and athletic interests or learning to work with their hands ..."[42] How *else* will they learn to *"work with their hands"?!?*

But it's not only right-wingers who can't stand the sexual pleasure of their fellow citizens. In 1984 (appropriately) radical feminists Catherine MacKinnon and Andrea Dworkin, who said that "there is no free speech and there never will be,"[43] pressured Indianapolis, Indiana legislators to ban *any* book, film, play or speech that a *single woman* reported to authorities as offensive. The ordinance stipulated: *"It is irrelevant ... whether the work has literary, artistic, political, or scientific value."* According to MacKinnon, who believes that "heterosexuality ... institutionalizes male sexual dominance and female sexual subversion" and "feminism stresses the indistinguishability of prostitution, marriage and sexual harassment"[44]:

- "If a woman is subjected, why should it matter that the work has other value?"[45]

---

* LaHaye and his wife graduated from Bob Jones University, which prohibited inter-racial dating until 2001, nearly four decades after the passage of the Civil Rights Act. Masturbation? *No!* White Supremacy? *Yes!*

- "The First Amendment absolutist position is very different from this position … the free speech of men silences the free speech of women."[46]

- "If pornography is part of your sexuality, then you have no right to your sexuality."[47]

- "The law of equality and the law of freedom of speech are on a collision course in this country."[48]

MacKinnon and Dworkin ridded Indianapolis bookstores, schools and libraries of such "pornography" as James Joyce's *Ulysses* and Homer's *Iliad*, which "both depict women as submissive objects for conquest and domination." The ordinance banned any photograph or film in which "women's body parts—including but not limited to vaginas, breasts, and buttocks—are exhibited,"[49] even if adults "consented to a use of the performance," "showed no resistance," "signed a contract," and were "paid or otherwise compensated."[50] In other words, *women had no freedom to make decisions about their own lives or bodies, which is the entire point of feminism.*

MacKinnon described Indianapolis as "a place that takes seriously the rights of women,"[51] but a higher court struck down the ordinance for violating the First Amendment. In the 1990s MacKinnon and Dworkin convinced Canadian legislators to pass a similar law; the first books that Canadian authorities seized were *Dworkin's,*[52] for her sexist proclamations such as:

- "Under patriarchy, every woman's son is her potential betrayer and also the inevitable rapist or exploiter of another woman."

- "Hatred of women is a source of sexual pleasure for men in its own right."

- "Violence is male; the male is the penis. ... What the penis can do it must do forcibly for a man to be a man."

- "In my view, rape is simply a matter of access. There is no qualitative distinction about men here. ... Men will rape women to whom they have access."

- "[S]ex and murder are fused in the male consciousness, so that the one without the imminent possibly of the other is unthinkable and impossible ... their DNA, in order to perpetuate itself, hurls them into murder and rape."[53]

According to the Ms. Foundation's Gloria Steinem: "In every century, there are a handful of writers who help the human race to evolve. Andrea is one of them."[54] If *that's* evolution, perhaps we should reconsider the merits of taking Genesis literally.

In 2004 students at Rutgers University received gender studies class credit for helping to ban a weekly campus news publication after it published artful nude photos. The student editor said, "When I found out this was part of a class, I thought, 'How can a teacher be encouraging something that is against the Constitution?'"[55]

According to *Ms.* magazine editor Robin Morgan, "Eighty-five percent to ninety percent of the feminist movement is involved in one way or another in the feminist campaign against pornography."[56] She proclaims, "Pornography is the theory, rape is the practice."[57] In Dworkin's words, "Pornography reveals that male pleasure is inextricably tied to victimizing, hurting, exploiting."[58] This is clearly bullshit:

- The U.S. National Research Council concluded that "empirical links between pornography and sex crimes in general are weak or absent."[59]

- The director of a sex-offender program in Connecticut admitted: "Pornography does not cause rape; banning it will not stop rape. In fact, some studies have shown that rapists are generally exposed to *less* pornography than normal males."[60]

- A doctor who works for the Child Sexual Abuse Treatment Program in Santa Clara, California says: "In contrast to common belief, a great number of men who turn to their children for sexual purposes are highly religious or morally rigid individuals who feel that this is 'less of a sin' than masturbation ..."[61]

The myth persists: the National Organization for Women declared in a press release, "NOW believes pornography violates the civil rights of women and children ... pornography harms women and children."[62] Is this the same NOW that directed funds to the legal defense of Andrea Yates, a Texas woman who *murdered* her five children?[63] (NOW President Patricia Ireland explained that Yates was the victim of a "patriarchal society" in which "women are imprisoned at home with their children."[64])

In 2007 a Democratic New York City lawmaker introduced a bill "making it illegal to look at someone's genitals without permission,"[65] as if every XXX video should come packaged with a signed legal release. The feminist author of *Against Pornography* defines the simple act of *viewing* erotic materials as "visual rape."[66]

However, only one in three thousand pornographic images contains violence, which is overwhelmingly directed toward *men*.[67] A journalist who interviewed a hundred and fifty male porn viewers concluded that the vast majority "do not find violence against women or domination of women sexy," and "are specifically turned off by such behavior."[68] For many of these men, masturbation is simply a relaxant "to rest, nap, or turn in for the night."[69]

These men's girlfriends and wives reported *enjoying* the sexual techniques depicted in porn.[70] According to a professional marriage counselor, "[I]t is common knowledge in my field that sexually explicit films and videos are often recommended as a mode of treatment for couples … with clinical sexual problems."[71] Earth to Republicans: porn *saves* marriages! No *wonder* feminists hate it.

Porn also saves *lives:* Australian researchers discovered in 2003 that men who masturbate five times per week are a third less likely to develop prostate cancer.[72] The fountain of youth tastes like salt water.

And get *this*, radical feminists: porn prevents *rape*. In nations where pornography is illegal, far more women are sexually assaulted; in nations where pornography is *legal*, rape transpires far less often.[73] After the Danish decriminalization of pornography in 1969, rates of sexual assault and child molestation plunged six hundred percent.[74]

It's the same story in the United States: "A 10 percent increase in Net access yields about a 7.3 percent decrease in reported rapes," according to a Clemson University researcher.[75] The Internet's hundreds of millions of pornographic websites did not exist before the 1990s, but since then sexual assault has subsided by more than seventy percent in the U.S.[76] Men are simply too busy masturbating to bother.

The fact is that Republicans' foreign policy is far more harmful to kids than their parents' naughty movies: the American Medical Association concluded that children in military families are forty-two percent more likely to experience abuse if their parents are deployed overseas.[77]

Whereas our troops fight for freedom, extremists on the Left and Right have more in common with the forces of tyranny:

• The Saudi king warned newspapers not to print *any* photographs of women because this could make young men horny.[78]

- Chinese authorities jail pornographers for life due to their "bad effect on youth and society."[79]

- Palestinian terrorists have bombed dozens of Internet cafes in the Gaza Strip for "keeping Muslims away from prayer and providing pornography."[80]

- Al-Qaeda in Iraq "dispatched one of their men to a local cinema with orders to blow it up because it was showing pornographic films," according to the *Atlantic*.[81]

The Ayatollahs of Iran execute pornographers, which "hardcore" activists of the Left and Right would love to do, but it turns out that human beings will risk their lives for sexual freedom. An Iranian teenager explains: "People have learned to do everything they want in society behind closed doors. We are human beings. It's natural."[82] Perhaps the U.S. military should airdrop tons of pornographic videos over the entire Middle East in order to win hearts and minds?

Liberation by masturbation!

★ ★ ★

Prohibition Nation vs. Intoxication Nation

PART ONE:
MARIJUANA

★ ★ ★

"The only power any government has is the power to crack down on criminals. Well, when there aren't enough criminals, one makes them ... you create a nation of law-breakers—and then you cash in on guilt."[83]

—AYN RAND

"It grows naturally upon our planet. Doesn't the idea of making nature against the law seem ... a bit unnatural?"[84]

—BILL HICKS

The U.S. government spends nearly $8 billion per year on anti-marijuana enforcement—it was less than a billion twenty years ago[85]—and jails half a million Americans for drug-related offenses,[86] more than the number imprisoned for *all* crimes in 1970.[87*] Police arrest nearly eight hundred thousand citizens per year for possession of marijuana,[88] more than the number arrested for murder, rape, robbery and assault combined.[89] This costs another $8 billion in legal expenses.[90]

Holy shit, man, we are *wound up.*

---

* According to a February 28, 2008 Associated Press story, one in every ninety-nine Americans is behind bars, a higher rate—and higher number at 2.3 million—than any other nation's prison population.

The Drug Enforcement Agency mocks the notion "that drug users are essentially normal people,"[91] but forty percent of American adults—including our presidents, congressmen and governors—have smoked marijuana.[92] More than half of Americans believe that it's no more harmful than alcohol;[93] more than sixty percent believe that it should be decriminalized;[94] more than eighty percent believe that doctors should have the ability to prescribe it for medical reasons.[95]

This country owes its *existence* to marijuana: colonial Virginia *required* "every household to grow" hemp for its shipbuilders. (Today the state punishes possession of a single marijuana plant with three decades in jail.[96]) Presidents George Washington and Thomas Jefferson cultivated ganja,[97] and Benjamin Franklin must have rolled a humongous blunt every morning. During World War II the U.S. government initiated the "Hemp for Victory" campaign, *begging* farmers to replace their crops with cannabis.[98] Is it any wonder that M&Ms were first sold in the 1940s?

But this changed when professional fear-mongers rose to power while everyone else was too stoned to notice. Between the 1930s and 1960s the U.S. Bureau of Narcotics warned that marijuana "consumed over any period of time, drives the user insane,"[99] and "gives man the lust to kill, unreasonably and without motive."[100] In 1943 a Tulsa prosecutor argued that marijuana gives otherwise law-abiding citizens "courage to kill," especially when the reefer is "mixed with tobacco …"[101] A Texas policeman said that marijuana led to a "lust for blood" and "superhuman strength," while "transforming healthy teenagers into sex-crazed maniacs."[102]

Leaving aside the fact that teenagers are *already* sex-crazed maniacs, the truth is that stoners are too docile to harm anyone. The New York Police Department's crackdown on marijuana smokers in the '00s caused no reduction in violent crime.[103] Smokers are just as likely as nonsmokers to hold full-time jobs; Americans who earn double the average national salary are far more likely to use marijuana.[104]

A 2002 Canadian government study concluded: "cannabis use presents no harmful consequences for physical, psychological, or social well-being in either the short or the long term."[105] The journal *American Psychologist* found that "adolescents who had engaged in some [marijuana] experimentation were the best-adjusted," and teenagers who "never experimented with any drug were relatively anxious, emotionally constricted, and lacking in social skills."[106] A 2007 Swiss study of five thousand teenagers concluded that those who smoke marijuana are "more socially driven," "significantly more likely to practice sports," "have a better relationship with their peers," "have the same level of good grades," and "are not more likely to be depressed."[107]

You would never know this from public service announcements that cost American taxpayers billions of dollars. These anti-drug commercials blame marijuana for bad grades, suicide, and even the transmission of HIV.[108] A Reagan Administration official believed that marijuana "leads to homosexuality … and therefore to AIDS."[109]

In 2006 the U.S. Government Accountability Office concluded that the anti-weed marketing campaign had generated zero "significant favorable effects," and *more* teenagers were "trying the drug after seeing the ads." The GAO recommended ending the campaign; the White House demanded "another $120 million for next year."[110]

In 2002 the White House Office of National Drug Control Policy, which admitted that it wasted $3.3 billion on "failed" programs,[111] declared that "legalization would be a nightmare," not only because "marijuana and violence are linked," but because it's "a gateway drug."[112] However, Americans are fifty times more likely to use marijuana than cocaine and six hundred times more likely than heroin.[113] The vast majority of smokers have never tried any other illegal drug.

Actually the *drug war* is more of a gateway drug: random drug tests in public schools have reportedly caused students to "switch from use of cannabis … that can be traced a relatively long time after use, to drugs that are cleared from the body much more quickly, including heroin,"[114] and "household chemicals" such as "glue and paint."[115]

Eighty-nine percent of American high school seniors in 1982 said that obtaining marijuana was "easy." Two decades later, after billions of wasted dollars, this figure *remained* at eighty-nine percent,[116] despite the fact that in 1998 Republicans in Congress "vowed to make America virtually drug-free by 2002."[117] The irony is that *decriminalization is apparently the most effective deterrent.* Just as the Danish legalization of pornography led to widespread "boredom" with dirty movies,[118] the Netherlands' 1976 curtailment of marijuana enforcement led to a huge decline in usage; only eight percent of its teenagers smoke weed.[119] (Most of the stoned people in Amsterdam are probably American tourists, or at least they were before the U.S. dollar collapsed like a *High Times* subscriber running from the law.)

In our crusade to exterminate the Evil Herb, we have significantly lowered our quality of life *and* death:

- The U.S. government forbids AIDS sufferers to smoke marijuana even though cannabis relieves symptoms in seventy-two percent of test cases, according to the medical journal *Neurology.*[120]

- The doctor of a California woman with a brain tumor said that marijuana was "the only medicine keeping her alive," but a federal court nixed her prescription. "If she obeys the law, she will die," explained the woman's lawyer.[121] That same year a Montana woman took her own life because she could not get a prescription, leaving a note that said: "Give me liberty or give me death."[122]

- Former New York Governor Eliot Spitzer refused to decriminalize marijuana for hospital patients who had terminal diseases even though he admitted to personal use.[123] In 2008 Spitzer resigned after fucking a hooker despite jailing plenty of people as attorney general for doing the same.

The Supreme Court ruled that federal authorities could apprehend patients in states that have legalized medical marijuana.[124] The majority of Americans oppose this draconian bullshit, but we live in a Dumbocracy, not a democracy. Even the American Association of Retired Persons called for legalization in its official magazine.[125] ("Hey Grandma, do you like my gravity bong?")

Why *wouldn't* the elderly want to blaze? In 2005 Swiss researchers discovered that cannabis "protects blood vessels from dangerous clogging" and "could lead to new drugs to ward off heart disease and stroke."[126] That same year Canadian researchers found chemicals in cannabis that serve as powerful antidepressants,[127] and increase memory capacity,[128] which could prevent the onset of Alzheimer's.[129] (Fun Factoid: President Reagan, Alzheimer's sufferer in his final decade, considered marijuana "the most dangerous drug in America today."[130])

Nevertheless former Speaker of the House Dennis Hastert, a Republican who lacks a medical degree but knows better than those who do, pronounced, "There is absolutely no sound scientific evidence that marijuana has any medicinal value."[131]

Complications from *legal* prescriptions kill a hundred thousand Americans per year and injure two million more.[132] The sedative Ritalin, which millions of American parents feed to their children, can reportedly cause "hallucinations that usually feature insects, snakes or worms."[133] The World Health Organization blames alcohol and tobacco, which are legal and taxed in the U.S., for a tenth of all deaths worldwide.[134] What harm does marijuana cause? Excessive Taco Bell consumption?

In the Bizarro World of Republican fascism, stoners are *terrorists*, prosecuted under the post-9/11 PATRIOT Act.[135] A Republican congressman has suggested padding drug charges with *support for terrorism*, even though "the government need not prove that the defendant knew that ... a designated foreign terrorist organization" profited from the sale.[136] However, Congress has repeatedly blocked legislation that would require *congressmen* to undergo drug tests.[137]

In 2002 the DEA exhibit "Target America: Drug Traffickers, Terrorists, and You" juxtaposed wreckage from the World Trade Center with photographs of stoners. *Reason* magazine editor Nick Gillespie summarized the exhibit's message thusly: "If you've smoked a joint, then you are implicated in one of the most horrific mass murders in world history. If you are against the drug war, then you are for the terrorists."[138]

But if the terrorists hate our freedom, as the GOP propaganda machine reminds us every day, they should *love* the War on Drugs. A drug-free America is a *freedom*-free America:

- Police officers have accidentally killed dozens of citizens in the last decade—including children, college students and grandparents—while raiding homes for drugs, often mistaking one address for another.[139] In 2003 the Supreme Court unanimously sanctioned these lethal "no-knock" raids, which police currently perform fifty thousand times per year.[140] (No surprise that they end in bloodshed; the chief of the Los Angeles Police Department said that casual drug users "ought to be taken out and shot" for "treason."[141])

- Police officers armed with submachine guns stormed through a South Carolina high school in 2003, forced all the students to lie facedown on the floor, searched everyone with drug-sniffing dogs and handcuffed any teenager who failed to comply "quickly enough." The officers found no drugs. A class-action lawsuit resulted in a $1.6 million settlement. However, the school principal refused to apologize: "I'll utilize whatever force I deem necessary to keep this campus safe and clean," the administrator boasted,[142] neglecting to mention that it already *was*.

- A 2006 congressional measure required *all* public schools to perform random drug tests in exchange for vital federal funding.[143] However, a two-year study by the *Journal of Adolescent Health* found that random testing has absolutely no effect on teenage drug use. Students actually partake in "greater risk-taking," possibly because they assume that they will get caught anyway.[144]

- Eighty-five percent of youths arrested for marijuana possession are racial minorities, but whites smoke the same amount per capita.[145]

- The U.S. forbids foreigners—including Canadians—to cross the border if they publicly admit to illegal drug use, even if it occurred *forty years ago*.[146]

- The White House wants to expand U.S. marijuana laws to cover traces in citizens' bloodstreams, not simply on their persons. When Sweden passed a similar law, police demanded a "tenfold increase in blood samples" from the populace.[147] (In 2008 the United Arab Emirates sentenced a British tourist to four years in jail over "a microscopic speck of cannabis stuck to the bottom of one of his shoes."[148])

- In 2005 the Supreme Court ruled that police could search citizens' garbage for evidence of drug use even if there is no "specific suspicion of illegal activity."[149] We don't require warrants for U.S. citizens suspected of terrorist sympathies; why require warrants for anyone else?

- In 2006 the federal government tested citizens' *sewage* for traces of cocaine.[150] That same year the Wisconsin Supreme Court ruled that forcing suspects to consume laxatives—in order to find drugs in their digestive tracts—does not qualify as an "unreasonable search."[151] Hey, the War on Drugs *is* shitty!

In the 1990s a Republican congressman proposed requiring the death penalty for all drug dealers. When police arrested his son for growing thirty marijuana plants, the boy received community service, not lethal injection.[152]

The hypocrisy never ends: Legalized reefer would provide the U.S. with an estimated $32 billion in tax revenues,[153] but the Partnership for a Drug-Free America—one of the most powerful special interests in the country—is sponsored by "manufactures of cigarettes, beer, coffee and tranquilizers,"[154] according to author Jacob Sullum, who explains: "A drug-free America is the last thing these companies want to see."[155]

Such a total bummer, man ...

What were we talking about?

★ ★ ★

PART TWO:
ALCOHOL

★ ★ ★

"The last thing the world needs is more drinkers, even moderate ones."[156]
—THE CENTER FOR SCIENCE IN THE PUBLIC INTEREST

"Alcohol may be man's worst enemy but the Bible says love your enemy."
—FRANK SINATRA

The failure of our War on Drugs should not surprise anyone who has studied Prohibition. In the early twentieth century a coalition of Jesus Freaks and freedom-hating socialists lobbied for a constitutional amendment to ban alcohol. The Christian fundamentalists hated physical pleasure of any kind; the latter wanted to improve the life of the common man by taking away the only thing that made it tolerable.

Jesus Freak lawyer William Jennings Bryan, who prosecuted a Tennessee schoolteacher simply for discussing evolution, compared "winning World War I to winning the national fight against alcohol."[157] Even the *Ku Klux Klan* demanded "obedience of state and national prohibition laws."[158] (Who else would prefer hangings to hangovers?)

Prohibition led to organized crime, the deaths of thousands from poisonous bootleg liquor, the arrests of thousands more, and

ultimately an amendment to overturn the original amendment.
Everyone realized that alcohol is wonderful. End of story, right?
Not so much:

- In 2005 the DEA proclaimed that "Prohibition *did* work" and
  "[a]lcohol use … causes major problems."[159]

- In 2006 a DEA administrator explained: "You only need to look
  at Prohibition to see that criminalizing an activity suppresses it,
  and legalization increases it."[160]

- The chief of the DEA in the 1990s said that adults who drink a
  single glass of alcohol are "not too smart."[161]

The U.S. government spends $14 million per year on anti-alcohol
public service announcements, $71 million per year to combat
teenage drinking, and $243 million to research the hazards of booze.
Local authorities spend tens of millions more.[162] In the past few
years several U.S. states and cities have banned advertisements for
alcoholic beverages, drastically hiked taxes on alcohol,[163] banned the
importation of wine,[164] outlawed *singing* while drinking[165] and *dancing*
while drinking,[166] investigated a bar for serving *frozen* drinks,[167]
ordered airlines to "cease and desist" serving drinks to passengers,[168]
and criminalized the sale of beer and liquor to *adults* "in an effort to
stop teenagers from drinking …"[169]

In 2005 Seattle legislators criminalized the sale of *cheap* beer to
save the poor from themselves.[170] The Russian government instituted
a similar ban on cheap vodka a year later, which resulted in dozens
of deaths and thousands of hospitalizations from the consumption of
"bootleg liquor laced with brake fluid, lighter fuel, disinfectants and
other poisonous agents."[171]

In 2003 and 2005 Virginia and Texas police officers, wearing "paramilitary" uniforms, raided more than twenty bars and arrested every patron inside who had consumed more than a single drink, even if they were adults and had no plans to drive.[172] An executive from Mothers Against Drunk Driving said: "In our view, law enforcement is doing its job. We consider [the] police to be everyday heroes."[173] Another MADD representative said: "A lot of people think it's OK to be drunk in bar, but it's illegal. ... Even after one drink, you aren't 100 percent."[174]

A spokeswoman for the Texas Alcoholic Beverage Commission defended the arrests—and by extension the "pre-crime" detectives of Philip K. Dick's dystopian *Minority Report*—because *some* of the drinkers "*might* have tried to drive."[175] This is an interesting legal precedent considering that anyone "might" try to do *anything*.

The founder of MADD says that the organization "has become far more neo-prohibitionist than I had ever wanted or envisioned," adding that "I didn't start MADD to deal with alcohol; I started MADD to deal with the issue of drunk driving."[176] The lady has a point:

- In 2000 MADD convinced Congress to withhold millions of dollars in federal funds from states that legally define intoxication as occurring after the consumption of approximately two drinks. But the vast majority of drunk drivers who cause fatal crashes have consumed around *nine* drinks.[177] Enforcing the lower limit costs taxpayers an extra $20 million per year.[178] A Massachusetts legislator who supported lowering the limit even further in 2008 is conveniently a "DWI (driving while intoxicated) defense attorney in private practice."[179]

- The National Highway Traffic Safety Administration, which works closely with MADD, has proposed a *single* drink limit,[180] an absurdity that Washington, D.C. police enforced in 2005.[181] "There is no safe blood alcohol level, and for that reason responsible drinking means no drinking," said MADD's president.[182]

- A MADD television advertisement declared: "If you think there's a difference between heroin and alcohol, you're dead wrong."[183]

- In 2007 a Florida sheriff's deputy—whom MADD honored for busting drunk drivers—was fired for allegedly jailing nearly sixty people who were not actually intoxicated.[184] A MADD representative earlier said, "I believe that most people would not mind the slight inconvenience of being arrested for a low blood-alcohol level, given the opportunity to prove their innocence … "[185]*

- The American Institute for Philanthropy has ranked MADD as one of the most corrupt and least effective charities in the country.[186]

For all its finger-wagging and moral posturing, MADD is *responsible* for drunk driving: the organization refuses to "support the use of personal alcohol tests to assist a driver in making decisions about his or her ability to safely operate a motor vehicle," according to an official position statement.[187] In 2003 a MADD official condemned free bus services that take drunks home because "[t]he fact that it's taking them to … drink in the first place is problematic."[188]

---

* This draconian attitude is common for activists who believe in collective punishment. The assistant dean of student life at Vassar College claimed "that men who are unjustly accused [of rape] can sometimes gain from the experience," according to the June 3, 1991 issue of *Time*, and added: "I think it ideally initiates a process of self-exploration. 'How do I see women?' 'If I didn't violate her, could I have?' 'Do I have the potential to do to her what they say I did?' Those are good questions." She said that wrongly accused males "have a lot of pain, but it is not a pain that I would necessarily have spared them."

That same year MADD scolded the Arizona Department of Public Safety for distributing thirty thousand "Alcohol Test" strips to teenagers so they could gauge whether they were too drunk to drive.[189] Even though such a sensible policy "may prevent death and injury on the road," said the president of MADD, "it sends a dangerous message to teenagers that it's okay to break the law."[190] Never mind that seventy percent of American teens *already* drink.[191] (MADD should get together with the equally unrealistic anti-condom crowd; unprotected sex at ninety miles per hour—on the wrong side of the road—is *amazingly* safe.)

The War on Booze, like the War on Drugs, leads to "death and injury" for the Bill of Rights:

- In 2006 the California Supreme Court ruled that authorities could break into citizens' homes at any time—without a warrant—in order to check their blood-alcohol levels.[192]

- A Washington law stipulated that if a citizen wished to challenge a Breathalyzer result, the trial must be held "in a light most favorable to the prosecution,"[193] contrary to the entire Western legal tradition. This was later ruled unconstitutional.

- A Seattle newspaper reported in 2007 that dozens of the city's policemen regularly drove drunk without fear of punishment.[194] A Los Angeles newspaper reported in 2008 that police rarely bust "thousands of public employees" for traffic violations because of special license plates that serve as a "signal that the drivers are 'one of their own' or related to someone who is."[195]

- The 2006 Defense Appropriations Bill for the War on Terror included $3.5 million for Breathalyzers.[196] Is Congress unaware that Islamist terrorists bomb Arab liquor establishments that operate "in the service of the Devil," and Iran punishes "immoral" alcohol consumption with dozens of lashes? [197]

- Prior to a 2007 appeals court ruling, judges across the country routinely forced booze offenders to join Alcoholics Anonymous, which orders members to "turn our will and our lives over to the care of God ..."[198] (Personally I turn my life over to Captain Morgan.)

- Numerous municipalities repossess the automobile of anyone suspected of drunk driving *even if they prove their innocence.*[199]

- In 2004 a Democratic New York assemblyman proposed requiring all drivers to pass a digital sobriety test *every twenty minutes* on the road.[200] In 2007 a Pennsylvania legislator argued for a similar ordinance.[201] A sober man who used the dashboard-mounted device claimed that he "blew so hard during one test ... that he fell unconscious and crashed into a tree ..."[202]

- In 2007 Vermont police cracked down on bartenders for not ensuring that drinkers were over the legal age. One bar owner would not let undercover cops inside without presenting proof of their ages, *so they arrested him for "impeding a police officer."*[203]

For Americans between the ages of eighteen and twenty-one, the War on Booze is *especially* insulting. They can join the military, vote in national elections and apply for marriage licenses, but a sip of alcohol warrants jail time. MADD has specifically objected to granting young soldiers the right to drink.[204] In 2008 the founder of MADD said that eighteen-year-olds haven't "developed, and that's exactly why the draft age is eighteen, because these kids are malleable." She continued to insult the troops in shockingly elitist language: "They will follow the leader, they don't think for themselves, and they are the last ones I want to say, 'Here's a gun, and here's a beer.' They are not adult—that's why they're in the military. They are not adults."[205] Perhaps she should create another organization: Mothers Against Operating Tanks While Tanked.

The U.S. has the highest drinking age in the world, and subjects its high school students to random Breathalyzer tests,[206] yet teenagers in Europe—where the legal age of consumption ranges from fourteen to eighteen—drink nearly ten percent *less* than American adolescents, and drink to intoxication twenty-five percent less often.[207] *Reason* magazine editor Radley Balko explains: "When something is illegal, you take as much of it as you can get, as fast as you can possibly get it."[208]

According to the Rutgers University Center of Alcohol Studies, raising the U.S. drinking age from eighteen to twenty-one "increased drinking-induced fatalities in the 21–24 age group, by about as much as it lowered fatalities for those aged 18–20." This is because "experience" leads to moderation, "not the age of the person drinking."[209] Is it any wonder that the average age of drivers killed while driving drunk is twenty-one?[210]

Neo-prohibitionists refuse to concede that anyone can drink responsibly because they don't *believe* in the <u>concept</u> of responsibility. In 2004 the mother of a nineteen-year-old sued the Coors Beer Company for millions of dollars because her son illegally consumed its product and then drove a car into a light pole at ninety miles per hour. By her logic, if Coors beer did not exist then her genius son would have lived.[211] Ever heard of Budweiser, lady? How about Survival of the Fittest?

Unlike this dead speed racer, eighty percent of American teenagers refuse to drink and drive,[212] but police across the nation apprehend *sober* teens for driving their intoxicated friends.[213] This law enforcement overreach is killing America's young people; according to a nineteen-year-old arrested twice for volunteering to serve as a designated driver: "it's stopping people from [getting] safe rides home. I know a lot of people ended up driving home that shouldn't have."[214]

An Indiana policeman rationalizes this: "Alcohol abuse is the problem, not the issue of whether or not you are going to drive."[215] The U.S. government concurs: "recommending a designated driver should be rated unacceptable."[216] Incidentally drunken driving deaths increased in the '00s for the first time in two decades.[217]

Parents are increasingly punished for allowing minors to drink at home,[218] but teenagers who are forced to drink "in the woods ... or at unattended homes" are far more likely to binge. Countries that allow parents to supervise adolescent imbibing have "the *lowest* binge drinking rates," according to the *Wall Street Journal.*[219]

Just like with pornography and marijuana, propagandizing teenagers on the dangers of alcohol is a surefire way to *increase* their consumption. Four-fifths of U.S. school districts implement the anti-alcohol curriculum D.A.R.E., which costs $1.3 billion per year, but a government study discovered that students exposed to D.A.R.E. "were *more* likely than others to drink, smoke and take drugs."[220] Young people are only drawn to liquor because paranoid grownups make such a *huge fucking deal* about it. In 2006 Spanish legislators proposed a crackdown on teenage drinking; twenty-five thousand adolescents "swarmed onto Spanish streets ... for mass drinking sessions," according to Reuters.[221]

Zero tolerance laws—*not* alcohol and drugs—destroy many young Americans' lives. In recent years U.S. public schools have suspended and expelled students as young as six for swigging mouthwash that contains alcohol,[222] ingesting the legal painkiller ibuprofen for headaches,[223] eating powdered sugar because it *looks* like cocaine,[224] eating parsley because it *looks* like marijuana,[225] and eating Jell-O because college students *mix* Jell-O with alcohol.

According to administrators: "it doesn't matter if it had alcohol in it or not."[226]

It's not even *necessary* to discourage children from drinking: in 2004 Virginia teachers mistook margaritas in the teacher's lounge for lemonade; when they accidentally served a class of eight-year-olds tequila, the children "sipped it and said that it didn't taste good."[227] Likewise in 2007 a California restaurant mistakenly served a margarita to a child, who reacted by "making funny faces and pushing away his cup."[228] (Kids, it will taste *amazing* once you are old enough to deal with a woman's bullshit on a daily basis.)

Another sick irony: we are teaching our children that drinking is a terrible vice when in fact it's *extremely healthy:* moderate alcohol consumption lowers the risk of early death by eighteen percent,[229] senility by twenty percent,[230] obesity by fifty-four percent,[231] rheumatoid arthritis by fifty-five percent,[232] fatal heart attacks by eighty percent,[233] and erectile dysfunction by a "significant" margin.[234] (How many *sober* people did you fuck in college?)

New research suggests that beer might drastically reduce the risk of cancer.[235] A daily glass of wine helps you to lose weight, lowers your blood pressure and bad cholesterol, and may increase your memory.[236] In 2007 researchers discovered that liquor "boosted the antioxidant nutrients" in various fruits.[237] The five healthiest U.S. states are those with the most drinkers per capita.[238] Social drinkers earn higher average salaries than non-drinkers,[239] and alcohol consumption increases at every level of corporate success.[240] The world's (formerly) oldest person, who died in 2007 at the age of a hundred and fourteen, drank alcohol every day.[241] You're not drinking yourself to death; you're drinking yourself to *life!*

Naturally the federal government forbids alcohol manufacturers to *advertise* these health benefits.[242] In fact, Congress has debated requiring alcohol manufacturers to warn customers that "[a]lcohol is injurious to the consumer's health,"[243] which is exactly what Hitler believed: "Today we no longer see the ideal of the German people in the beer drinker of former days, but in men and women who are healthy to the core."[244]

Prohibition is to Nazism what alcoholism is to *Americanism*. British taxes on molasses—necessary to manufacture rum—led to widespread support for the American Revolution.[245] George Washington and Thomas Jefferson brewed their own beer. Washington distributed a hundred and sixty-four gallons of alcohol to residents of a Virginia town,[246] and Jefferson declared that taxing alcohol was a "condemnation" of "our citizens." The party monster Benjamin Franklin praised fermentation as "proof God loves us and wants to see us happy."[247]

Not only is the War on Booze treasonous, it's *blasphemous:* the Bible describes wine as "the dew of Heaven," which "gladdens God and men," and allows us to "put troubles out of mind." Jesus commands, "Drink ye all of it," and Paul elucidates: "Be no longer a drinker of water, but use a little wine ..." The Old Testament proclaims: "One in whose house wine does not flow like water is not blessed."[248]

God says: "Chug! Chug! Chug!"

Who the fuck are you to argue?

Postscript

Last night I blew fifty dollars on two amber ales, a gin & tonic, a shot of Bacardi 151, a muddy orgasm (Amaretto/Bailey's/Jäger) and three shots of Basil Hayden's bourbon to make up for the super-gay muddy orgasm. My girlfriend failed to appreciate my singing, staggering, stench-ridden self when I arrived at home.

"If you keep being obnoxious," she said, trying to sleep, "I'm going to punch you in the balls."

Naturally I assumed that she was PMS-ing as usual. So I kept singing, staggering and otherwise acting like a complete asshole. And then the bitch knocked my gonads deep into my intestines.

"Fuck you," I squealed, trying to breathe as I writhed on the bedroom floor. "I'll *cheat* on you for this and I'll *never* tell you when. Ha! Ha! Ha!"

Ahhhhhhhhhhhhhh, I love *drinking*. Fuck Love! *Booze* is my bride! She lifts my spirits when I'm down, keeps me honest—sometimes *too* honest—and never punches me in the fucking testicles. So the next time you see me facedown in the gutter, hair caked with vomit, lips chapped and eyes bloodshot, various biological stains on my trousers, drilling my fingers into my temples, a used condom stuck to my forehead for some reason, just remember: I'm fucking *happy* and you're *dead* inside.

★ ★ ★

Prohibition Nation vs. Oral Fixation Nation

PART ONE:
CIGARETTES

★ ★ ★

"There is nothing better than enjoying a smoke with amiable companions."[249]

    —*GENTLEMAN'S GUIDE TO GROOMING AND STYLE*

"If I cannot smoke in heaven, then I shall not go."

        —MARK TWAIN

Cigarettes are heinous little fuckers. I say this as a former smoker who craves nicotine at every moment. They make you stink like a charbroiled corpse, cost you a fortune and then kill you, but tyrannical anti-smoking activists want to revoke your right to commit suicide. Some things are worse than death.

Five million people die from smoking-related illnesses per year, according to the United Nations,[250] including between a hundred thousand and four hundred thousand Americans.[251] This is not breaking news. Ninety percent of Americans in 1954 were aware that cigarettes might cause cancer.[252] One in five American adults currently smoke, down from *half* in 1953.[253] Nevertheless a minority of smokers sue tobacco manufacturers for billions of dollars, feigning ignorance of the health risks despite warnings on every pack.[254] In 2006 the Massachusetts Supreme Court ruled that smokers can sue manufacturers even if they *know* the health risks because "there can be no *non*-unreasonable use of cigarettes," meaning that smokers are legally incapable of making their own decisions.[255]

When the citizenry relinquishes self-control, politicians control everyone. Half of Americans live in a city or state that bans smoking indoors at public places such as bars, restaurants and offices.[256] An elderly man died in 2007 from hypothermia thanks to such a law,[257] and a 2008 *Journal of Public Economics* study found that indoor smoking bans are responsible for drunken driving crashes because smokers travel to bars in friendlier, smoke-free-*free* jurisdictions.[258]

It makes sense to shield nonsmokers—especially children—from secondhand carcinogens, but the Health Nazis have in many cases gone beyond protecting nonsmokers to *persecuting* smokers:

- In 2006 the U.S. Surgeon General said that he would "support the abolition of all tobacco products."[259] Officials from the Environmental Protection Agency and the Food and Drug Administration have suggested similar crackdowns.[260]

- Three California cities have banned outdoor smoking, *even if nobody else is around*, and in many cases smoking inside private homes. An early version of one bill mandated "a jail sentence of up to six months" for lighting up in privacy.[261]

- In 2007 Tennessee state troopers announced that they would arrest citizens who purchase "large quantities of cigarettes."[262] That same year a Pittsburgh policeman used a stun gun on a fifty-year-old man for smoking at an outdoor bus stop.[263]

- In 2005 San Francisco lawmakers forbade public use of chewing tobacco even though it creates no secondhand smoke.[264]

- A Maryland lawmaker helped ban smoking inside private homes "to change the social norm concerning tobacco use," by his own admission, not merely shield nonsmokers.[265]

- In 2007 former New York City Mayor Ed Koch wrote: "Let's save smokers from themselves ... Let's ban the manufacture and sale of tobacco products in the United States."[266]

- In 2005 the Federal Bureau of Alcohol, Tobacco and Firearms pressured credit card companies to refuse payments for online sales of cigarettes, even if customers proved their legal age.[267]

- Sixty colleges throughout the U.S. have banned smoking on campus.[268] So much for mixing opium with hookah on the quad.

- In 2007 the British National Health Service ruled that smokers could not receive any form of surgery "for conditions that are not immediately life-threatening."[269] This was devastating for U.K. transsexuals who can't kick the habit.

Cigarettes are taxed at higher rates than any other product, and those taxes have tripled over the last fifteen years despite the fact that "no other federal tax hurts the poor more than the cigarette tax," according to the nonpartisan Tax Foundation.[270] Federal authorities recently proposed raising the national cigar tax by twenty *thousand* percent, which a lifelong stogy manufacturer derided as the single largest tax increase "in the history of man."[271]

The World Health Organization recommends a worldwide

increase of such taxes and a ban of tobacco advertising.[272] British authorities proposed requiring citizens to apply for an expensive "smoking permit" before they could purchase tobacco products.[273] In 2008 China appointed one hundred thousand "smoking inspectors" to spy on its citizens.[274] Public health activists in the U.S. have compared the "self-perceived" right to smoke with "terrorism," "rape," "anarchy" and "people's self-perceived rights to urinate [and] defecate ... in public."[275]

Our government engages in similar hyperbole: in 2006 the U.S. Surgeon General warned "there is no risk-free level of exposure to someone else's drifting smoke," and blamed *momentary* exposure— not long-term—for "cancer," "blood clots," "heart attacks and strokes."[276]

However, a fifth of lung cancer patients have "never lit a cigarette," according to the Associated Press.[277] In 2005 *Time* magazine reported: "If you're 30 years old and a lifelong smoker, you can almost completely eliminate your risk of lung cancer by quitting ... it's almost a negligible increased risk."[278] That same year U.S. researchers announced that *daily bathing* might cause major health problems due to pollutants in the water.[279] Should our government wage a multibillion-dollar War on Showers? Should *everyone* stink like cigarette smokers?

Politicians such as President Blow Job and Senator Ted Kennedy have blamed "cynical" tobacco advertisements for cigarette-smoking teenagers. But the youth smoking rate remained steady after Camel retired its widely criticized Joe Camel cartoon mascot.[280] It's worth noting that Kennedy, who proposed the highest cigarette tax increase in history, killed a young woman after driving drunk; the bloated Irishman's alcoholism has caused one more death than your cigarette habit.

The very *existence* of a youth smoking crisis is questionable: teenagers constitute only three percent of the U.S. smoking population;[281] a third of teenagers smoked in 1975 and the same ratio smoke today despite countless taxpayer-funded anti-smoking campaigns.[282] The wave of smoking bans and higher cigarette taxes in the past few years has similarly accomplished nothing: a fifth of Americans smoked in 2004 and a fifth smoked in 2007. Naturally the federal researchers who conducted this study concluded that the government "must spend more to persuade people to kick the habit."[283] Why not kick the habit of spending more on federal researchers?

Washington spent millions of dollars in 2005 to inform teenagers that "kissing a smoker is just as gross" as smooching "a dead rat or a dead fish," as if this weren't obvious.[284] Considering that male smokers are forty percent more likely to suffer from erectile dysfunction,[285] perhaps we should *require* smoking in high schools to reduce teenage pregnancy. You don't *support* teenage pregnancy, do you?

Or do you support *Islamists?* The Taliban orders its followers to "refrain from smoking cigarettes."[286] Religious authorities in Somalia punish smokers with flogging in order to "impos[e] a fundamentalist version of Koranic law."[287] Many moderate Muslims enjoy tobacco, of course, but in the 1600s the Ottoman Empire *executed* more than twenty-five thousand "suspected smokers."[288]

Or do you support the *monarchy?* King James, who considered smoking as sinful as lechery, imposed a four thousand percent tax on tobacco.[289] France funded the Revolutionary War in exchange for tobacco from the American colonies.[290] No Cigarettes? No U.S.A.

Or do you support the *Nazis?* During World War II the U.S. Army urged soldiers to smoke for relaxation, and Congress allocated $10 million to ship cartons to the troops,[291] but Germany *banned* cigarettes.[292] Guess who won?

Easy: the Nazis. They won because we have adopted so many of their goddamned attitudes and policies. In the Hitler years

German filmmakers were forbidden to feature cigarettes in their movies. Today the American Medical Association, the American Lung Association, the American Heart Association, the American Academy of Pediatrics, the World Health Organization, the Los Angeles Police Department and the New York State Department of Health collectively endorse a proposal to forbid moviegoers younger than eighteen to view any film that depicts smoking, unless A) their parents are in attendance, or B) the film "unambiguously reflects the dangers and consequences of tobacco use ..."[293] In 2007 the Motion Picture Association of America, which rates the vast majority of films in the U.S., acquiesced to the activists' demands, and many Hollywood studios agreed to chuck cigarettes.[294] James Bond actor Daniel Craig complained: "I can blow off someone's head at close range and splatter blood, but I can't light a good Cuban."[295]

The Health Nazis want to create an alternate reality in which tobacco has never *existed*. Cigarettes have been digitally removed from official photographs of James Dean, Paul Simon, Jackson Pollack and the Beatles "in a bid to fit in with more health-conscious times." Franklin Delano Roosevelt's famous cigarette holder "vanished" from a memorial statue in Washington, D.C.[296] A broadcaster censored many classic Hanna-Barbera cartoons such as *Tom and Jerry*, *The Flinstones* and *Scooby-Doo* after a single complaint from a British "media regulator."[297]

Just like the Wars on Porn, Drugs and Booze, the crusade to save young people from cigarettes has *worsened* the behavior: teenagers' number one reason for smoking is that *"it's against the rules."*[298] In 2007 University of Georgia researchers discovered, "The more exposure middle school students have to anti-smoking ads, the more likely they are to smoke ..."[299] This is basic psychology, not rocket science. Teenage boys dive into swimming pools far more often when "No Diving" signs are posted.[300]

Author Tara Parker-Pope explains: "cigarettes have emerged as a torch of individuality ... the very act of smoking now represents a backlash against the sanctimonious tone of the public health crusaders and anyone else who would threaten the right to life, liberty and pursuit of pleasure."[301] And sometimes that means the right to death.

★ ★ ★

PART TWO:
FOOD

★ ★ ★

"If more of us valued food ... it would be a merrier world."[302]

—J. R. R. TOLKIEN

"Tell me what you eat, and I shall tell you what you are."[303]

—JEAN-ANTHELME BRILLAT-SAVARIN

I f Americans told Brillat-Savarin what we eat, his reply would be:
"You are giant sacks of shit."

We are *disgusting*. More than half of the U.S. population is
overweight, including a quarter of children, doubling the 1960s
figure.[304] The average American eats three hamburgers and four
orders of fries every week,[305] and drinks nearly sixty gallons of soda
every year.[306] Ninety percent of American children regularly dine at
McDonald's.[307] We are the fattest fuckers on the planet.

This costs hundreds of thousands of lives and hundreds of billions
of dollars in health care expenses.[308][*] Overeating is "deadlier than
smoking," according to medical researchers.[309] Our addiction to fast
food leads to widespread heart disease, high blood pressure, diabetes,

---

[*] In a February 14, 2008 *Slate* column, Daniel Engber argued that smokers and over-
eaters *save* the rest of us money because they die at younger ages from rapid afflic-
tions, whereas long-term medical care for senior citizens is far more expensive.

cancer, zits, poop and ugly. Our sausage thighs, elephantine derrières and cascading layers of flab are inexcusable, but naturally we would rather blame *others* for our lack of willpower:

- In 2005 the State of California sued McDonald's, Burger King, Wendy's Old-Fashioned Hamburgers, and Kentucky Fried Chicken for serving unhealthy food.[310] Why not sue millions of California residents for *choosing to eat it?*

- In recent years lawyers have filed lawsuits against major fast food chains on behalf of their obese clients, including a man who weighed nearly three hundred pounds, suffered two heart attacks and *continued to eat fast food.* Also: the mother of a fifteen-year-old who weighed four hundred pounds. The mother had "always believed McDonald's was *healthy* for my son."[311] Did she begin to suspect the opposite around pound *three* hundred?!?

- The Secretary of the U.S. Health and Human Services has blamed corporate executives for the fact that "[w]e are too fat and don't exercise."[312] Yes, it's the fault of CEOs that gluttons consume sixteen thousand calories and then refuse to get off the couch.

The Center for Science in the Public Interest, a well-funded lobbyist group that the *Washington Post* describes as "left-leaning,"[313] claims that "[o]besity is not merely a matter of individual responsibility,"[314] and has either sued or threatened to sue Kentucky Fried Chicken and Starbucks over the fats in their foods,[315] Kellogg over its Pop-Tarts breakfast snack,[316] and Coke & Pepsi over the sugar in their drinks.[317] But the CSPI president has said, "I'd like to get rid of ... diet soft drinks completely," even though these contain no sugar.[318] This man craves "taxes on butter, potato chips, whole milk, cheeses [and] meat," boasts that "CSPI is proud about finding something wrong with practically everything,"[319] and believes that the U.S. government should warn citizens who purchase ice cream: "just know that you're going to kill yourself."[320]

Other health activists have claimed that fast food produces "addictive effects on the brain ... the same way as nicotine and heroin,"[321] and "Americans cannot help but ingest the calories present in the environment all around us," which therefore necessitates the implementation of "policies ... to reduce calorie pollution," akin to air pollution, only more delicious.[322] A doctor wrote in the *New York Times:* "Is the freedom to choose unhealthy food that difficult to forfeit?"[323]

Numerous states and cities have imposed taxes on unhealthy food,[324] and legislators are proposing similar taxes "all over the country," according to the *Washington Times.*[325] Health activists believe that taxes could magically "save thousands of lives each year,"[326] but the truth is that people are far more likely to shed pounds when *paid* for eating nutritiously instead of *charged* for eating poorly.[327] Does the U.S. need Weight Watchers Welfare?

Sixty percent of Americans oppose taxing junk food, and only three percent follow the government's nutrition guidelines,[328] but Democratic senators have proposed forcing junk food providers to warn consumers of health risks anyway. Liberals can't sleep unless the government scolds us exactly like our parents did when we were children, assuming that our parents didn't perish from ingesting a plethora of pork rinds.

The minds of children are the primary battleground. Junk food companies spend tens of billions of dollars marketing to kids,[329] who subsequently believe that anything wrapped in McDonald's packaging tastes better.[330] But the director of Yale University's Center for Eating and Weight Disorders, who supports taxes on unhealthy foods,[331] admits that the "very utilitarian reason for focusing on children, of course, is then you get away from these arguments about personal responsibility."[332]

Congress has banned unhealthy food in schools.[333] Connecticut and California administrators "take away from students any non-nutritious foods such as ... chips, sugary snacks, soda, etc.," even if parents approve of these items.[334] However, after Sweden banned unhealthy snacks from its public schools, childhood obesity declined only six percent over four years.[335] A thorough review of the billion-dollar U.S. crusade against childhood obesity discovered "mostly failure."[336]

Never mind the *facts*; we have to save the *children*. An Illinois school district banned fruit juice because it's not *as* nutritious as unprocessed fruits.[337] A Virginia middle school suspended an eighth-grade student, and kicked him off the baseball team, for eating a single cookie.[338] A Connecticut eighth-grader was "suspended for a day, barred from attending an honors dinner and stripped of his title as class vice president after he was caught with a bag of Skittles candy," according to the Associated Press.[339] Massachusetts public schools have banned birthday cupcakes; instead "each birthday kid will get a birthday pencil."[340] (*Wow!* A fucking *pencil?* This is the best birthday *ever!*)

In 2005 Hawaii lawmakers proposed requiring teachers to stay slender if they wish to keep their jobs.[341] Schools have forfeited millions of dollars in vending machine sales that "paid for field trips, marching bands and other programs,"[342] and no longer reward overachievers with pizza and donuts.[343] The anti-candy crusade has created a black market in public schools, the goods trafficked by clandestine "sugar pushers."[344]

Democratic lawmakers have suggested including students' body mass index alongside their grades on quarterly report cards.[345] A Pennsylvania elementary school initiated this policy, which spread "fear" throughout the student body, and a six-year-old girl refused to eat *anything* because she was terrified of punishment.[346] A similar policy in Colorado caused students to cry.[347] The *New York Times* reported that "families with anorexic and bulimic children identified middle school health classes, which focus on weight, as the No. 1 trigger for their teenagers' disorders."[348] Conversely the Boston University School of Medicine reports: "strict disciplinarians are far more likely to wind up with children who are fat by age six, perhaps because the youngsters over-eat as a reaction to stress."[349]

Our obsession with physical fitness is leading to mental trauma. The Associated Press reports that "baby exercise classes" are available for infants "as young as two months."[350] The author of *Itsy Bitsy Yoga* explains: "Fit baby equals fit toddler equals fit child equals fit teen equals fit adult."[351] In 2007 a pair of health-conscious parents received lifelong jail sentences after their underfed infant died.[352] Is baby bulimia a sign of cultural *progress?*

In 2005 the beloved children's TV character Cookie Monster exchanged his cookies for fruits and vegetables because the government-funded Public Broadcasting System wanted to encourage healthy behavior.[353]* The United Kingdom has banned advertisements for unhealthy food to protect children,[354] a policy that some U.S. congressmen have endorsed.[355] Senator Hillary Clinton believes that fast food companies "will be implanting chips in our children to advertise directly into their brains."[356]

However, researchers have found that corporate marketing has far less of an impact on a kid's body than the "diet, weight, and activity level of that child's parents."[357] For every hour that a parent works per week, her children are one percent more likely to be overweight;[358] overworked parents would rather "just go out to McDonald's" than "cook nutritious meals."[359] Another factor is that children *and* adults

---

* STOP RAPING MY CHILDHOOD, FOOD FASCISTS!!!!!! COOKIE MONSTER EATS *COOKIES*, NOT *TOFU!!!!* HE IS NOT *TOFU* MONSTER!!!! *YOU* ARE THE MONSTERS!!!!!! JESUS CHRIST CREATED *HELL* FOR YOU AND YOU WILL BUUUUUURNNNNNNNN!!!!!!

expend a third fewer calories per day than in previous decades because of computers.[360]

But why choose to get off our enormous posteriors when the government can decide everything *for* us?

- The *Washington Times* reports that "mainstream" health activists are pressuring child welfare departments across America to remove plump kids from their parents' custody.[361] In 2007 a Texas judge forbade the overweight to adopt.[362]

- Police in Washington D.C., "under heightened security because of the continuing threat of terrorism," arrested a woman for eating a candy bar near a subway station. A police chief explained: "if she had just stopped for the issuance of a citation, she never would have been locked up."[363]

- In 2008 Mississippi lawmakers introduced legislation to "make it illegal for state-licensed restaurants to serve obese patrons."[364]

- The chairman of the New York City Health Committee and members of the Los Angeles City Council have proposed using the power of the law to rid their cities of fast food restaurants.[365]

This is not simply an American obsession; in the past few years the Scottish Health Minister threatened to revoke the license of any restaurant that serves unhealthy food,[366] British legislators voted to criminalize ice cream vendors,[367] New Zealand forbade citizenship to overweight immigrants,[368] Japan mandated obesity screening for all citizens over the age of forty,[369] and the World Health Organization recommended the implementation of global "regulatory policies" and "surveillance systems" to curb overeating,[370] whatever *that* means.

Perhaps it's similar to how British authorities monitor citizens with video cameras and warn offenders "via a loudspeaker" that they detract from "a healthy, clean environment."[371] In 2007 Prince Charles proposed banning McDonald's.[372] Many British legislators believe that overweight citizens should not receive any public health care.[373] Incidentally British schoolchildren believe that "being fat" is worse than "dying" when asked to identify "the very worst thing in the world."[374]

As the U.K. has learned, it's a slippery slope from health advocacy to autocracy. In 2005 British authorities dragged a twenty-three-year-old man to a mental hospital for weighing more than the government deemed suitable. He sobbed as police raided his home (over the objections of his family) and forced him into an ambulance, but officials considered the institutionalization necessary "in the interests of that person's health."[375]

In 2007 British authorities threatened to remove an overweight eight-year-old boy from his mother's custody.[376] That same year British Airways suspended an employee for eating a muffin.[377] A British health official proposed forcing companies to institute daily hour-long exercise regimens for workers, which he admitted was a "form of paternalism."[378]

When George Orwell depicted mandatory exercise in *1984*, it was a *criticism* of the notion, but public health crusaders have a soft spot—not in their slenderized midsections—for tyranny:

- Junk food critic Morgan Spurlock, director of the Academy Award-nominated documentary *Super-Size Me*, praises Communist Cuba because it's not "flooded with American consumer crap,"[379] and encourages "high-fiber, plant-based diets" like those in "[t]he non-industrial world," where millions of people *starve to death*.[380]

- After visiting Communist North Korea, ultra-liberal CNN
  founder Ted Turner said of the famine-ridden dictatorship:
  "I had a great time there. ... There weren't a lot of fat people
  walking around. They were all thin. And being thin is healthier
  than being fat."[381]

- According to the author of *Stolen Harvest: The Hijacking of the
  Global Food Supply*, "Food for humans is increased at the cost of
  food for cows and earthworms. Reclaiming food democracy in
  food production implies reclaiming the rights of all species to
  their share of nutrition ..."[382] Yes, the human race should perish
  so that *earthworms* may prosper.

Extreme leftist protesters have bombed, torched and robbed
McDonald's franchises around the world.[383] In 2005 the chairman
of the U.S. Senate Environment Committee accused the activist
organization People for the Ethical Treatment of Animals of directing
funds to domestic terrorists.[384] A PETA official said: "it would be great
if all of the fast-food outlets ... exploded tomorrow ... Hallelujah to
the people who are willing to do it."[385]*

Furthermore the War on Fat is unhealthy for reasons that *aren't*
related to explosives. Researchers have discovered that moderate
pudginess—up to thirty excess pounds—does not cause early death,[386]
overweight patients are more likely to survive life-threatening
diseases,[387] and a dozen extra pounds "seemed to protect male drivers
from dying in car crashes ..."[388] If our excess poundage is so life-
threatening, why is our average lifespan—three times longer than a
hundred years ago—at an all-time high?[389]

It's partly *thanks* to "unhealthy" food. According to researchers at
Harvard, Johns Hopkins and other universities:

---

* According to the Center for Consumer Freedom, *USA Today* quoted PETA founder
  Ingrid Newkirk as saying, "Even if animal research resulted in a cure for AIDS,
  we'd be against it."

- Chocolate consumption lowers the risk of fatal heart disease by nearly fifty percent,[390] and "may boost brain function."[391]

- Sugar boosts the human immune system. Sweeteners in diet sodas and fat-free snacks fail to achieve this effect.[392]

- Caffeine lowers the risk of colon cancer by twenty-five percent, diabetes by more than half, and Parkinson's disease and liver problems by four-fifths.[393] Nevertheless the mayor of San Francisco wants to tax caffeine in order to cut "obesity," which is nonsensical considering that it *boosts* metabolism.[394]

- A "fat-rich diet" may help fight many cancers;[395] pizza appears to "lower the risk of cancer, heart disease and other ailments";[396] women who eat a daily serving of ice cream "gain less weight than women who don't," according to the *American Journal of Clinical Nutrition.*[397]

- Obese men are forty-two percent *less* likely to commit suicide, which "may be related to their higher production of ... hormones that affect mood."[398] (Or perhaps the nooses snap.)

Just as the Wars on Porn, Drugs, Booze and Cigarettes exacerbate the problems, many Americans consume fast food to feel *liberated* from the "nutrition Nazis," according to the CEO of Burger King, who authorized a marketing campaign that links the Whopper hamburger to macho nonconformity.[399]

"I don't think it's my job to tell Americans what they should eat," the BK CEO told *Newsweek*. "We might as well go back to communism."[400] The CEO of fast food chain Hardee's likewise says: "Every time [nutritionist critics] come out with something, it helps us advance the impression of the brand."[401]

The critics are known as "nutrition Nazis" for a reason. In the 1940s German propaganda proclaimed: "Your body belongs to the nation! Your body belongs to the Fuhrer! You have the duty to be healthy! Food Is Not a Private Matter!"[402]

In 2006 the New York City health commissioner said, "When anyone dies at an early age from a preventable cause in New York City, it's my fault," not their own.[403] What a bunch of totalitarian bullshit. In the words of nineteenth century French philosopher Frederic Bastiat:

> "If the natural tendencies of mankind are so bad that it is not safe to permit people to be free, how is it that the tendencies of these organizers are always good? Do not the legislators and their appointed agents also belong to the human race? ... I accept people as they are. I desire only to study and admire ... for liberty is an acknowledgement of faith in God and His works."[404]

This raises a tiny question: *does God exist?*
Let's fly to Israel and discover the truth!
Or get killed in a vicious terrorist attack!
Or *both* at the very same wacky time!

III.

THE PROMISED LAND

★ ★ ★

Part One:

YOUNGSTERS OF ZION

★ ★ ★

July 2007

Amerrican political discourse revolves around religion, especially with controversial issues such as abortion, gay marriage, the War on Terror, sex education and the teaching of evolution. I wanted to understand the mind of the True Believer, so I traveled to the Holy Land.

Before I could look for God, however, I had to attend a conference whose organizers paid for my plane ticket. (I'm a Jew *and* journalist; you think I'm covering the tab myself?)

Miraculously my invitation stood to the Jerusalem-based ROI ("Return on Investment") Global Summit for Young Jewish Innovators after I posted this profile on the ROI website:

> *"MARTY BECKERMAN, 24: I write books for a living, although sometimes the living is more like starving to death. ... I figured that if I suck up to the Zionist-controlled media, I might get some work."*

Apparently the staff believed that this was a *joke* of some kind. Ha! Ha!

A certain mystique surrounded the Global Summit. The website was alternately vague ("forging new frontiers in ... contributing to the evolution of Jewish identity") and psychedelic ("create a hub in time and space in Jerusalem—THE hub of time and space—for intensive engagement and collaboration ... forming a dynamic, eclectic, and international pod of leaders"). Huh?

This sounded shadowy and exhilarating. Perhaps I would observe the inner mechanics of the Jew World Order, which conspiracy theorists have obsessed over for centuries. Plus I could hardly turn down a free ticket halfway around the world, *especially* if I might get to join the Illuminati. (Get ready for an injection of *sexxxiness*, Masons!)

When I learned that I had been signed up for a series of sessions called "Content Delivery," however, I panicked and called a staff member.

"Listen, you Jew bastard," I said, "I'm an *objective journalist*. I can't distribute pro-Israel press releases to my media contacts whenever the IDF* bulldozes some goddamned hippy, as much as I enjoy the thought of crushed, bloodied vegans. Are you trying to ruin my career? Are you trying to make me into a shill?"

"No, it's not like that," said the staffer. "Think of ROI as a networking and brainstorming session ... You'll make some great contacts. Trust me. Just do it."

"Okay, you Jew bastard," I said. "Let's skull-fuck this bitch."

The flight to Tel Aviv is grueling. You lose touch with reality after so many hours in an airplane, especially if you're surrounded by people who have *already* lost touch with reality. At seven o'clock in the morning Orthodox Jews awaken me to recite prayers that I do

---

* Translation for the *goyim:* Israeli Defense Forces.

not know nor care to learn. Against my protestations they strap a leather band around my arm, which seems better suited for kinky S&M foreplay than communicating with the Almighty.

"It is *tefillin*," explains a stocky bearded man with a heavy accent. "When I was a commander in the Israeli army, I tried to tell my men to pray with *tefillin* every morning, but they would not do it. *I* would pray with *tefillin*, but they never would. When Arabs ambushed us with grenades, I was the only one who lived. So you will pray with *tefillin?*"

"Whatever, dude," I say, consenting to the bondage, but only because if the plane crashes, I don't want *him* to be the only one who survives.

When I arrive at the Jerusalem hotel I'm infuriated to discover that the editors of the ROI profile booklet, which includes a welcome message from the Israeli prime minister, have changed one of my answers:

- The question: "What keeps you up at night?"

- Their answer: "Attitudes Toward Intermarriage."

- *My* answer: "The Orthodox screaming at me for dating a *shiksa.** She doesn't eat pork so get off my back and let me finish what Hitler started (by mixing my seed into forbidden, un-chosen fruit), you frummer-than-thou motherfuckers."†

---

* Translation for the *goyim:* non-Jewish female.

† Translation for *goyim:* "holier-than-thou." It's a cliché in Jewish circles to say that marrying a gentile is "finishing what Hitler started," as it supposedly contributes to the demise of our people.

The woman at the registration booth forces me to sign a waiver, which stipulates that if terrorists kill me during the conference then my family can't sue the organizers. Furthermore if I engage in "illegal drug use or excessive alcohol consumption," I'll get sent back to the U.S. immediately on my own dime.

"Could you please *define* 'excessive'?" I ask the woman, who has *no* sense of humor.

Fortunately the first ROI event is a wine tasting on the hotel veranda. Unfortunately the wine is kosher, which means that it's awful saccharine goop. I try to drink myself into oblivion, but only manage to drink myself into heartburn. I'll get diabetes long before I get drunk.

Over the next hour I shake hands with the other hundred and nineteen future Jewish leaders. I'm hoping for a diabolical cabal of global power players with ties to occultist secret societies that sacrifice human children to Moloch, demon lord of the Phoenicians, but the ROI attendees are considerably less exciting: youth leadership directors of Jewish Community Centers, campus Hillel organizers, pro-Israel activists and other professional bullshit artists who want to "make a change."

While these people are *nice*, I don't know how to speak their language. They speak of "community with a big 'C,'" "incubating pilot programs," "building a coalition," and "changing the world" with "vision" and "solidarity," but it's unintelligible mush. Every third word is "empowerment." Their lips are moving—they are projecting *sound*—but it doesn't *mean* anything. The conspiracy theorists would be shocked: the organized forces of Zionism aren't monsters; they're simply *zombies*.

The activists are not amused when I recount how I once accidentally urinated on the Israeli embassy when I lived in Washington, D.C. (It's a long story, but basically I was very drunk.) They are also not amused by the story of when I urinated on a Tel

Aviv beach—a few days before the ROI conference—while waving my U.S. passport and screaming, "You can't arrest *me!*"

"Why are so many of your stories about pissing on things?" asks another attendee.

I have no good reply.

Plenty of the other attendees are sanctimonious goddamned hippies: activists for "gender equality and social justice," organic-lifestyle "ecological farmers" who believe that "feeling the earth here is really special," the Lesbian/Gay/Bisexual/Transgender Coordinator of the International Union of Socialist Youth, an "enthusiastic eco-activist" representing Bicycles for Jerusalem, and other bleeding hearts who hope for "world and inner peace," "integrating social justice into that effort," blah blah blah blah. And they are happier than pigs in shit, although they would never dream of eating pork.

Case in point: we're forced to wake up at six-thirty a.m., which is difficult when your internal clock hovers somewhere over the Atlantic—or when it's *actually* six-thirty a.m.—so that we can spend the day cleaning bird sanctuaries and planting "community gardens." A middle-aged female hippy explains that "developing a community garden is definitely an empowering experience," because "you can feel healthy in it" and "make a difference." An ROI official explains without any humor that the Hebrew word for "service" is the same word as "punishment for white collar crime." Sounds like fun!

We are crammed into buses like European Jews into Nazi trains, and taken to perform our community service. The Jerusalem Bird Sanctuary is a mosquito-ridden swamp that smells like animal feces and is equally pleasant to walk around in. (A conservationist explains that preventing development here was a "victory" for environmentalists, proving once again that environmentalism *is* shitty.)

We're forced to pull thorny plants from the ground without any gloves; I wind up with more pricks in me than the "actresses" of *Campus Fuck Fest*, a terrific porno film that deserves your hard-earned money. For some reason I'm the only one *unhappy* with this situation; the other participants are *enjoying* themselves. A girl from Chicago *swears* that she doesn't see the trillions of mosquitoes sucking harder than the "actresses" of *College Fuck Fest*, which—once again—is fantastic.

"This place should be turned into something useful," I say to a female hippy who wears a SAVE DARFUR t-shirt. "I'm thinking either a highway or a wildfire. You have any ideas, babe?"

No, she does not.

At the end of the torture session, the conservationist thanks us for helping to make the bird sanctuary that much cleaner.

"Noooooooooo," the stupid hippies say in union. "Thank *youuuuuu.*"

This is a surefire symptom of collective mental illness. Our people escaped from slavery in Egypt thousands of years ago. There is no good reason to replace the Pharaohs with the *pigeons*.

We're given two hours to shower and prepare for a fancy dinner at the Jerusalem Museum, but the woman at the hotel's front desk fails to effectively explain when my laundry will be finished—and since she's a stereotypically ungracious Israeli, she blames *me* for misunderstanding her instead of apologizing for the miscommunication—so I'm forced to wear dirty jeans and a short-sleeved shirt. Everyone else is wearing dress clothes. This is humiliating until the fourth glass of wine takes away the shame, as alcohol tends to do for people with zero dignity.

A lady with quite a bit of dignity (and money!), Lynn Schusterman—who funded the ROI conference—addresses us before the dinner. She praises our "infectious energy and enthusiastic vision." She seems nice; I briefly meet her later and thank her for all the free shit.

However, I leave the dinner early with my homosexual friend James. We find a downtown bar and knock back beers. (You'll get a pint faster in the Negev desert than an Israeli pub. Apparently nobody in the Jewish nation's service industry *expects* a tip.)

"I don't understand Christians," I say, drunk enough to wonder if I'm going to experiment with my sexuality tonight. "They think that the Old Testament is invalid when it comes to pork and shellfish—because Jesus says that what comes out of your mouth matters more than what goes in—but they rail against your brand of degeneracy, which is *also* forbidden in the Old Testament."

"What comes out matters more than what goes in?" James asks. "So Jesus *would* be down with cock-sucking?"

James invites me to a Jerusalem gay bar, which would only seem more out of place at Disneyland, but I must save my energy— and my anal integrity—for tomorrow.

Well, okay, just my energy.

We are awakened for ROI-mandated Talmud study at nine in the morning. I can't bring myself to debate the Oral Torah before I've digested breakfast—especially with my vicious hangover—so I stagger to the men's room and nap on the cold, bacteria-ridden floor. (Yes, I feel a pang of nostalgia for my college experience.)

When I drag myself back to the conference room, the rest of

the attendees are enthusiastically discussing the passage:

- "So like, what is *our* holy of holies?"

- "Life is the *journey*."

- "It's like the audacity of *hope*, which is a phrase that Senator Barack Obama uses."

- "We are so lucky to meet in a city where we can forge our *own* destinies."

- "You can't go into the Holy of Holies *physically* but you can go there *spiritually*."

Why is nobody else *kvetching?** What the fuck is *wrong* with these happy people?

We break into smaller groups: Content Delivery, Community Service, Environmental Activism, Youth Programming and Israel Advocacy. The Content Delivery session is a discussion of how the Internet has impacted Old Media.

"It always helps to look at pornography to see where the next tech boom will come from," says the group leader.

"It always just helps to look at pornography," I contribute.

A group member complains that many "American Jews don't even *know* what Hamas is," referring to the bloodthirsty terrorist organization.

"Isn't that what you eat with pita and falafel?" I jest to no one's amusement.

Another member informs us that he had a baby six months ago.

"*Mazel tov*, man," I say. "The kid didn't have any birth defects

---

* Translation for the *goyim:* "complaining."

or Down syndrome or anything, did it?"

"*No.*" He stares at me in disgust. "Did you really just *ask* me that?"

Despite their atrocious manners, Israelis are *gorgeous.* I've made it approximately sixty hours without masturbating in the Holy City, which is not easy when the local female population is comprised of olive-skinned goddesses armed with semiautomatic weapons; for some reason this makes them a thousand times hotter.

Why do I desperately want to make love to these women who could kill me in endless ways? You know, if Jewish American Princesses weren't so reflexively horrified by the Second Amendment and skin cancer—and if Jewish American nebbishes looked anything like our muscular IDF counterparts—perhaps the American intermarriage rate wouldn't be quite so devastating.

Speaking of which, the conference attendees are definitely not fans of miscegenation. At one session, titled "Jewish Continuity in 2020," the young activists rail against mixed breeding; you see, every impure child "cuts off a thousand generations of Jews." (Fun Factoid: I attended the "2020" session because I wanted to discuss flying cars, and also because showing up to "Kosher Sex" might have given people the impression that I'm some kind of pervert.)

"Why *should* Jews survive?" I ask to my own surprise. "Like, if it's just about breeding for the *sake* of breeding, what's the point? And even if Judaism *does* die out, billions of people are still going to worship our God, right?"

The other attendees gawk at me with eyes like daggers. (For the record: I'm not a self-hating Jew; I'm a *self-loving asshole.*)

"Oh, I'm just fucking with you," I say. "We survived Pharaoh, the Romans, the Diaspora, Hitler and the Bacon Double Cheeseburger.

The fact that WASPs finally let us bang their daughters is not exactly the most daunting crisis that we've ever faced."

"It *is* a crisis." "It's the crisis of *freedom*." "You are *clearly* misinformed."

Some of the Israeli ROI attendees, who are much gruffer than the rest of us—mandatory army service will do that to you—complain that American Jews are pathetic, neurotic dweebs who refuse to perform any manual labor and analyze our identities to no end. None of the American Jews protest these hurtful stereotypes because they are a hundred percent accurate.

This gets me thinking: if secular American Jews and secular Israeli Jews don't have a shared religion *or* culture, what *do* we have in common besides a distant family tree?

But there I go analyzing my identity like a weakling American Jew who enjoys laughter, knows how to stand in a line without cutting and doesn't dress like a European disco addict or flamboyant homosexual.

We enjoy dinner and more free wine—this time really *good* free wine; I help myself to nine glasses—along the Tel Aviv port. Lynn Schusterman announces a $100,000 grant for ROI participants' projects, but I'm too busy getting loaded off her booze to pay much attention.

The next couple of hours are hazy in my memory. Apparently I reminisced about seeing a live porn shoot in Los Angeles (the working title was *Atomic Ass Whores*), sang stunning renditions of Beatles and Elvis Costello tunes (as everyone tried to sleep on the bus back to Jerusalem), and when I overheard a hippy chick from California say, "I just love animals so much and want to help them in any way possible," I replied, "Yeah, I like to help them into a bowl of honey barbeque sauce."

Everyone thanks God when I lose consciousness.

Amazingly I do not have a hangover, but I *am* sickened when the hotel charges me *thirty-five dollars*—in American currency, not Israeli shekels—for my late laundry. (I was expecting to pay six bucks at the max.) The desk clerk won't let me check out until I've signed the bill.

Without getting too dramatic, this worthless hotel is the only place in Israel that I hope Palestinian terrorists incinerate on the condition that only the desk staff is killed.

A closing ceremony follows lunch. A top ROI staffer suggests that we make *aliyah*,* and asks us to stand for "Hatikvah," the Israeli national anthem. Apparently I'm the only person in the room who does not know the lyrics. (I would make a snide comment about how I'm a proud fucking *American*, except that I don't remember most of the words to the Star-Spangled Banner either.)

After the closing ceremony everybody hugs goodbye and swears that ROI has changed their lives. As for me, I'm Jewed out. All I've heard for a week straight is Jewish this, Jewish that—Jewish Jewish Jewish Jewish *Jewish*—and I need a vacation.

I don't want to talk about Jews anymore.

I don't want to *think* about Jews anymore.

---

* Translation for the *goyim:* a permanent move to Israel.

I certainly don't want to *look* at Jews anymore.

You *hear* me? I'm *done* with *Jews*.

So I say goodbye to my fellow Future Jewish Leaders, take one last look at the Jewish Promised Land and leave for the airport so I can get back home ...

To Jew York City.

Fucker.

Part Two:

JEW-BOY LOOKS FOR GOD, FINDS DRUGS INSTEAD

★ ★ ★

But I cannot leave Israel. Not yet. Not until I have discovered the answer to one little question: *does God exist?* I reschedule my flight, take a train back to midtown Tel Aviv, and walk aimlessly with my suitcase. The temperature is at least a hundred degrees Fahrenheit. Sweat pours down my face. I sit cross-legged on the sizzling sidewalk with my head buried in my arms.

"What am I *doing?*" I ask myself. "Where am I going to *sleep* tonight?"

"Shalom," says an Israeli woman who seems to take pity on my perceptible homelessness. "Ckkkkkkkkkkkh, Akkkkkkkkkkkkh, Ckkkkkkkkkkkh, Bakkkkkkkkkkkkh?"

"Sorry, ma'am," I say, trying to convey that I can't speak my language of heritage. "Do you know English?"

"A little bit, yes." She smiles. "Why do you have this sad face?"

"I was supposed to go back to America but I canceled my flight without making any hotel reservations. I don't know where I'm *staying*—where I'm *going*—and I didn't bring much money."

"Why did you *come* to Israel?"

"I'm ... well ... looking for God."

"You should *never* have *left* your *home*," the woman barks. "You will find *nothing*. There is *no* God, only *sheep people* who will make *you* one of the sheep people. Do you *see* God? There is *no* God to see. You waste your *time* in Israel."

Disoriented and dehydrated, I find the nearest bar.

"American, yes?" the bartender asks, uncapping my beer. "What are your plans?"

"I don't *have* any plans," I say. "I'm … just … trying to figure out if God exists."

"You chase a *fairy tale*." The bartender grimaces. "The Palestinians killed my best friend. God would not have *let* him die. No God exists."

"A few of my best friends also have di—"

"Have you fucked any Israeli girls yet?"

"Actually I have a girlfriend back in the States."

"You do not *cheat?* Are you *married?* Oh my friend, you have not *fucked* a woman until you fuck an *Israeli* woman. Your girlfriend on the other side of the world does not need to *know*. You must be a *man*. You must *live*."

"She would see the guilt in my eyes and hear it in my voice," I say. "And I enjoy having testicles attached to my body."

I finish the beer and leave the bar. Since I'm looking for God it makes sense to go back to Jerusalem, but I'd rather not take a public bus considering that terrorists ignite these on a semi-regular basis. (And I want to *find* God, not *meet* Him.)

So I take a far more expensive group taxi with two young Jews and an old bearded man whom I've never met. I silently ask God to send me a sign that I'm not wasting my time.

The two young passengers debate astrology.

"I read this book in college that said it *does* affect your personality and the way—"

"*Bullshit*, it's all pop-psychology that applies to anyone *with* a personali—"

"It *is* real," says the old bearded man, who identifies himself as Matityahu Glazerson, *Judaism's foremost Zodiac expert.* He has written more than thirty books on astrology. "Oh, yes, it is *very* real."

Wow, this is freaky. This is *really* freaky.

"You are looking for the *truth*," Glazerson says, suddenly turning in my direction and peering into my eyes. "You are *burning* for the truth. You cannot *sleep* until you *find* the truth. This is why you have come to *Eretz Yisrael*."*

We have officially gone from "freaky" to "holy *shit*."

The taxi arrives in Jerusalem. I hunt for a cheap place to stay, ultimately finding a *yeshiva*—a Jewish religious school—that gives young Americans free beds and meals in exchange for attending lectures. The man at the front desk asks for an identification card; I give him my driver's license.

"It says 'Organ and Tissue Donor,'" the man says with a frown. "Do you know that this violates Jewish law?"

"Huh?" I say. "If I die then somebody else can use the spare parts. What's wrong with charity?"

"If somebody loaned you a cell phone, would you return it with a missing battery?"

"I … uh … don't *think* so."

"All right, God loans you a *body*. When the *Moshiach*† comes to resurrect the dead, it won't work if your organs are in different people."

"Why couldn't God … like … create *new* body parts?"

The deskman sighs and directs me to my bedroom. My bunkmate is a twenty-year-old Orthodox Jew who needs many years of therapy.

"You need to learn to feel *disgusted* at sexual thoughts," the bunkmate says. "When a pretty girl approaches, you should look *away*

---

* Translation for the *goyim:* "the Biblical land of Israel."

† Translation for the *goyim:* "messiah."

because the thought of sex is so terrible. You should want to *vomit* when you see pretty girls and you should *beg* God for forgiveness when you have these thoughts. Getting to this point of revulsion is difficult—I know, I know—but we are all working on it."

"What are you *talking* about?" I ask. "What about *marriage?* Shouldn't you find your *wife* attractive? How do you fall in love with ugly chicks?"

"There is no such *thing* as love; it's a silly *Western* idea. Arranged marriages are best. The rabbis know what they're doing. *They* know what works; *you* know nothing. You only need to meet your wife *once* before you marry her. You can get to know her *after* the wedding."

Another male *yeshiva* scholar sounds like the technology-fearing Unabomber: "*Moshiach* will never come until we *reverse* this society. We have electricity, automobiles, money. These distract us from God and prayer and Torah study. If Jews want the God of the Bible to return to us, Jews must return to the *times* of the Bible."

No thanks, buddy, I'd rather *keep* the air conditioning and Penicillin.

This Orthodox cult is unlike anything that I've ever associated with Judaism. I was raised in a Reform community of liberal, secularized Jews who believe in science, equality, and lobster bisque. My friends and I had bar mitzvahs and believed in God, sure, but we weren't *fucking psychotic.*

However, the *yeshiva* youths dress alike (black suits, white fringe and big circular hats), pray alike (this weird jerky motion called *davening*) and *think* alike—or refuse to think at all.

"If you see a Christian missionary, you should *kill* him because he's a blasphemer and in the Torah blasphemers are *killed*," says one scholar. "If a *goy* tries to study Torah, he must be put to death."

"Are you *serious?*" I say. "You can't *kill* people over rules in a book that's three thousand years old!"

"The Torah is forever—it's for *all* generations!"

Some of their behaviors are more reminiscent of obsessive-compulsive disorder than conventional religion.

"Why don't you flick your cigarette?" I ask a *yeshiva* student who smokes with me outside. "You have two inches of *ash* dangling off."

"It would be symbolic of destroying the Temple," the student explains. "We cannot extinguish the Eternal Flame."

"Sometimes a cigarette is only a cigarette, bro!"

"It makes sense when you learn the entire law. Ask the rabbis."

So I attend a theology class. This week's Torah portion describes an elixir that poisons adulterous wives but spares faithful wives.

"*That* sounds scientific," I snicker to a student.

"What do you mean? It's true—it's in the Torah."

"Come *on*, man, that's scientifically *impossible.*"

"It was during the Time of Miracles. When God rebuilds the Temple, the miracles will happen again."

In the *yeshiva* library I discover a book titled *The Path of the Just*, which informs me: "There is a small organ on a man which, when it is satiated, hungers, and which, when made to hunger, is sated."

My *stomach* is hungrier than my "small organ," which by the way is an enormous organ, so I ask a *yeshiva* student to help me find a pizza parlor. He orders a cheese slice and I order pepperoni.

"There isn't *pepperoni* in *Jerusalem.*" The student laughs at my ignorance. "You can't mix *beef* and *milk*—it's not kosher. And pepperoni is mostly *pork* anyway."

"Okay, whatever, I'll have *chicken* pizza."

"You can't mix *any* meat with *any* milk."

"*Seriously?* Can chickens even *make* milk?"

"It's a rabbinical decree. We don't question the rabbis here. If the rules don't make sense to us, it's because they are too complex for our understanding—*not* because we're too complex for the rules. Nobody is as wise as the rabbis. Nobody's *mind* is on their *level.*"

"Do you follow *every* rule? Isn't there some law against touching your *dick* when you take a *piss?* You can't *possibly* observe *that* one!"

"We *do* observe it here." The student blushes. "You can maneuver your belt strategically to aim. Why *touch* it? It's a filthy part of the body, plus the Talmud says, 'The hand that reaches below the navel should be chopped off.'"

Shockingly I'm *not* jacking it in Jerusalem. If this *is* the house of God, I'd feel guilty for staining the sheets.

> "*Not one of them who took up in his youth with this opinion that there are no gods ever continued to old age faithful to his conviction.*"
>
> —PLATO, *LAWS*

> "*All men have need of the gods.*"
>
> —HOMER, *THE ODYSSEY*

What are we?

How are we?

Why are we?

These questions have haunted Mankind since the dawn of civilization. Those who claim to know the Answers—and feel the need to force their conclusions on others—are responsible for unspeakable bloodshed throughout history; it matters not if their conclusion is Godliness or Atheism. A fundamentalist is a fundamentalist, a butcher is a butcher, and an asshole is an asshole.

What we *do* know: a speck of energy once exploded, creating the elements, the stars, the planets and the Black Forever. World-renowned physicist Stephen Hawking observes: "Many people do not like the idea that time has a beginning, probably because it smacks of divine intervention."[1]* Life developed on a single planet in the Milky Way Galaxy, the odds of which—as Yale physicists and Nobel Prize winners have calculated—are equivalent to rolling "100 trillion consecutive double sixes" with a single pair of dice, or "a tornado sweeping through a junkyard" and assembling "a Boeing 747 from the materials within."[2]

Yes, the Universe is a crazy place where bizarre, frightening and possibly unnatural events transpire, somewhat like the average fraternity house party. A mere sixth of our species—including six percent of Americans—lack any faith in the supernatural,[3] but those who have blind faith are often hostile to intellectual pursuits. Which side is intelligent? Which side is ignorant?

Faith in God declines dramatically as education increases,[4] but the director of the U.S. National Human Genome Research Institute claimed that he had seen a "glimpse at the workings of God," and blamed "the shrill voices that occupy the extremes of this spectrum" for "this impression that ... science and religion have to be at war."[5]

Religious extremists *started* the war. The Catholic Church forced Galileo Galilee to renounce his evidence that the earth revolves around the sun, which was "dangerous," "heretical" and would "harm the Holy Faith by rendering Holy Scripture false," according to a cardinal in 1615.[6] Two hundred and fifty years later the Vatican condemned the notion that "sciences ought to be perused in such a spirit of freedom that one may be allowed to hold as true their assertions, even when opposed to revealed doctrine."[7]

In 2007 a Catholic archbishop said that governments should not tolerate "ridicule of the sacred" as "free expression,"[8] and the Vatican's official newspaper accused a comedian of "terrorism" for "criticizing the Pope."[9] They aren't the only ones who wish to

---

* You wouldn't believe in God either if you were Hawking.

silence blasphemous opponents: the Associated Press reported in 2008 that "leaders of the world's Muslim nations are considering taking legal action against (Westerners) that slight their religion or its sacred symbols."[10]

Theological absolutism has resulted in countless gallons of spilled blood for generation after generation. The Islamist barbarians of our time are no different than Roman Christians who punished adultery and prostitution with amputation and eye gouging. In the late 1300s Spanish Catholics "dragged Jews to the baptismal fronts and forced them, on pain of death, to convert to Christianity," according to historian Karen Armstrong. The Catholics then killed thirteen thousand of these *converts* who did not appear to sufficiently love the Prince of Peace.[11] Catholics and Protestants massacred each other in the name of God when they weren't busy drowning and burning suspected witches.

However, the Inquisition backfired: theocratic violence led to "the first declarations of secularism and atheism in Europe," according to Armstrong,[12] along with doubts about the divine right of kings, papal authority and scriptural authenticity.

The Enlightenment was based on principles of reason and liberty, but the former eventually led to the dismissal of the latter. Whereas Judeo-Christian theology purports that Man possesses God-given free will, three major European thinkers in the 1800s challenged this notion:

- Charles Darwin postulated that species designations are "purely subjective inventions of the taxonomist."[13]

- Sigmund Freud hypothesized that the *sub*conscious controls human behavior. He considered the notion of God "foreign to reality" and "patently infantile."[14]

- Karl Marx envisioned a new form of government that could alter human nature. He considered religion "the opiate of the masses," and believed that free will was an illusion because "it is not the consciousness of men which determines their existence, but, on the contrary, it is their social existence which determines their consciousness."[15] (This makes more sense after the ingestion of *massive* opiates.)

The Communist Manifesto inspired twentieth century Russian malcontents—led by Vladimir Lenin, Joseph Stalin and Leon Trotsky—to overthrow their government, kill the Tsar and his ministers (Woo! Woo!), criminalize religious expression, force women to work in the fields, and imprison or execute hundreds of thousands of "counterrevolutionaries."

Just as Christian fundamentalists abhor the freedom of the individual, *anti*-Christian fundamentalists forced their ideology on millions of people. Soviet administrators disciplined adolescents for *not* sleeping with numerous comrades.[16] "Love was outlawed," and those who preferred monogamous romance over randomized copulation "were attacked as 'destroyers of communist ethics,'" according to socialist Wilhelm Reich.[17]

The *Atlantic Monthly* reported on Russia in 1926: "It was not an unusual occurrence for ... a girl of [twenty years old] to have had three or four abortions."[18] Lenin *boasted* of this in 1925: "At present, the position of the woman in the Soviet Union is such that even from the standpoint of the most progressive nations it would have to be called ideal."[19] Another Soviet official explained that as communist policies are implemented, "[t]he patriarchal family disintegrates."[20]

Many on the American Left cheered the Soviet Revolution, including National Education Association president John Dewey, *New York Times* reporters, and feminist author Tillie Olsen, who described the USSR as "heaven ... brought to earth in Russia."[21]

However, the prominent freethinker Bertrand Russell visited the USSR in 1920 and reported back to the States: "Bolshevism is a closed tyrannical bureaucracy, with a spy system more elaborate and terrible than the Tsar's. No vestige of liberty remains, in thought or speech or action."[22]

This was unsurprising to anyone who did *not* have his idealistic head stuck up his Ivy League asshole. "Socialists demand the *strictest* control," according to Lenin. "It is true that liberty is precious—so precious that it must be rationed."[23] He initiated "a series of restrictions of liberty," and ensured: "[T]here is no liberty, no democracy. We have neither a parliament, nor the freedom to call meetings."[24]

Just as Christian authoritarians had censored artists and authors for centuries, Soviet artists could not paint landscapes, only portraits of the communist revolution; Soviet authors could not pen love stories, only tales of overturning traditional society.[25]

The equal distribution of wealth was hardly a consolation; there wasn't any to distribute: Soviet citizens had to work four times longer than Americans to afford bread, twelve times longer to afford an automobile, a hundred times longer to afford clothes, a hundred and fifty times longer to afford sugar, a hundred and twenty times longer to afford tea, and—cruelest of all—four times longer to afford vodka.[26]

Soviet citizens had four times less living space than Americans, consumed five times less food,[27] and occasionally *were* the food: after agricultural reforms starved five million Soviets to death, some turned to cannibalism for survival.[28] (Mutually ensured *digestion?*)

It wasn't enough that the Bolsheviks had their own country; they wanted the entire planet. Lenin lusted for world domination and believed that the notion of socialist countries existing "side by side with Christian states … is unthinkable—one or the other must triumph in the end."[29] Same bullshit, different day.

★ ★ ★

JERUSALEM | At Sabbath dinner I encounter one of the most dazzling young women whom I have ever had the pleasure to ogle. Her name is Sarah. She wears a pink poncho over a black dress. She is a brunette—I *crave* brunettes—with a perfect smile and Ample Breasts. Yes, I love her.

"Hey ..." I extend my hand to shake, kiss and sodomize hers. "My name is Mart—"

"Don't *touch* me," Sarah shrieks. "Sorry, I never touch boys except for my family members—or eventually my husband."

No. No. No. God. Please. *No. No.* **NO**.

"Not even a *hand* job?" I ask. "I mean, *hand*shake, hand*shake!*"

"I shook hands a couple years ago but now I'm *shomer negiah*."*

"*Marry* me, Sarah. We'll make beautiful genetically pure Jewish babies together."

"*No.*" She laughs seductively. "I don't even know your *name.*"

"That doesn't *matter.* I'm Jewish, you're Jewish—doesn't that mean *anything* to you?"

Then I remember: *Orthodox Judaism forbids oral sex.* Never mind, you Cock-Teasing Jew Bitch.

Speaking of bitches, the *yeshiva* students are *furious* when I talk about my *goy* girlfriend back in the States: "Could you *live* with yourself if you marry a *shiksa?*" "How could you end your lineage forever?" "Your heritage, *gone with your generation!*" "You should be *ashamed* of yourself!" "Intermarriage is what *Hitler* would have wanted!"

"Wasn't *genetic purity of his race* what Hitler wanted?" I respond on more than a few occasions.

On a temperate evening I tour the Old City with a scrumptious female Israeli solider.

---

* Translation for the *goyim:* "observant of not touching the opposite sex."

"You know something?" I say. "The U.S. Constitution means more to me than the Torah."

"*Why?*" the soldier scoffs. "Your country is so *racist;* it *lets* people be racists."

"You mean free speech? Well, if the government makes one opinion illegal, it can throw people in jail for *any* opinion, you know?"

"Racism isn't an 'opinion,' it *hurts* people. Just look at *our* country; if bigots spread hatred, people are going to die."

No use arguing. Safety is (understandably) far more important to Israelis than freedom. Everyone is drafted into the army at eighteen years old. The only exemption is for Orthodox youths studying in the *yeshivas,* and they aren't exactly pluralistic civil libertarians.

"We haven't had a draft in America for thirty-five years," I say to a twenty-one-year-old IDF intelligence officer as we drive along the countryside. "Isn't that kind of like *slavery?*"

"You see this gas station?" The soldier points through the lowered window. "Two years ago a suicide bomber killed twenty-seven people right there. Hamas would kill us if they could. Syria would kill us if they could. Iran would kill us if they could. There is no complaining about Army service because how else could we *survive?* Americans cannot understand because Canada and Mexico are your *friends.* They do not wish to kill everyone in your country."

"Huh," I say, wondering for the first time if Americans believe in liberty because we *have* the liberty. "Have you ever *met* a Canadian?"*

Even by post-9/11 American standards, Israeli security measures are daunting: guards with enormous weapons examine *everyone* who enters shopping malls, nightclubs, movie theaters and coffee shops. As I dine at a falafel joint, a female soldier lays her machine gun on a

---

* A 2004 survey of Canadian youths found that forty percent considered the U.S.
"evil." What are you going to *do* about it, sissies?

table pointing toward my face. She notices my anxiety and rotates the gun so its crosshairs instead point toward a baby carriage.

Jerusalemites' obsession with security is nothing compared to their obsession with God. A rabbinical student from the *yeshiva* walks me through the ancient City of David.

"Tell me, Martin," the Future Rabbi says. "*Why* are you looking for God?"

"I don't *know*, man," I say. "I've been agnostic since high school but all of my friends who committed suicide—or *tried* to commit suicide—didn't believe in God either. Maybe that's not a coincidence."

"God is a mirror reflecting reality back at you. Everything in existence is a *part* of God, including *you*. Not being in touch with that is *exile*. It's tough for Americans because we're so individualistic, but we have to give ourselves away to become a part of something greater."

We enter an excavation site on the side of the road.

"You see, Martin," the Future Rabbi says, "there are five levels of pleasure. We would trade *all* of a lower one for a *taste* of a higher one. So what is the *lowest* level of pleasure?"

"Hmmm ..." I say. "Fucking?"

"Yes, *sensory* pleasures: sex, food, alcohol. What would we trade all of the sex in the world for the littlest bit of?"

"Love?"

"Exactly." The Future Rabbi smiles. "What would we trade all of the *love* in the world for?"

"*Fucking!*"

"No, Martin, the answer is *goodness*. You would jump in front of a speeding car to save a child playing in the street—even if it meant never seeing your wife or girlfriend again."

"I wouldn't be so sure of that."

"Yes, Martin, you *would*. Now what is the *ultimate* pleasure? What would you trade all of the *goodness* in the world for?"

"Not burning in hell forever? *Should* I accept Jesus as my personal savior?"

"You have a very Jewish sense of humor." The Future Rabbi rolls his eyes. "The answer is *absolute truth*. We would trade all our good acts to know that God loves us and that God created us *because* He loves us. Therefore the highest level of pleasure is that which *God* receives from giving *us* pleasure."

"*We* don't get the highest pleasure? That's a gyp, huh?"

"If we could truly get pleasure from a giant *fireball* rising into the sky, or *flowers* growing, or our *hearts* beating, or our lungs *breathing*, we would *cry* with joy—but we learn to *ignore* God's creation and focus on *ourselves*. When we are finally reunited with God in the World to Come, our lives will bring *infinitely* more pleasure than *any* earthly experience."

Suddenly the Future Rabbi removes his clothes and walks into a dark cave.

"*Excuse* me," I say. "*Why* are you naked?"

"This is a *mikvah*. It's a pool for purifying your body and soul. This one is three thousand years old! King *David* bathed here! Come in!"

"Uh ... I don't have a *towel*, dude ... and I'd rather *not* follow a naked stranger into a dark pool."

"Nobody's *looking*. I'll dunk in first and then you can go—it's *amazing* how different you feel afterward! This is something that Jews have done for *millennia*. You're getting in touch with your *heritage!*"

The Naked Future Rabbi dives into the water and resurfaces. I turn away to avoid glancing at his Hairy Jew Dong.

"That was *great*," the Naked Future Rabbi shouts. "Are you *ready?*"

"Jesus Christ, whatever ... why doesn't anyone take 'no' for an answer here?" I remove my shirt, jeans and underwear, dive into the FREEZING water, and rocket back to the surface, gasping for air.

"Wow, that *does* feel pretty awe—"

Forty Japanese tourists stand in the historic *mikvah* entrance, snapping photographs of my dripping naked body.*

"My gay friend says that Jewish guys have four *inches* on Asians," I explain to the Future Rabbi. "Nothing to be ashamed of."

"Martin," says the Future Rabbi with a friendly smile, "you have shrinkage."

> "*Fascism does not consider that 'happiness' is possible upon earth ... It has limited useless or harmful liberties and preserved those that are essential. It cannot be the individual who decides in this matter, but only the State. ... In the Fascist State religion is looked upon as one of the deepest manifestations of the spirit; it is, therefore, not only respected, but defended and protected.*"[30]
> —BENITO MUSSOLINI, *THE DOCTRINE OF FASCISM*, 1932

> "*[F]anatics of all kinds are actually crowded together at one end. It is the fanatic and the moderate who are poles apart and never meet. ... [T]he reactionary and the radical have more in common than either has with the liberal or the conservative.*"[31]
> —ERIC HOFFER, *THE TRUE BELIEVER*, 1951

For activists of the Left and Right, any tactic—including the brainwashing of children—is justified in the name of Victory.

Three-fourths of Republicans want creationism taught in public schools,[32] despite the fact that human DNA is ninety-six percent identical to chimpanzee DNA.[33] We get the leaders that

---

* This actually happened. If God exists, He has a wretched sense of humor.

we deserve: only forty percent of Americans believe in evolution,[34] and eleven percent believe that the sun revolves around the earth.[35] If God created our bodies, why do so many theists refuse to utilize their *brains?*

The Republican House Majority Leader, a devout Christian, blamed the Columbine High School shootings on the fact that "our school systems teach our children that they are nothing but glorified apes who have evolutionized out of some primordial mud."[36] *Evolutionized?*

Recent evidence that *we* are the Stupid Apes:

- The Kansas Board of Education banned the teaching of evolution and instead told students that the earth is less than ten thousand years old, the Grand Canyon could have formed "in hours or days," and "dinosaurs lived very recently and coexisted with man."[37] A $27 million Kentucky creationism theme park, which attracts thousands of Americans per day, also posits this hypothesis.[38] (Apparently *Jurassic Park* is one of Spielberg's *historical* films.)

- A Missouri legislator compared biology teachers to *terrorists*: "It's like when the hijackers took over those four planes on September 11 and took people to a place where they didn't want to go ... this is *our* country and we're going to take it back."[39] (Surely the psychotic Islamists *loved* Charles Darwin.)

- A Pennsylvania school board member said: "This country wasn't founded on ... evolution. This country was founded on Christianity, and our students should be taught as such."[40] (Thomas Jefferson: "Christianity neither is, nor ever was, a part of the common law.")

- In 2007 a Texas Republican representative ridiculed "the Big Bang, fifteen-billion-year, alternate 'creation scenario' of the Pharisee religion."[41] (You read it here: astronomy is the *Jews'* fault.)

- Nearly two hundred thousand American public school students learn "of the literal truth of the biblical text" concerning the earth's orbit, thanks to the National Council on Bible Curriculum.[42]* (Wow, evangelical astronauts are in for a big fucking surprise!)

A decade-long study on the efficacy of billion-dollar pro-abstinence programs, ushered in during the era of the Republican Congress, revealed that the money was completely wasted: there is "no evidence" that communities with anti-sex education have lower rates of teen pregnancy *or* STD transmission.[43] However, the *Journal of Adolescent Health* found that teenagers "who received comprehensive sex education were fifty percent less likely to become pregnant than those who received abstinence-only education."[44]

Curricula in twenty-five states erroneously claimed that "half the gay male teenagers in the United States have tested positive for the AIDS virus," fingering a female "can result in pregnancy," a six-week-old fetus is a "thinking person," "AIDS can be spread via sweat and tears," and "[c]ondoms fail to prevent HIV transmission as often as thirty-one percent of the time ..."[45] Never mind that condoms, when used properly, reduce the transmission of HIV by nearly a *hundred* percent, and fingering a female can only result in a urinary tract infection. And possibly sex, if you're dexterous enough!

Federal curricula further informed teenagers:

---

* When the media reported in 2008 that a Minnesota public elementary school was teaching the Koran and leading students in Islamic prayers, Republicans went ballistic. No competing for theocracy!

- "We actively seek to eliminate terrorism from our land; please help us actively seek to eliminate this corruptive terrorism that is stealing our children's future." (Weapons of Mass *Dick-Suction?*)

- "While a man needs little or no preparation for sex, a woman often needs hours of emotional and mental preparation." (Before *sex?* No. Before *dinner?* Yes.)

- "Sexual relationships often lower the self-respect of both partners—one feeling used, the other feeling like the user. ...This depression may lead to attempted, or successful, suicide."[46] (Hey, I wanted to kill myself in high school because I *couldn't* get laid.)

Even in the God-fearing states, a zippered approach to sex education has proved useless: the Texas Board of Education rejected textbooks for mentioning condoms and *breast cancer*—the Jesus Freaks don't want their daughters to screen themselves for *fucking cancer!*—opting instead to inform students that the best way to avoid STDs is to "get plenty of rest," "respect yourself," and "go out as a group."[47] (Group sex *never* leads to herpes!)

Incidentally Texas has one of the five highest teenage birthrates in America,[48] twice as many per capita as Heathen Massachusetts.[49] In 2007 the U.S. government's "leading advocate of abstinence-only programs" resigned after reporters discovered his name was on the client list at a D.C. escort service.[50]

Activists on the other side are no better: ultra-leftist teachers and administrators have reportedly forbidden students to say, "Thank you, God, for my food";[51] wear Santa Claus costumes,[52] cross necklaces[53] and "What Would Jesus Do?" bracelets;[54] thank God in graduation speeches;[55] and recite the Pledge of Allegiance with the phrase "one nation under God."[56] In 2005 Colorado students were instructed to pledge their allegiance to "one nation *under my belief system* ..."[57]

Richard Dawkins, author of the bestseller *The God Delusion*, questions whether parents should have the right to raise their *own* children with religion: "Is there something to be said for society stepping in? What about bringing up children to believe manifest falsehoods?"[58]

Who needs parents anyway? The State can reengineer human nature and construct a utopian society: "Under a 'perfect' system no one needs goodness," wrote influential behaviorist B.F. Skinner. "Hormones may be used to change sexual behavior, surgery—as in lobotomy—to control violence, tranquilizers to control aggression, and appetite depressants to control overeating." All society needs is a "benevolent dictator," *not* "the defenders of freedom and dignity."[59]

In 1972 a Harvard psychiatrist reportedly told the Association of Childhood Education:

> *"Every child in America entering school at the age of five is mentally ill because he comes to school with certain allegiances to our Founding Fathers, toward our elected officials, toward his parents, toward a belief in a supernatural being, and toward the sovereignty of this nation as a separate entity. It's up to you as teachers to make all these sick children well—by creating the international child of the future."*[60]

There is more leftist lunacy on the fringes of the environmental movement. Activists have condemned "Western democracy" for its "perceived liberties,"[61] proposed that "a limitation be put on how many squares of toilet paper can be used in any one sitting,"[62] threatened to "audit" and spy on citizens who don't recycle,[63] demanded control over citizens' home thermostats,[64] proclaimed that humans are "the

AIDS of the Earth" and "[f]reedom to breed will bring ruin to all,"[65] suggested that governments should "radically and intelligently reduce human populations" to a sixth of the current number,[66] and announced their intent to murder scientists who question whether global warming is a manmade phenomenon.[67]

This is the same fanatical hatred that drives right-wingers who believe that "we need to execute ... prominent liberals who are trying to demoralize the country," as a young Republican woman told a reporter for the U.K. *Independent,* adding: "Just take a couple of these anti-war people off to the gas chamber for treason to show, if you try to bring down America at a time of war, that's what you'll get."[68] This unhinged seething is inevitable when you believe—in the words of a Utah Republican legislator—that "Satan" is responsible for Mexican immigrants, and that Democrats want to "destroy Christian America."[69]

These extremists of the Left and Right have *nothing* in common with mainstream Americans, and *everything* in common with one another. Pat Robertson and Jerry Falwell *agreed* with Osama bin Laden that America deserved 9/11 for our moral freefall. Right-wing author Dinesh D'Souza admitted: "the political right and the Islamic fundamentalists are on the same wavelength on social issues."[70] At the same time leftists such as Ward Churchill and Noam Chomsky agree with Islamic militants that 9/11 was an understandable response to American foreign policy. Militants on both sides believe that the U.S. *deserves* destruction. No American moderate—liberal nor conservative—would ever volunteer such a juvenile masochistic tirade.

The media feeds us a narrative that America is comprised of two camps, Red and Blue, but extremism is by *definition* divergence from the center. The stereotypes only hold true for the freaks on the fringes:

- Nearly the same percentage of Republicans and Democrats believe in the afterlife and "pray daily or more often."[71]

- Not all conservatives are greedy: religious Americans donate far more food, clothing and money to the needy.[72] Not all liberals are anti-family: nonreligious Americans hold the lowest divorce rate of any demographic.[73]

- The vast majority of Americans would vote for a qualified African-American, Hispanic, Mormon or woman. More than half would vote for a qualified homosexual or atheist.[74]

The extremists are a very loud minority. And a very *deluded* minority: neuroscientists discovered in 2006 that Democratic and Republican loyalists were "quick to spot inconsistency and hypocrisy—but only in candidates they opposed," and did not "use the rational regions of [their] brain to think ..."[75] In 2008 the *Economist* reported that "extremists of both sides are happier than moderates ... because they are certain they are right," but "this often leads them to conclude that the other side is not merely wrong, but evil."[76] An Emory University psychologist who wrote a book titled *The Political Brain* found that extremists on both sides enjoy outrage in the same way that "drug addicts get their 'fix,' giving new meaning to the term political junkie."[77]

The vast majority of left- and right-wingers are convinced that the objective mainstream media is hostile to their beliefs, as if there *were* a "biased liberal media" or "right-wing corporate media."[78] The shocking truth about journalists—I say this after ten years of experience in newsrooms—is that we are simply *lazy*. And often intoxicated.

Free speech is intolerable to extremists, whether it's right-wingers who can't stand pacifism or left-wingers who can't stand prejudice, for example the Reverend Al Sharpton and the chairwoman of the Congressional Black Congress, who want the government to punish the airing of racist speech, according to the *Los Angeles Times*.[79]

However, the Founding Fathers believed that coercion is *always* immoral. Thomas Jefferson, who admittedly would have enslaved and fucked the chairwoman of the Congressional Black Congress, loathed the kind of thugs who comprise the modern Republican base:

- "The legitimate powers of government extend only to such acts as are injurious to others. But it does me no injury for my neighbor to say there are twenty gods, or no God."

- "The clergy converted the simple teachings of Jesus into an engine for enslaving mankind ... these clergy, in fact, constitute the real Anti-Christ."

- "History, I believe, furnishes no example of a priest-ridden people maintaining a free civil government. ... In every country and in every age, the priest has been hostile to liberty."

James Madison believed that churches had never acted as "guardians of the liberties of the people," and insisted that "[r]eligion and government will both exist in greater purity the less they are mixed together." John Adams ratified a treaty, written during the Washington Administration, which proclaimed: "the Government of the United States of America is not in any sense founded on the Christian religion."

Despite their opposition to organized religion, the Founding Fathers passionately viewed God as a torchbearer of freedom:

- "Rebellion to tyrants is obedience to God," according to Jefferson, because "God hath created the mind free."

- Benjamin Franklin said, "If men are so wicked ... *with religion*, what would they be *if without it?*"

- George Washington believed that religion makes citizens "greater and happier than they already are."

- John Adams warned that the "Constitution was made only for a moral and religious people; it is wholly inadequate for the government of any other."

So the problem isn't *faith*; it's *intolerance*. Republicans tried to ban doctor-assisted suicide after a majority of Oregon residents voted to legalize it,[80] simply because the right-wingers could not tolerate values others than their own. Congressional Democrats want to force pro-life taxpayers to fund abortions for poor women,[81] and require conservative radio stations to broadcast left-wing viewpoints.[82]

Theocracy is morality without freedom.

Socialism is equality without freedom.

But given the choice—if there *is* such a thing as choice—the majority of Americans opt for emancipation.

"I have no fear but that the result of our experiment will be that men may be trusted to govern themselves without a master," Jefferson wrote. "Could the contrary of this be proved, I should conclude either that there is no God or that he is a malevolent being."[83]

JERUSALEM | One week in the Holy City and I've lost all faith in organized religion. I keep breaking commandments and mores that I had no idea *existed:* sitting at the same table as a female, using my cell phone on the Sabbath, ripping *toilet paper* on the Sabbath. The ultra-Orthodox nuts shake their fists and curse me for my ignorance.

It's not only *Jews* who are freaking me out. A shopkeeper in Jerusalem's Muslim Quarter explains that "Islam means *peace*," while his assistant—a burly juggernaut—blocks the doorway.

"Let us get this over with," the shopkeeper says. "One thousand shekels."

The juggernaut clearly differs on the meaning of Islam. I grudgingly forfeit a couple hundred U.S. dollars worth of Israeli currency.

When I speak to fundamentalists of each religion, I hear exactly the same things: hardcore Jews say that God does not hear the prayers of Muslims or Christians; hardcore Muslims say that God does not hear the prayers of Jews and Christians; hardcore Christians say that God does not hear the prayers of Jews and Muslims. *If God is everywhere*, I want to scream, *doesn't He hear everything?*

"All of my friends who have killed themselves or tried to kill themselves were atheists," I say to a Christian. "But I hope they were wrong, you know?"

"Why do you hope they were *wrong?*" the Christian asks. "If God exists, they're in hell."

A bearded man approaches me at the Western Wall, Judaism's holiest site, and describes the Coming Apocalypse: "Can you imagine *lightning bolts* striking every *inch* of the earth's surface at once? At *once*, you understand?"

"The sky looks pretty clear tonight," I say.

"Not *tonight*—no, not *tonight*—but *soon*."

A sixty-year-old Hippy Rabbi from San Francisco invites me to dinner at his townhouse.

"Dad, can I go down to the *Kotel* and *daven* before dinner?" the Hippy Rabbi's fifteen-year-old son asks. "Please?"*

"There's no *time*," says the Hippy Rabbi. "We have to start the blessings."

---

* Translation for the *goyim:* "go down to the Western Wall and pray."

"*Daaaaaaaaaaaaaaad,*" the kid squeals. "Stop *controlling* me!"

Is this Orthodox Jewish teenage rebellion? I wonder with horror.

After blessing God for our food, the Hippy Rabbi pours a thick green substance into my glass.

"This is *khat* juice from Yemen," the Hippy Rabbi says. "It's illegal in the States so you better enjoy it while you can. *Sip!*"

"Uh ..." I raise the glass. "It's not like *LSD*, right?"

"No, no, trust me, it's *soothing*—you'll feel *relaxed.*"

"Yes sir." I chug the liquid, which tastes like sour kiwi juice. "Wow, I've never met a drug-dealing *rabbi* before!"

The Hippy Rabbi refills my glass. I drink obligingly and then pour myself *another* two glasses. The whole family begins to look concerned.

"Oh ... damn ..." I say, chugging my fifth glass. "That's ... really ... ah ... holy *shit* ..."

Suddenly I cannot stop *giggling.* I apologize and scurry outside.

"*Thanks for creating DRUGS, God!*" I howl into the Night Sky, staggering like a maniac through the stone(d) Jerusalem streets.

Even if I *weren't* tripping on Yemeni narcotics, I'd have to concede that something *powerful*—something *primal, ancient, elevating*—permeates this city. Is it me projecting my awe onto the stones? Or the stones projecting their awe onto me?

The *yeshiva* deskman wakens me at four-thirty in the morning.

"It's *Shavuot,*" the deskman explains. "We celebrate this holiday by studying Torah from sundown until the next afternoon. Get out of bed and go to the library."

Fuck this bullshit. If there *is* a God who desires my happiness—*or* my beauty sleep—He would never force me to live with these maniacs. So I take a taxi back to Tel Aviv, where I spend a week on the beach smoking as much Hebrew hashish—and drinking as much *khat* juice—as I can afford. Every drugged-up, chemically blessed evening I marvel at the cantaloupe, honeydew and lavender sunsets over the Mediterranean. I ponder whether *coincidence* could have created anything so gorgeous. (This is the same question that I ask myself whenever I look into a mirror.)

And it strikes me: if there *is* a God, I'll discover the truth when I'm dead and buried. Yes, I want to believe, but I also want to *live*. Yes, I could agonize over the meaning of life like the *yeshiva* zombies, but then I'd *sacrifice* a meaningful life. The orthodox of all persuasions— Jews and Christians and Muslims, theists and atheists, leftists and rightists—get so wrapped up in their eternal quests, their conversion campaigns, their apocalypses and their utopias, the Rapture and the Revolution, that they forget to *enjoy* their infinitesimal time on earth. They forget *life*, *love*, *laughter* and *liberty*. Why would anyone make that mistake?

God only knows.

"A young man is not a proper hearer of lectures on political science—for he is inexperienced in the actions that occur in life … And, further, since he tends to follow his passions, his study will be vain and unprofitable … And it makes no difference whether he is young in years or in character."

—ARISTOTLE

"Whenever you find yourself on the side of the majority, it is time to pause and reflect."

—MARK TWAIN

"Freedom is something that dies unless it's used."

—HUNTER S. THOMPSON

★ ★ ★

Postscript:

MY ODYSSEY FROM TEENAGE COMMUNIST TO COLLEGE REPUBLICAN TO SO FUCKING ASHAMED

★ ★ ★

When I entered college I was a diehard liberal—I believed in a maximum wage, racial quotas, the inherent evil of money, and censorship of right-wing preachers—but then I witnessed the tyranny of academic leftists: every little joke was cause for a moral panic; sensitivity-enforcing speech codes stifled honest debate; and I received a bad grade on a paper because I used the phrase "girly man," which apparently is a "manifestation of patriarchal hetero-normative bigotry," or whatever my professor said.

In response to this P.C. B.S., I befriended a bunch of College Republicans because they were the enemies of my enemies. Soon I was reading right-wing books, getting my news from biased conservative media outlets, and only conversing with people who kept the echo chamber buzzing. I began to wonder: maybe the legalization of gay marriage *will* destroy society; maybe torture and domestic spying *will* keep America safe; maybe receiving oral sex *will* secure the wrath of God.

Like drinking and screwing, religious devotion is healthy in moderation and a sickness in excess. If you ask me, excessive religious devotion is anything that gets in the way of drinking and screwing. When you worry that oral sex somehow aids the Godless International Communist Conspiracy, it's seriously time to relax. *With a Blow Job!*

At one point I actually considered joining the Army, despite the fact that as a Jewish pipsqueak with Irritable Bowel Syndrome I would be more useless on the battlefield than a mute Quaker paraplegic.

The College Republicans convinced me that Abraham Lincoln, Franklin Roosevelt and Martin Luther King, Jr. were power-hungry tyrants instead of liberators and civic heroes. One of the young conservatives told me: "Killing homosexuals shouldn't count as murder because it's not like fags are human beings." Terrific joke, old sport!

This venomous loathing of the Weak became everyday background noise. I forgot that *moderate* liberals existed; in my mind *all* liberals became monsters under the bed: power-hungry Stalinists that steal everyone's money, destroy the traditional family, eradicate babies by the truckload, support anti-American terrorists and encourage five-year-olds to fornicate. Of course, there *are* left-wing lunatics, but I forgot that most people fall into the middle. I forgot that most people are basically good.

When you view scientists, journalists and teachers—society's voices of reason—as co-conspirators in Marxism, the world becomes a desperate ideological showdown of Us versus Them. Naturally God favored "Us." Right-wing propaganda constantly reminds GOP acolytes that the Lord is On Their Side. Who needs humility and introspection when you have a Divine Mandate?

It took a few years for me to realize that Republican leaders *talk* like libertarians—freedom this, freedom that—but only *support* liberties that involve worshipping the Judeo-Christian God, stockpiling ammunition and discriminating against various minorities. After 9/11 the entire country swerved too far to the right, just as it swerved too far to the left in the humorless, hypersensitive '90s, but the pendulum has swung back to the center—as it always does—because the American people are the most moderate in the world.

There are intelligent and decent Americans on both sides of the spectrum: not all Democrats are loony bohemians; not all Republicans are mutant troglodytes. Reasonable liberals ask, "Why can't we do better?" They want our species to improve its circumstances, insisting upon the greatest good for the greatest number, which is surely noble. Reasonable conservatives ask, "Why *can't* we do better?" They recognize the limits of our human capacities and fear the abuses that occur whenever we forget that government cannot alter our nature.

Both are necessary questions for a healthy national discourse, but *un*reasonable activists have hijacked this conversation and transformed it into a demagogic battle of infotainment gladiators. My sin was mistaking their lucrative show business and deceptive propaganda for something that actually *matters*, something worth basing our friendships upon, something for which we should live and die.

Left-wingers are like marijuana smokers: incomprehensible, lovey-dovey and full of silly ideas, but essentially harmless if they aren't placed in positions of responsibility. However, right-wingers are like *alcoholics:* angry, violent, impulsive and full of bile. I've found myself at both extremes, and neither is conducive to enlightenment nor happiness.

Nevertheless this political journey—from Left to Right and finally back to the Center—was much like experimenting with a bounteous cornucopia of mind-altering substances when I was a teenager: I wouldn't do it again today, but I definitely learned a lot about myself from the experience. And luckily I didn't lose my mind forever.

Here's the solution:

Think for yourself.

It's better this way.

★ ★ ★

History and Acknowledgements

★ ★ ★

I have gone to hell and back for this book. *Dumbocracy* was originally titled *Retard Nation: America's Sexxxiest Young Journalist Exposes the Bastardly Forces Keeping You Stupid*. A major corporate publisher scheduled it for a 2006 release. For legal reasons I can't disclose the story of what happened, but essentially I received one of the hardest ass-fuckings in publishing history. After months of lies from my editor, the book was unceremoniously canceled.

When I first heard the news I sat at my desk for an hour, completely numb, and then walked to the nearest bar and guzzled alcohol until the pain went away, which is what I kept doing for the next two years. I spent hours and hours on my futon over the ensuing weeks, writhing with horrible pains in my stomach. The physical symptoms were like those that accompanied the worst breakups of my life. I considered quitting the journalism profession. I considered jumping from my tenth floor balcony. Worst of all I considered law school.

Suddenly the manuscript that I had spent thousands of hours researching and completing over two years was just that: a stack of paper on my desk, collecting dust. We tried to sell the book to other publishers—I offered to change the title and remove the funniest jokes—but a dozen editors passed. It was hopeless.

The former publisher demanded that I return the money. My bank account dried up. I had to take loans from my parents, which did not feel terrific in my mid-twenties. I moved to an apartment in a neighborhood that most people would refer to as the Ghetto—police sirens blared all night, a few people were murdered down the block, and even the graffiti was graffitied. (Compare this to my situation a couple years earlier: after the success of my book *Generation S.L.U.T.*, including a lucrative Hollywood option, I toured Los Angeles in the back of a limousine, drinking champagne for hours.)

Retard Nation's cancellation destroyed my life. My buzz from *S.L.U.T.* died and I couldn't get any work. Neither could I walk into a bookstore without anger and mourning. I took a bartending class, which indicates how I wanted to fill my days. (Holy shit, how do homeless people *afford* alcoholism?)

And then I got an email from Gary Baddeley of Disinformation: "Marty, I think it's time for you to send the book to us."

Maybe it was all supposed to happen this way. The guys at Disinfo completely understood what I was trying to say and encouraged me to say it *louder*. They actually offered to let me keep the title *Retard Nation*, but I decided that—even though I'm all about offending political extremists—hurting the feelings of handicapped kids and their families is a little much. Even for a professional asshole like me.

The book's cancellation was the greatest professional defeat of my life. I was in a godforsaken place spiritually and financially for two years but the struggling and the suffering have partly forged me into a Man. There is grittiness in my voice that did not exist before. My face is harder; my *heart* is harder. If you think this sounds like bullshit, you have never survived a complete breaking. But if you have survived one, you know that nobody can ever break you in the same place again.

By the way, it's not like I'm totally sober; I'm just tired of waking in pools of my own puke. Who over the age of twenty-four *isn't?*

Dumbocracy could not have happened without Gary Baddeley, Ralph Bernardo, James Fitzgerald, Greg Stadnyk, Devin Ranck, Ian Walters, Mark Ebner, David Abitbol, Robyn Schneider, Francisco Vieira, Jessica Webb, and Mom & Dad. Thanks to *Radar* and *Playboy* for permission to republish the CPAC pieces, and *Jewcy* for "Youngsters of Zion." Special acknowledgement is made to the work of Eric Schlosser, Andrew Sullivan, Jacob Sullum, Radley Balko and *Reason* magazine.

This book is dedicated to the memory of Dr. Steven Edgell (1942–2005) for bringing me back to earth when I had lost my mind. We just didn't know it at the time.

This book is *also* dedicated to God Almighty. Next time You create "intelligent" life, please try harder.

Notes

INTRODUCTION: DOUCHE BAG NATION

1   *Communism, Fascism and Democracy: The Theoretical Foundations*, edited by Carl Cohen, Random House, 1962, p. 7

I. ADVENTURES WITH ACTIVISTS

1   Polls from the *Los Angeles Times,* January 2005; CBS News, March 2005; Gallup/CNN/*USA Today*; *Los Angeles Times,* January 2005; CBS News, March 2005; Gallup/CNN/*USA Today*, May–November 2005. Quoted from ReligiousTolerance.org and PollingReport.com

2   "Which phrase best describes your view of stem cell research?" CNN.com, poll of 46,000 readers, April 11, 2007; "[Retard] vetoes stem-cell funds bill," BBC News, June 20, 2007

3   "Interested Persons Memo: Ban on Safe Abortion Procedures: The So-Called 'Partial Birth Abortion Ban Act of 2003,'" American Civil Liberties Union, ACLU.org, June 18, 2003

4   "Parental involvement in minors' abortions: State Policies in Brief," Alan Guttmacher Institute, August 15, 2005

5   "Where the Rubber Meets Roe," William Saletan, Slate.com, Sept. 30, 2006

6   "The Grassroots Abortion War," Nancy Gibbs, Time.com, Feb. 15, 2007

7   "Facts on Induced Abortion in the United States," Alan Guttmacher Institute, January 2008

8   "1 in 5 pregnancies worldwide and 1 in 3 in Europe ends in abortion," Dr. Gilda Sedgh, Alan Guttmacher Institute, quoting the *Lancet*, October 11, 2007

9   "Ask Dr. Cullins," PlannedParenthood.org, 2003. No longer online. Quoted from *National Review,* NationalReview.com, May 13, 2005

10   *Woman and the New Race,* Margaret Sanger, Brentano's Press, New York, 1920

11   *The Pivot of Civilization,* Margaret Sanger, Brentano's Press, New York, 1922

12   "Editorial Comment," *Birth Control Review,* Volume IV, Number 6, June 1920; *The Pivot of Civilization*

13   *The Pivot of Civilization*

14   Ibid.

15   "Book Review: *Woman of Valor: Margaret Sanger and the Birth Control Movement in America,*" Michael Flaherty, *National Review,* August 17, 1992

16   "Response to caller 'a serious mistake,' says Planned Parenthood of Idaho," Sandra Forester, *Idaho Statesman,* IdahoStatesman.com, February 28, 2008

17 "A White Lie," Michael K. Flaherty, *American Spectator,* August 1992

18 *The Nazi Connection: Eugenics, American Racism, and German National Socialism* by Stefan Kühl, Oxford University Press, 1994, p. 61–63 of the 2002 edition

19 "Condom testing reveals best brands: Planned Parenthood condom performs worst," Reuters, January 4, 2005

20 "The living industry of death," Hans Zeiger, WorldNetDaily.com, December 16, 2003

21 "Planned Parenthood's Feldt Looks Back," Cynthia L. Cooper, Women's eNews, WomenseNews.com, March 31, 2005

22 "A Superhero for Choice," Planned Parenthood Golden Gate, PPGG.org. Removed from website after media scrutiny in August 2005. Author viewed the cartoon before its removal.

23 "Women in Germany," Margaret Sanger, *Birth Control Review,* December 1920

24 "The Family Un-Planner," Amanda Schaffer, Slate.com, November 21, 2006; "Right to Lie," William Saletan, Slate.com, April 24, 2007; "Induced and Spontaneous Abortion and Incidence of Breast Cancer Among Young Women," *Archives of Internal Medicine,* Vol. 167, Number 8, American Medical Association, April 23, 2007

25 "How will we raise our children in the year 2000?" *Saturday Review of Education,* March 1973, p. 30

26 "Women Are Never Front-Runners," Gloria Steinem, *New York Times,* January 8, 2008

27 "For Young Earners in Big City, a Gap in Women's Favor," Sam Roberts, *New York Times,* August 3, 2007; "Female U.S. corporate directors out-earn men: study," Martha Graybow, Reuters, November 7, 2007; "Big (Wo)Man on Campus," Nick Gillespie, *Reason,* Reason. com, March 27, 2007

28 "Interview: Patricia Ireland," Public Broadcasting Service, PBS.org, 1998

29 *Life So Far: A Memoir,* Betty Friedan, Simon & Schuster, 2000, p. 41

30 *The Feminine Mystique,* Betty Friedan, W. W. Norton & Company, originally published 1963, p. 305 of the 2001 reissue

31 "I'm considering a revolution," *Guardian,* October 10, 2007, Music.Guardian.co.uk

32 "Before *Roe v. Wade,* did 10,000 women a year die from illegal abortions?" Cecil Adams, Straight Dope, StraightDope.com, May 28, 2004

33 "Abortion Surveillance—United States, 1999," *Morbidity and Mortality Weekly Report,* U.S. Centers for Disease Control and Prevention, November 29, 2002

34 Appearance on *The Oprah Winfrey Show,* quoted from "Hysterical women for Kerry," Michelle Malkin, Creators Syndicate, October 20, 2004

35 "Marriage," Sheila Cronan, 1970, quoted from *Radical Feminism,* edited by Anne Koedt, Ellen Levine, and Anita Rapone, Quadrangle Books, 1973, p. 375–376

36 "The Declaration of Feminism," Nancy Lehmann and Helen Sullinger, 1971, quoted from *The Death of the West: How Dying Populations and Immigrant Invasions Imperil Our Country and Civilization,* Patrick J. Buchanan, St. Martin's Press, 2002, p. 41

37 "It's surviving and healthy," Dolores Barclay, *Tulsa Sunday World,* August 21, 1977

38 *The New Victorians: A Young Woman's Challenge to the Old Feminist Order,* Rene Denfeld Warner Books, 1995, p. 102

39 *Domestic Tranquility: A Brief Against Feminism*, F. Carolyn Graglia, Spence Publishing Company, 1998

40 *The Dialectic of Sex: The Case for Feminist Revolution*, Shulamith Firestone, Farrar Straus Giroux, 1970, p. 52, 216 of the 2003 reissue

41 Quoted from *Reweaving The Web of Life: Feminism and Nonviolence*, Pam McAllister, Consortium Books, 1982, p. 271–284

42 "Abortionist Caught on Tape," Students for Life of America, StudentsForLife.org; "Late-Term Abortionist Admits to Aborting 1 Day Before Delivery," Lawrence Jones, *Christian Post*, ChristianPost.com, March 22, 2008

43 *Brainwashed: How Universities Indoctrinate America's Youth*, Ben Shapiro, WND Books, 2004, p. 64

44 "Princeton Bioethics Professor Debates Views on Disability and Euthanasia," Paul Zielbauer, *New York Times*, October 13, 1999; Peter Singer interview with Johann Hari, *Independent*, January 7, 2004

45 "Blow to machismo as Spain forces men to do housework," Giles Tremlett, *Guardian* (U.K.), April 8, 2005

46 "Schyman in equality policy shock: tax men," Andy Butterworth, *Local Europe*, TheLocal.se, October 5, 2004

47 "Murder in Families," U.S. Department of Justice, July 1994

48 "I thought urinals were for men!" Ben Shapiro, Creators Syndicate, June 23, 2004

49 Ibid.

50 *The War Against Boys*, Christina Hoff-Sommers, Simon & Schuster, 2000, p. 56

51 "It's a Female Dog, or Worse. Or Endearing. And Illegal?" Michael Grynbaum, *New York Times*, August 7, 2007

52 "Santas warned 'ho ho ho' offensive to women," Agence France-Presse, November 14, 2007

53 "Police: Idaho Teen Is Tied Up and Scalped," Associated Press, February 8, 2005

54 "Sex, Society, and the Female Dilemma: A Dialogue Between Simone de Beauvoir and Betty Friedan," *Saturday Review*, June 14, 1975, p. 17–20

55 "Enemies of the State?" Hannah Beech, *Time* magazine, September 19, 2005

56 "Report: China led world executions in 2007," Associated Press, April 14, 2008

57 *Oprah* episode quoted from "Abetting coercion in China," *Washington Times*, October 10, 1989

58 "Abortionist accused of eating fetuses," WorldNetDaily.com, June 14, 2005

59 *Communism, Fascism and Democracy: The Theoretical Foundations* edited by Carl Cohen, Random House, 1962, p. 207, 256

60 "Study: Abortion increases suicide risk," WorldNetDaily.com, December 2, 2005, quoting the *British Medical Journal* and *Southern Medical Journal*

61 "The Terrorists Who Aren't in the News," Jennifer L. Pozner, *Newsday*, October 8, 2006

62 "Terry preaches theocratic rule," *News-Sentinel* (Fort Wayne, Indiana), August 16, 1993, p. 1A

63 "Randall Terry Censured By Church," Hanna Rosin, *Washington Post*, February 12, 2000, p. C01

64 "Family Values: Randall Terry Fights Gay Unions. His Son No Longer Will," Michael Powell, *Washington Post*, April 22, 2004, p. C01

65 "Appalling appeal?" Lynn Vincent, *World* magazine, WorldMag.com, June 14, 2003

66 *Freakonomics: A Rogue Economist Explores the Hidden Side of Everything*, Steven Levitt and Stephen Dubner, HarperCollins, 2005

67 "Abortion just as common where it's illegal," Associated Press, October 12, 2007

68 *Diverse Sexuality and Schools: A Reference Handbook*, David Campos, ABC-CLIO, 2003, p. 22

69 "Jury Awards Father $2.9M in Funeral Case," Associated Press, October 31, 2007

70 Debate at Casper Open Bible Church in Casper, Wyoming, October 13, 2002, GodHatesFags.com

71 Ibid.

72 Letter to Russian President Boris Yeltsin, July 5, 1997, quoted from the Anti-Defamation League, ADL.org

73 *The Broken Hearth: Reversing the Moral Collapse of the American Family*, William J. Bennett, Random House, 2001, p. 137

74 "Gay to Wed," *Newsweek*, May 23, 2005

75 "Abortion and Rights of Terror Suspects Top Court Issues: Strong Support for Stem Cell Research," Pew Research Center for the People and the Press, August 3, 2005; "U.S. Majority Supports Same-Sex Unions," United Press International, November 8, 2007

76 "Hamilton College Hot Button Issues Poll: Guns, Gays and Abortion," Zogby International, January 2006

77 *Diverse Sexuality and Schools: A Reference Handbook*, David Campos, ABC-CLIO, 2003, p. 23

78 Ibid., p. 3

79 Ibid.

80 "The gay marriage slump," Caren Chesler, Salon.com, February 22, 2008

81 *Gay and Lesbian Educators: Personal Freedoms, Public Constraints*, Karen M. Harbeck, Ph.D., Amethyst Press, 1997, p. 152–153

82 *Diverse Sexuality and Schools: A Reference Handbook*, p. 50

83 *Crimes Without Victims: Deviant Behavior and Public Policy*, Edwin M. Schur, Prentice-Hall, 1965, p. 78

84 *Diverse Sexuality and Schools: A Reference Handbook*, p. 57

85 "The Man Upstairs Is in the House," Dana Milbank, *Washington Post*, July 19, 2006

86 "GOP Mailing Warns Liberals Will Ban Bibles," Associated Press, September 17, 2004

87 "The Rove Less Traveled," Marcus Baram, *Radar Online*, RadarOnline.com, September 5, 2006

88 "Texas bans gay foster parents," Agence France-Presse, April 20, 2005

89 "All Happy Families," Julian Sanchez, *Reason* magazine, Reason.com, January 18, 2005

90 "Utah Family Values," Andrew Sullivan, AndrewSullivan.com, October 5, 2007

91 "U.S. divorce rate falls to lowest level since 1970, but why?" The Associated Press, May 10, 2007

92 "Debate Over Gay Foster Parents Shines Light on a Dubious Stat," Carl Bialik, *Wall Street Journal*, WSJ.com, April 28, 2005

93 *Child Sexual Abuse: New Theory and Research*, David Finkelhor, Free Press, 1984, p. 27

94 "Pope Calls Gay Marriage Part of 'Ideology of Evil,'" Reuters, February 22, 2005; "Pope Says Abortion, Gay Marriage Are 'Obstacles' to World Peace," Francis X. Rocca, Religion News Service, December 11, 2007

95 "Cousins' marriage highlights relationship controversy," Associated Press, April 5, 2005

96 "First Trio 'Married' in The Netherlands," *Brussels Journal*, BrusselsJournal.com, September 27, 2005

97 *The Battle and the Backlash: The Child Sexual Abuse War*, David Hechler, Lexington Books, 1988, p. 294–295

98 "Sweden highlights bestiality problem," Agence France-Presse, April 29, 2005

99 *The Broken Hearth: Reversing the Collapse of the American Family*, William J. Bennett, Random House, 2001, p. 115

100 *Make Love, Not War: The Sexual Revolution: An Unfettered History*, David Allyn, Little, Brown and Company, 2000, p. 86

101 "Marriage in the March of Time," Colbert I. King, *Washington Post*, February 12, 2005

102 *Make Love, Not War: The Sexual Revolution: An Unfettered History*, p. 85

103 *Queering Elementary Education: Advancing the Dialogue about Sexualities and Schooling*, William J. Letts IV and James T. Sears, Rowman & Littlefield, 1999, p. 7

104 "Womb environment 'makes men gay'," BBC News, June 27, 2006

105 "Same-sex Attraction Is Genetically Wired In Nematode's Brain," *Science Daily*, ScienceDaily.com, October 26, 2007

106 "Science told: hands off gay sheep," Isabel Oakeshott and Chris Gourlay, *Times of London*, December 31, 2006

107 "Is Your Baby Gay? What If You Could Know? What If You Could Do Something About It?" Albert Mohler, AlbertMohler.com, March 2, 2007, quoted from AndrewSullivan.com

108 "A Surgeon General Who Will 'Cure' Gays?" DailyKos.com, June 1, 2007

109 "Ex-Gay Camp Investigation Called Off," ABCNews.com, June 28, 2005; "Turning off gays," Mark Benjamin, Salon.com, July 18, 2005

110 "3 former leaders of ex-gay ministry apologize," Rebecca Trounson, *Los Angeles Times*, June 28, 2007

111 *Being Homosexual: Gay Men and Their Development*, Richard A. Isay, M.D., Farrar Straus and Giroux, 1989, p. 112

112 Ibid., p. 18–19, 23

113 *The Homosexual Matrix* (second edition), C.A. Tripp, Ph.D., Meridian/McGraw-Hill, 1987, p. 275; AndrewSullivan.com, December 13, 2006

114 "Future Shock," Patricia Nell Warren, *Advocate*, October 3, 1995

115 *Queering Elementary Education: Advancing the Dialogue about Sexualities and Schooling*, p. 112

116 Ibid., p. 111, 115

117 Ibid., p. 9–10

118 Ibid., p. 102

119 Ibid., p. 97–98

120 *Persecution: How Liberals Are Waging War Against Christianity*, David Limbaugh, Perennial, 2004, p. 98–100

121 *Queering Elementary Education: Advancing the Dialogue about Sexualities and Schooling*, p. 201

122 "The survey says what? Sexual-orientation questions cause stir at Port high school," Tom Kertscher, *Milwaukee Journal Sentinel*, May 15, 2006

123 *Persecution: How Liberals Are Waging War Against Christianity*, David Limbaugh, Perennial, 2004, p. 78

124 Ibid., p. 100

125 Ibid., p. 101

126 Ibid., p. 99

127 "Dog bites man," Hendrik Hertzberg, *The New Yorker*, May 5, 2003

128 Quoted from "The Queer Heterosexual," Tristan Taormino, *Village Voice*, April 30, 2003

129 *Gay and Lesbian Educators: Personal Freedoms, Public Constraints*, Karen M. Harbeck, PhD., Amethyst Press, 1997, p. 49

130 Quoted from "Robertson apologizes for remark," *Chicago Sun-Times*, August 25, 2005

131 "Hawaii state senate candidate Robb Finberg supports executing gays," QueerDay.com, October 27, 2004

132 "We have to protect people," *Guardian*, December 9, 2004

133 "Alabama Bill Targets Gay Authors," CBSNews.com, April 27, 2005

134 "Gay book ban goal of state lawmaker," Kim Chandler, *Birmingham News*, December 2, 2004; "Alabama Bill Targets Gay Authors," CBSNews.com, April 27, 2005

135 "Victimization For Sexual Orientation Increases Suicidal Behavior In College Students," *Science Daily*, ScienceDaily.com, September 25, 2007

136 *Diverse Sexuality and Schools: A Reference Handbook*, p. 13

137 "GOP Lawmakers Balk At Gay Provision In Bully Law," 365Gay.com, March 8, 2005

138 "There Won't Be Blood," Steve Robles, 10ZenMonkeys.com, February 12, 2008

139 "FDA to Implement Gay Sperm Donor Rules," Associated Press, May 5, 2005

140 "Pentagon Lists Homosexuality As Disorder," Lolita Baldor, Associated Press, June 19, 2006

141 "Hundreds of military officers, health care professionals discharged under gay policy," Lolita Baldor, Associated Press, January 25, 2006

142 "Report: 'Don't Ask, Don't Tell' Cost $363M," Liz Sidoti, Associated Press, February 13, 2006

143 "55 Fewer Arab Linguists in the Military," Andrew Sullivan, AndrewSullivan.com, July 28, 2006; "U.S. military continues to discharge gay Arab linguists, and Congress members seek hearing," Associated Press, May 23, 2007

144 "Quote for the Day," AndrewSullivan.com, July 20, 2007

145 "Pentagon: 'Sex Bomb' Et Al Mostly Folly," Kelley Beaucar Vlahos, FoxNews.com, February 2, 2005

146 "Gays flee as religious militias sentence them all to death," Daniel McGrory, *Times* of London, May 17, 2006

147 "U.S. Nixes Gay Inclusion At UN," Doug Windsor, 365Gay.com, January 24, 2006

148 *Diverse Sexuality and Schools: A Reference Handbook*, p. 71

149 "A white supremacist admits he killed a gay couple, but claims the Bible made him do it," Gary Debsohn and Sam Stanton, Salon.com, November 8, 1999

150 "Murder suspect says he was doing God's work," Paige Hewitt, *Houston Chronicle*, July 15, 2007

151 "Florida man gets 30 years for fatal beating of 3-year-old son," Associated Press, August 20, 2005

152 *Diverse Sexuality and Schools: A Reference Handbook*

153 "FBI reports hate crimes rose 8 percent in 2006," Associated Press, November 19, 2007

154 *Diverse Sexuality and Schools: A Reference Handbook*, p. 19

155 Ibid., p. 4

156 *San Francisco Examiner*, February 14, 1999

157 "Four arrested in attack on gay man," Associated Press, *Newsday*, October 11, 2006

158 "'Bible as hate speech' signed into law," WorldNetDaily.com April 30, 2004; "'Bible as hate speech' bill passes," WorldNetDaily.com, September 18, 2003; "You Can't Say That," David E. Bernstein, *National Review*, December 2, 2003

159 "Mandatory Niceness," Jacob Sullum, *Reason* magazine, May 2008

160 "New law means anti-gay comments could lead to seven years in jail," Steve Doughty and James Slack, *Daily Mail*, October 8, 2007

161 DrudgeReport.com, November 11, 2006, quoting the *Observer Monthly Music Magazine*

162 "France outlaws sexist and anti-gay insults," *Guardian*, December 24, 2004

163 "Arrested father had point to make," Maria Cramer and Ralph Ranalli, *Boston Globe*, April 29, 2005

164 *Persecution: How Liberals Are Waging War Against Christianity*, p. 103

165 "Christianism Watch," Andrew Sullivan, AndrewSullivan.com, February 5, 2008

166 *Persecution: How Liberals Are Waging War Against Christianity*, p. 133

167 Ibid., p. 132

168 "A Ladies' Room of One's Own," Wendy Shalit, *Commentary* magazine, Volume 100, August 1995

169 *Freefall of the American University: How Our Colleges Are Corrupting the Minds and Morals of the Next Generation*, Jim Nelson Black, WND Books, 2004, p. 121

170 *U.S. News & World Report*, December 5, 1995, quoted from *Freefall of the American University: How Our Colleges Are Corrupting the Minds and Morals of the Next Generation*, Jim Nelson Black, WND Books, 2004, p. 14

171 *Persecution: How Liberals Are Waging War Against Christianity*, p. 376

172 *Diverse Sexuality and Schools: A Reference Handbook*, p. 60, 65

173 "Hate-crimes law worries pastors," WorldNetDaily.com, June 30 2004

174 "Prosecutor: Bible is 'fighting words,'" WorldNetDaily.com, December 16, 2004

175 "Judge drops all charges against Philly Christians," WorldNetDaily.com, February 17, 2005

176 "Paul leads in donations from military voters, with Obama next," Bennett Roth, Richard Dunham and Chase Davis, *Houston Chronicle*, October 18, 2007

177 "Some bring wrong stuff to the party," *New York Daily News*, September 1, 2004

178 "Coming to a Convention Near You: Scary Anarchist II," Sarah Ferguson, *Village Voice*, August 26, 2004

179 "Fortress Big Apple: Will the President Escape From New York?" Nicholas Turse, Alternet.org, July 21, 2004

180 "Republicans venture behind enemy lines," *Financial Times*, April 7, 2004

181 *Los Angeles Times*, September 4, 2004, quoted from TheocracyWatch.org

182 "The Presidential Debate Beyond the Edge of Forever," David Weigel, *Reason*, Reason.com, September 18, 2007

183 "Texas governor's religious remarks slammed," United Press International, November 6, 2006

184 "Convention Blog," Michael Crowley, *The New Republic*, TheNewRepublic.com, August 30, 2004

185 *National Journal: Convention Nightly*, August 30, 2004

186 Ibid., August 31, 2004

187 "McCain in NH: Would Be 'Fine' To Keep Troops in Iraq for 'A Hundred Years,'" David Corn, *Mother Jones*, MotherJones.com, February 25, 2008

188 "Jerry Falwell's Hit Parade," Timothy Noah, Slate.com, May 15, 2007

189 "Senator John McCain Defends 'Don't Ask, Don't Tell,' Calls Gay Troops an 'Intolerable Risk,'" Servicemembers Legal Defense Network, SLDN.org, May 3, 2007

190 "McCain: No Muslim president, U.S. better with Christian one," Helen Kennedy, *New York Daily News*, September 29, 2007

191 "McCain says al Qaeda might try to tip U.S. election," Reuters, March 14, 2008

192 "FBI pays $2 million to U.S. Muslim in terror-suspect case," Tom Regan, *Christian Science Monitor*, CSMonitor.com, November 30, 2006

193 "Get to know the real Jerry Falwell," Marc R. Masferrer, *Lufkin Daily News*, Cox Texas Newspapers, LufkinDailyNews.com, August 6, 2004; *Finding Inner Peace and Strength*, Jerry Falwell, Doubleday, 1982, p. 2, 4, 26, 41; *America Can Be Saved!* Jerry Falwell, Sword of the Lord Publishers, 1979, p. 52–53; *Architects of Fear: Conspiracy Theories and Paranoia in American Politics*, George Johnson, Houghton Mifflin, 1983, p. 156; *Finding Inner Peace and Strength*, Jerry Falwell, Doubleday, 1982, p. 46, 27, 28; "The Falwell Follies," Americans United for Separation of Church and State, AU.org, May 2000; "A Disciplined, Charging Army," Frances Fitzgerald, *New Yorker*, May 18, 1981, p. 53–141; "Falwell cleared in election statement," Bob Lewis, Associated Press, July 20, 2005

194 *Time* magazine poll quoted from *The President of Good and Evil: The Ethics of George W. [Retard]*, Peter Singer, Dutton, 2004, p. 202–203

195 "Secret Pentagon Briefing," Michael Drosnin, TheBibleCode.com, 2003

196 *The 1980's: Countdown to Armageddon*, Hal Lindsey, Bantom Books, 1980, p. 60

197 "Christianism Watch," Andrew Sullivan, AndrewSullivan.com, October 17, 2006, quoting the *Sacramento Bee*

198 *A History of the End of the World: How the Most Controversial Book in the Bible Changed the Course of Western Civilization,* Jonathan Kirsch, HarperCollins, 2007

199 "Script doctors wanted," John Leo, *U.S. News & World Report,* November 17, 2003

200 "A heartening response from atheists," Robyn Blumner, *St. Petersburg Times,* August 15, 2004; "Address to the Nation on the Situation in Somalia," December 4, 1992

201 "The [Retard] Beat," Ward Harkavy, *Village Voice,* VillageVoice.com, October 28, 2004; "The Greatest Gift," Edward E. Plowman, *World* magazine, February 15, 2003

202 "Top General: Could It Be Satan?" The Associated Press with CBSNews.com, October 17, 2003

203 "Academy removes Christian banner," Associated Press, November 20, 2004

204 "Not so fast, Christian soldiers," Michael L. Weinstein and Reza Aslan, *Los Angeles Times,* August 22, 2007

205 "US military accused of harboring fundamentalism," Agence France-Presse, February 14, 2008; "Atheist soldier says Army punished him," John Milburn, Associated Press, March 5, 2008

206 "God Is on Our Side. Does That Mean War?" ABC News, ABCNews.com, March 27, 2007

207 "The evolving James Robison," Darren Barbee, Knight Ridder Newspapers, June 11, 2003

208 "[Retard] says God chose him to lead his nation," *Observer,* November 2, 2003

209 *The Battle for God: A History of Fundamentalism,* Karen Armstrong, Ballantine Books, 2001, p. 311

210 "Cop stomping suspect caught in same clothes," *New York Daily News,* September 1, 2004

211 *Village Voice,* September 28, 2004

212 "Canadian law firms compete to attract lucrative U.S. deals," *Globe and Mail,* Shawn McCarthy, December 29, 2003

213 Office of the New York Governor Press Release, "HUDSON RIVER PARK TRUST ISSUES RFEI FOR HUDSON RIVER PARK PIER 57," October 14, 2003

214 *On the Justice of Roosting Chickens: Reflections on the Consequences of U.S. Imperial Arrogance and Criminality,* Ward Churchill, AK Press, 2003

215 Quoting BBC News, BBC.co.uk, "How Iraqis Feel," Andrew Sullivan, AndrewSullivan.com, September 10, 2007

216 "Death could await Christian convert," CNN.com, March 22, 2006

217 White House transcript of speech delivered to United Bethel UME Church, New Orleans, Louisiana, January 15, 2004

218 "Takin' it to the street," Corky Siemaszko, *New York Daily News,* September 1, 2004

219 *Words That Won the War: The Story of the Committee on Public Information 1917–1919,* James R. Mock and Cedric Larson, Princeton University Press, 1939, p. 134

220 *Freethinkers: A History of American Secularism* Susan Jacoby, Metropolitan Books, 2004, p. 239

221 *Words That Won the War: The Story of the Committee on Public Information 1917–1919,* p. 9

222 *Freedom of Speech in the United States: Fourth Edition,* Thomas Tedford and Dale Herbeck, Strata Publishing, 2001, p. 47

223 *Words That Won the War: The Story of the Committee on Public Information 1917–1919*

224 *Freethinkers: A History of American Secularism*, p. 289

225 *Conscientious Objectors and the Second World War*, Cynthia Eller, Greenwood Publishing Group, 1991, p. 23

226 "Thousands of Christians hold anti-war service in D.C.," Associated Press, March 17, 2007

227 "Trespass charges dropped against [Retard] protesters," Associated Press, July 15, 2004; "Getting Busted for Wearing a Peace T-Shirt," Mike Werner, CounterPunch.com, July 1, 2006; "Sic 'em With the Rally Squad," Dahlia Lithwick, Slate.com, August 20, 2007; "White House Manual Details How to Deal With Protesters," Peter Baker, *Washington Post*, August 22, 2007

228 "F.B.I. Watched Activist Groups, New Files Show," Eric Lichtblau, *New York Times*, December 20, 2005; "ACLU Report Shows Widespread Pentagon Surveillance of Peace Activists," ACLU press release, January 17, 2007; "Police spies chosen to lead war protest," Demian Bulwa, *San Francisco Chronicle*, July 28, 2006; "City Police Spied Broadly Before G.O.P. Convention," Jim Dwyer, *New York Times*, March 25, 2007

229 "Antiwar Sermon Brings IRS Warning," Patricia Ward Biederman and Jason Felch, *Los Angeles Times*, November 7, 2005

230 "Branded," James Moore, *Huffington Post*, HuffingtonPost.com, January 4, 2006; "US no-fly list vexes travelers from babies on up," Reuters, December 15, 2005; "Enemy of the People," Andrew Sullivan, AndrewSullivan.com, April 8, 2007

231 "Quarantining dissent," James Bovard, *San Francisco Chronicle*, January 4, 2004

232 "Scientists worried by riot control ray gun," Reuters, July 20, 2005

233 "Air Force chief: Test weapons on testy U.S. mobs," Associated Press, September 12, 2006

234 "[Retard] military bird flu role slammed," CNN.com, October 5, 2005

235 "Would You Believe 'Possible Cause'?" Tim Cavanaugh, *Reason*, Reason.com, May 7, 2006

236 "Gingrich defends free speech curbs," Riley Yates, *Union-Leader* (New Hampshire), December 16, 2006

237 "Anti-War Shirt Banned," Radley Balko, *Reason*, Reason.com, July 12, 2007

238 "Demagoguery emboldened: Attacks on dissent since 9/11," Brendan Nyhan, Spinsanity.org, September 30, 2004

239 Ibid.

240 "[Retard] to Democrats: Don't Chide Iraq Policy," Jennifer Loven, Associated Press, January 10, 2006

241 "Lake Worth man accused of 'political attack' on girlfriend," *South Florida Sun-Sentinel*, October 27, 2004; "Teen pleads guilty to attacking girlfriend for her Kerry support," Missy Stoddard, *South Florida Sun-Sentinel*, March 31 2005

242 "High school political debate leads to assault," Associated Press, November 10, 2004

243 "Man Kills Another in Dispute Over War, Press and Police Call It a First," *Editor and Publisher*, August 6, 2005

244 "Spy Agency Data After Sept. 11 Led F.B.I. to Dead Ends," *New York Times*, January 17, 2006

245 "Congress Report: TSA Broke Privacy Laws," Associated Press, July 22, 2005; "FBI Finds It Frequently Overstepped in Collecting Data," John Solomon, *Washington Post*, June 14, 2007;

"Gonzales Was Told of FBI Violations," John Solomon, *Washington Post*, July 10, 2007

246 "Justice Dept.: FBI Misused Patriot Act," Lara Jakes Jordan, Associated Press, March 9, 2007

247 "Airport screeners could see X-rated X-rays," Joe Sharkey, *New York Times*, May 24, 2005

248 "Zogby Poll: 9/11 + 5 Reveals Dramatic Partisan Split," Zogby International, Sept. 5, 2006

249 Poll of 140,000 readers, CNN.com, April 28, 2004

250 "Subcommittee on International Organizations, Human Rights, and Oversight," U.S. House of Representatives, April 17, 2007

251 "In U.S., fear and distrust of Muslims runs deep," Reuters, December 1, 2006

252 "Terror Suspect Treatment," David Morris and Gary Langer, ABCNews.com, May 27, 2004

253 "US detainees 'murdered' during interrogations," Associated Press, October 25, 2005

254 "Mock Executions of Iraqi Detainees Cited by Army," Mark Mazzetti and John Hendren, *Los Angeles Times*, May 18, 2005

255 "Documents show US military in Iraq detain wives," Will Dunham, ABC News, January 27, 2006

256 "The Conscience of the Colonel," Jesse Bravin, *Wall Street Journal*, March 31, 2007

257 "Report: Flagstaff soldier killed self in protest," Larry Hendricks, *Arizona Sun*, November 2, 2006

258 "Sources: Top Bush Advisors Approved 'Enhanced Interrogation,' " Jan Crawford Greenburg, Howard Rosenberg, Ariane de Vogue, ABC News, ABCNews.com, April 9, 2008

259 "Soldier Who Reported Abuse Was Sent to Psychiatrist," R. Jeffrey Smith and Josh White, *Washington Post*, March 5, 2005; "'Aiding the Enemy'?" Andrew Sullivan, AndrewSullivan.com, April 26, 2007; "The Abu Ghraib whistleblower's ordeal," Dawn Bryan, BBC News, August 5, 2007

260 "The Shadow War, In a Surprising New Light," Barton Gellman, *Washington Post*, June 20, 2006; "Torture Is Counterproductive," Anne Applebaum, Slate.com, March 20, 2007

261 "ON INTERROGATION POLICY," Rich Lowry and Kate O'Beirne, *National Review*, NationalReview.com, September 12, 2006

262 "Soldier Who Reported Abuse Was Sent to Psychiatrist," R. Jeffrey Smith and Josh White, *Washington Post*, March 5, 2005

263 "Americans Review Conspiracy Theories," Angus Reid Global Monitor, Angus-Reid.com, August 7, 2006, polling conducted by Scripps Howard News Service / Ohio University

264 "Feeding the Military Machine," Claire Schaeffer-Duffy, *National Catholic Reporter*, March 28, 2003

265 "Recruiting the Class of 2005," David Goodman, *Mother Jones*, January/February 2002

266 "Feeding the Military Machine," Claire Schaeffer-Duffy, *National Catholic Reporter*

267 *Making Soldiers in the Public Schools: An Analysis of the Army JROTC Curriculum*, American Friends Service Committee, 1997

268 *Education as Enforcement: The Miltarization and Corporatization of Schools*, edited by Kenneth J. Saltman and David A. Gabbard, RoutledgeFalmer, 2003, p. 135

269 "Army targets youth with video game," Eric Gwinn, *Chicago Tribune*, November 7, 2003

270 Ibid.; "Draft Notices," Central Committee for Conscientious Objector, September–October 2002

271 "Virtual Reality Prepares Soldiers for Real War," Jose Antonio Vargas, *Washington Post*, February 14, 2006

272 Ibid.

273 "Army Recruits Video Gamers," CBS News, CBSNews.com, March 30, 2004

274 "Virtual Reality Prepares Soldiers for Real War," Jose Antonio Vargas, *Washington Post*, February 14, 2006

275 *Education as Enforcement: The Miltarization and Corporatization of Schools*, p. 282

276 Ibid., p. 11

277 *Communism, Fascism and Democracy: The Theoretical Foundations* edited by Carl Cohen, Random House, 1962

278 *No More Heroes: Madness and Psychiatry in War*, Richard Gabriel, 1987, Farrar, Straus and Giroux, p. 42

279 Ibid., p. 55

280 "Army: Mental ills worsen after troops return," John J. Lumpkin, Associated Press, July 29, 2005

281 "Army hiring more psychiatrists," Pauline Jelinek, Associated Press, June 14, 2007

282 "Army: Psychiatrists needed on warfronts," Pauline Jelinek, Associated Press, March 6, 2008

283 "Report Details Low U.S. Army Morale, Suicide in Iraq," Will Dunham, Reuters, March 26, 2004

284 "US soldier suicides at highest level for 26 years," James Orr, *Guardian*, August 16, 2007; "Army: Psychiatrists needed on warfronts," Pauline Jelinek, Associated Press, March 6, 2008

285 "Christianism in the Military," Andrew Sullivan, AndrewSullivan.com, November 13, 2007

286 "Absolutely Not," Christian Lowe, *Doublethink*, September 5, 2004

287 "Pentagon weighs changing sodomy law," Lou Chibbaro, Jr., *Houston Voice*, April 29, 2005

288 "Soldiers Once ... And Young," Tai Moses, AlterNet.org, October 12, 2004.

289 "Homeless Iraq vets showing up at shelters," Mark Benjamin, United Press International, December 7, 2004

290 "Wounded Soldier: Military Wants Part Of Bonus Back," Marty Griffin, KDKA TV, local CBS affiliate, KDKA.com, November 19, 2007

291 "National Guard Troops Denied Benefits After Longest Deployment Of Iraq War," Rhonda Erskine, WCSH6.com, local NBC affiliate, October 3, 2007

292 "Forgotten casualties," Lynn Harris, Salon.com, Sept. 22, 2004

293 "Soldier on leave in N.Y. charged in shooting death," CNN.com, December 30, 2005

294 "U.S. soldier gets 100 years for Iraq rape, killings," Associated Press, February 23, 2007

295 "Cops: Army vet confesses to shooting student," Desiree Hunter, Associated Press, March 12, 2008

296 "Police: Man Fatally Slashes Son In Front Of Neighbors, Kills Wife," WKMG News, LOCAL6.com, June 17, 2006

297 "Prosecutors say soldier stabbed his wife 71 times," Michael Gilbert, *News Tribune* (Tacoma, Washington), TheNewsTribune.com, January 11, 2006

298 "The Guilt-Free Soldier," Erik Baard, *The Village Voice*, January 22–28, 2003

299 Ibid.

300 *The Psychology of War*, Lawrence LeShan, Noble Press, 1992, p. 38

301 "Web site: U.S. troops traded Iraq photos for porn access," CNN.com, September 28, 2005

302 "Webmaster For Site With Iraqi Corpse Photos Arrested," Associated Press, October 8, 2005

303 "Judge says NY surveillance data can be made public," Daniel Trotta, Reuters, May 4, 2007

304 "GOP has dol-fun with Dems," Lloyd Grove, *New York Daily News*, August 29, 2004; "Donnie McClurkin, Ready to Sing Out Against Gay 'Curse,'" *Washington Post*, August 29, 2004

305 "Obama and the Jews," Jon Wiener, *Nation*, TheNation.com, March 3, 2008

306 "NOAM CHOMSKY ATTACKS 'TERRORIST STATE' U.S., ISRAEL WHILE VISITING HEZBOLLAH LEADER," *Drudge Report*, DrudgeReport.com, May 11, 2006

307 "Political Radar," ABC News, ABCNews.com, September 7, 2007

308 *Campus Support for Terrorism* edited by David Horowitz and Ben Johnson, Center for the Study of Popular Culture, 2004 (back cover)

309 The George Washington University *Hatchet*, September 6, 2005

310 "Free Alan," Rory McCarthy, *Guardian*, April 12, 2007

311 *Brainwashed: How Universities Indoctrinate America's Youth*, Ben Shapiro, WND Books, 2004, p. 163

312 "Nothing Left," Michael Young, *Reason*, Reason.com, February 28, 2008

313 "Allah Says: Don't Tread on Me," Jacob Sullum, *Reason*, Reason.com, July 10, 2007

314 *Brainwashed: How Universities Indoctrinate America's Youth*, p. 112

315 "Tensions Change Dress Code At Local Middle School," Mike Hooker, CBS4Denver.com, April 3, 2006

316 "H.S. BANS DISPLAY OF AMERICAN FLAG," MichelleMalkin.com, April 1, 2006

317 "High School Bans American Flag," WNCN, local NBC affiliate, NBC17.com, September 11, 2007

318 "Colo. School Bans Flags Amid Protests," Associated Press, April 1, 2006

319 "Hevron Arabs Ask Jews For Help in Banishing Leftist Activists," Ezra HaLevi, IsraelNN.com, November 23, 2005

320 "From Orthodox Jewish Education to Hebron; Scripture Distorted," Alan W. Miller, *New York Times* (letter to the editor), March 9, 1994

321 *Beyond Good and Evil*, Friedrich Nietzsche, 1886

322 "10 Reasons Why Abortion is Wrong," Tradition Family Property, TFP.org

323 *Whistleblower*, Volume 17, Number 1, January 2008

324 *Campus Report*, Accuracy in Academia, Volume XXII, Number 12, December 2007

325 "This is war," Ann Coulter, *National Review*, NationalReview.com, September 13, 2001

326 Interview with Brian Lamb, CSPAN, archived at Booknotes.org, August 11, 2002; "New Idea for Abortion Party: Aid the Enemy," Ann Coulter, November 23, 2005; *Slander*, Ann Coulter, Crown, 2002, p. 5–6; "That was no lady–That was my husband," Ann Coulter, TownHall. com, June 28, 2007

327 "Exclusive Interview: Coulter Says Book Examines 'Mental Disorder' of Liberalism," Lisa De Pasquale, HumanEvents.com, June 6, 2006

328 "Coulter courts Gainesville," Jessica Riffel, *Independent Florida Alligator*, Alligator.org, October 21, 2005

329 "An appalling magic," *Guardian*, May 17, 2003

330 "Columnist Ann Coulter Shocks Cable TV Show, Declaring 'Jews Need to Be Perfected by Becoming Christians,'" Fox News Channel, FoxNews.com, October 11, 2007

331 "Quote of the Day," AndrewSullivan.com, September 5, 2006

332 "Homegrown Islamic Terrorism," Martin Mawyer, Christian Action Network, 2008

II. PROHIBITION NATION

1 *Basic Writings of Bertrand Russell*, Bertrand Russell, Routledge, p. 560 of the 2001 edition; *Freethinkers: A History of American Secularism*, Susan Jacoby, Metropolitan Books, 2004, p. 206

2 "Is porn good for society?" BBC News Online, May 14, 2002

3 *Reefer Madness: Sex, Drugs and Cheap Labor in the American Black Market*, Eric Schlosser, Houghton Mifflin, 2003, p. 113–114

4 *Sex for Sale: Prostitution, Pornography, and the Sex Industry* edited by Ronald Weitzer, Routledge, 2000, p. 2; Kaiser Family Foundation, quoted from "10 Things Your Teen Son Won't Tell You ... but He Did Tell Me," Doug Donaldson, HealthyKids.com, March 2005

5 "Addiction to porn destroying lives, Senate told," Associated Press, November 18, 2004

6 "Porn on Trial," Kerry Howley, Reason magazine, Reason.com, November 3, 2006

7 "Networks' naked truth: Fear of the FCC," Associated Press, January 26, 2005

8 "Congress Increases Indecency Fines Tenfold," Jim Abrams, Associated Press, June 7, 2006

9 "Senate OKs Higher Fines for Indecency," Associated Press, June 23, 2004

10 "11th Circuit Nixes Sex Toys, Sex Rights," Jonathan Ringel, *Fulton County Daily Report*, July 29, 2004

11 "[Retard] transition office releases Ashcroft's remarks at Bob Jones University," CNN.com, January 12, 2001

12 "Feds Seek To Gag D.C. Madam," TheSmokingGun.com, March 7, 2007; "Senator's Number on Escort Service List," Associated Press, July 10, 2007

13 "Sex in the U.S.A.," Belisa Vranich, *Men's Fitness*, MensFitness.com, 2005

14 "Ashcroft's Porn Wars Come to Texas," *Austin Chronicle*, October 1, 2004

15 "Recruits Sought for Porn Squad" by Barton Gellman, *Washington Post*, September 20, 2005

16 Speech at the Hoover Institution, February 28, 2005, quoted from Radley Balko, TheAgitator. com, March 3, 2005

17 "Porn, Prosecutors, and Priorities," Radley Balko, *Reason*, Reason.com, March 19, 2007

18 "Senator: Decency Rules Should Apply to Pay TV, Radio," Reuters, March 1, 2005

19 "FCC's Powell disappointed in 'MNF,'" Associated Press, November 17, 2004

20 "FCC Warns Cable, Satellite: Clean Up TV Raunch," Fox News Channel, FoxNews.com, November 29, 2005

21 "TV viewers tune out govt control," *Hollywood Reporter*, November 29, 2005

22 "Saving Janet's Nipple," Radley Balko, *Reason*, Reason.com, September 24, 2007

23 "BBQ owner, city divided over mural of nude pigs," *Seattle Times*, December 30, 2004

24 *Freedom of Speech in the United States: Fourth Edition*, Thomas Tedford and Dale Herbeck, Strata Publishing, 2001, p. 118, 121

25 Ibid., p. 35

26 *Reefer Madness: Sex, Drugs and Cheap Labor in the American Black Market*, p. 120

27 Ibid.

28 Ibid., p. 119

29 Ibid., p. 120

30 *Make Love, Not War: The Sexual Revolution: An Unfettered History*, David Allyn, Little, Brown and Company, 2000, p. 137

31 Ibid., p 138–139

32 Ibid., p. 139

33 Ibid. p 137–138

34 *Reefer Madness: Sex, Drugs and Cheap Labor in the American Black Market*, p. 121

35 Ibid., 2003, p. 134

36 *Freedom of Speech in the United States: Fourth Edition*, p. 137

37 *Reefer Madness: Sex, Drugs and Cheap Labor in the American Black Market*, p. 135

38 Anti-Defamation League press release, March 1, 2002

39 *Nudes, Prudes and Attitudes*, Avedon Carol, New Clarion Press, 1994, p. 67; *Defending Pornography: Free Speech, Sex, and the Fight for Women's Rights*, Nadine Strossen, Scribner, 1995, p. 12

40 *Reefer Madness: Sex, Drugs and Cheap Labor in the American Black Market*, Eric Schlosser, Houghton Mifflin, 2003, p.200

41 *Pornography: Private Right or Public Menace?* edited by Robert M. Baird and Stuart E. Rosembaum, Promethus Books, 1991, p. 179–182

42 Ibid., p. 178–182

43 "William F. Buckley Jr., 1925–2008," Salon.com, February 28, 2008

44 "Feminism, Marxism, Method, and the State: An Agenda for Theory," Catharine A. MacKinnon, *Signs*, Vol. 7, No. 3, Feminist Theory, Spring, 1982, p. 515–544; *Feminism Unmodified: Discourses on Life and Law*, Catharine MacKinnon, Harvard University Press, 1987, p. 59

45 *American Booksellers v. Hudnut*, U.S. Seventh Circuit Court of Appeals, No. 84-3147, decided August 27, 1985

46 *Feminism Unmodified*, Catharine MacKinnon, Harvard University Press, 1985, p. 140, 156

47 *Defending Pornography: Free Speech, Sex, and the Fight for Women's Rights*, Nadine Strossen, Scribner, 1995, p. 161

48 Ibid., p. 30

49 Quoted from *Sex Wars: Sexual Dissent and Political Culture*, Lisa Duggan and Nan D. Hunter, Routledge, 1995, p. 65

50 Ibid., p. 66–67

51 *Defending Pornography: Free Speech, Sex, and the Fight for Women's Rights*, p. 78

52 Ibid., p. 238

53 *Domestic Tranquility: A Brief Against Feminism*, F. Carolyn Graglia, Spence Publishing Company, 1998; "Woman's Hating: The misdirected passion of Andrea Dworkin," Cathy Young, *Reason*, Reason.com, April 19, 2005; *Feminism Unmodified: Discourses on Life and Law*, Catharine MacKinnon, Harvard University Press, 1987, p. 79; *Pornography: Men Possessing Women*, Andrea Dworkin, Perigee Books, 1981, p. 19 of the 1989 edition; *Intercourse*, Andrea Dworkin, Free Press, 1987; *Defending Pornography: Free Speech, Sex, and the Fight for Women's Rights*, Nadine Strossen, Scribner, 1995, p. 107, 109, 110, 113, 196–197, 218; Andrea Dworkin, *Letters from a War Zone*, Lawrence Hill Books, p. 21, 114, 142 of the 1993 edition.

54 "Feminist author Andrea Dworkin dead at 58," Associated Press, April 11, 2005

55 "Suppressing Free Speech for Credit," Fox News Channel, FoxNews.com, November 26, 2004

56 *The New Victorians: A Young Woman's Challenge to the Old Feminist Order*, Rene Denfeld, Warner Books, 1995, p. 91

57 *Going Too Far: The Personal Chronicle of a Feminist*, Robin Morgan, Random House, 1968, p. 169 of the 1977 edition

58 *Watching Sex: How Men Really Respond to Pornography*, David Loftus, Avalon Publishing Group, 2002, p. 266

59 *Defending Pornography: Free Speech, Sex, and the Fight for Women's Rights*, p. 251

60 *The New Victorians: A Young Woman's Challenge to the Old Feminist Order*, Rene Denfeld, Warner Books, 1995, p. 103

61 *Nudes, Prudes and Attitudes*, Avedon Carol, New Clarion Press, 1994, p. 119

62 *The New Victorians: A Young Woman's Challenge to the Old Feminist Order*, p. 97–98

63 "NOW creates coalition to raise funds for Yates," Lisa Teachey, *Houston Chronicle*, August 23, 2001

64 "Rallying Around a Baby-Killer," Wendy McElroy, Fox News Channel, FoxNews.com, August 31, 2001

65 "Legislating us to death," Keith Ervin, *amNY*, amNY.com, August 27, 2007

66 *The New Victorians: A Young Woman's Challenge to the Old Feminist Order*, p. 65

67 *Watching Sex: How Men Really Respond to Pornography*, p. 263

68 Ibid., p. xii

69   Ibid., p. 81

70   Ibid., p. 143

71   *Defending Pornography: Free Speech, Sex, and the Fight for Women's Rights*, p. 163

72   "Masturbation 'cuts cancer risk,'" BBC News, July 16, 2003

73   *Defending Pornography: Free Speech, Sex, and the Fight for Women's Rights*, p. 255

74   "Is porn good for society?" BBC News, May 14, 2002

75   "How the Web Prevents Rape," Steven E. Landsburg, Slate.com, October 30, 2006

76   "Is pornography a catalyst of sexual violence?" Steve Chapman, *Reason*, Reason.com, November 5, 2007

77   "Kids often mistreated when parents sent to war," Canadian Television, CTV.ca, July 31, 2007

78   "King warns Saudi media over women," Reuters, May 16, 2006

79   "China Threatens Internet Porn Merchants with Life," Reuters, September 6, 2004

80   "In chaotic Gaza, the Internet is a target," Bloomberg News, March 4, 2007

81   "The Short, Violent Life of Abu Musab al-Zarqawi," Mary Anne Weaver, *Atlantic*, July/August 2006

82   "Anger grows among children of Iran's 25-year-old revolution," Dan De Luce, *Guardian*, February 9, 2004

83   *Atlas Shrugged*, Ayn Rand, 1957

84   *Love All the People: Letters, Lyrics, Routines*, Bill Hicks, Soft Skull Press, 2004, p. 130

85   "Marijuana Arrests For Year 2003 Hit Record High, FBI Report Reveals," NORML, October 25, 2004

86   "Feature: Drug War Prisoner Count Over Half a Million, US Prison Population at All-Time High," Drug Reform Coordination Network, citing U.S. Bureau of Justice Statistics, October 28, 2005, StopTheDrugWar.org

87   *Reefer Madness: Sex, Drugs and Cheap Labor in the American Black Market*, p. 36, 57

88   "Pot Prisoners Cost Americans $1 Billion a Year," Paul Armentano, AlterNet.org, February 10, 2007, reprinted from the *Washington Examiner*

89   "Marijuana Arrests For Year 2003 Hit Record High, FBI Report Reveals," NORML, October 25, 2004

90   "Pot Prisoners Cost Americans $1 Billion a Year," Paul Armentano, AlterNet.org, February 10, 2007

91   *Saying Yes: In Defense of Drug Use*, Jacob Sullum, Putnam, 2003, p. 20

92   "Pot Prisoners Cost Americans $1 Billion a Year," Paul Armentano, AlterNet.org, February 10, 2007

93   *Saying Yes: In Defense of Drug Use*, p. 57

94   *Reefer Madness: Sex, Drugs and Cheap Labor in the American Black Market*, p. 67

95   "Should medical marijuana be legalized?" CNN.com poll of 35,000 readers, October 5, 2006

96   *Reefer Madness: Sex, Drugs and Cheap Labor in the American Black Market*, p. 29

97 Ibid., p. 19

98 Ibid., p. 34

99 *Saying Yes: In Defense of Drug Use*, p. 140

100 Ibid., p. 202

101 Ibid., p. 201

102 *Reefer Madness: Sex, Drugs and Cheap Labor in the American Black Market*, p. 19

103 "Smoking Joints and Broken Windows," Jacob Sullum, *Reason*, Reason.com, December 15, 2006, quoting "Reefer Madness: Broken Windows Policing and Misdemeanor Marijuana Arrests in New York City, 1989–2000," *Criminology and Public Policy*, 2007

104 *Saying Yes: In Defense of Drug Use*, p. 115

105 Ibid., p. 113

106 Ibid., p. 14

107 "Swiss Study Has Some Surprises on Marijuana Use," Reuters, November 5, 2007

108 "Dirty Needles Aren't the Only Way Drug Use Spreads AIDS, Campaign Argues," Isaac Wolf, Scripps Howard Foundation, November 29, 2005

109 *Reefer Madness: Sex, Drugs and Cheap Labor in the American Black Market*, p. 24

110 "Auditors Fault Anti-Drug Ad Spending," Kevin Freking, Associated Press, August 25, 2006

111 "Another one bites the dust," Ten Galen Carpenter, NationalReview.com, August 12, 2004

112 *Reefer Madness: Sex, Drugs and Cheap Labor in the American Black Market*, p. 225

113 *Saying Yes: In Defense of Drug Use*, p. 130

114 "Here's Your Cup, Junior," Paul Armentano of the NORML Foundation, LewRockwell.com, October 12, 2005

115 "Report: Young Teens Favor Inhalants to Get High," Fox News Channel, FoxNews.com, March 14, 2008

116 *Reefer Madness: Sex, Drugs and Cheap Labor in the American Black Market*, p. 71

117 "House republicans vow to make U.S. drug-free," Joanne Kenen, Reuters, May 2, 1998

118 *Reefer Madness: Sex, Drugs and Cheap Labor in the American Black Market*, p. 203

119 *Saying Yes: In Defense of Drug Use*, p. 276

120 "Medical Marijuana Milestones," Jacob Sullum, *Reason*, Reason.com, February 12, 2007

121 "Dying Woman Loses Marijuana Appeal," Dan Kravets, Associated Press, March 14, 2007

122 "Medical marijuana advocate kills herself," Michael Moore, *Missoulian*, October 27, 2007

123 "I'm So High Right Now, I Don't Even Know Who I'm Prosecuting," David Weigel, Wonkette.com, July 26, 2006

124 "Specter favors Rx Grass," *Philadelphia Daily News*, June 21, 2005

125 "Prisoners of Pain," Barry Yeoman, *AARP: The Magazine*, September & October 2005

126 "Cannabis compound benefits blood vessels," Roxanne Khamsi, Nature.com, April 6, 2005

127 "Cannabis acts as antidepressant," BBC News, October 13, 2005

128 "Study turns pot wisdom on head," Dawn Walton, *Globe and Mail*, October 14, 2005

129 "Marijuana may stave off Alzheimer's," Reuters, October 5, 2006

130 *Reefer Madness: Sex, Drugs and Cheap Labor in the American Black Market*, p. 24

131 "Quote of the Day II," AndrewSullivan.com, April 28, 2007

132 "Prescription drug reactions kill more than 100,000 a year," Associated Press, April 15, 1998

133 "Panel Advises Disclosure of Drugs' Psychotic Effects," Gardiner Harris, *New York Times*, March 23, 2006

134 "WHO: Legal drugs pose greatest health threat," Reuters, March 18, 2004

135 "Marijuana smuggling case first local use of Patriot Act provision," Maureen O'Hagan, *Seattle Times*, July 30, 2004

136 H. R. 3199, Sponsor: Representative Henry Hyde, July 21, 2005

137 *Reefer Madness: Sex, Drugs and Cheap Labor in the American Black Market*, p. 51

138 "Is your bong breeding terrorists?" Nick Gillespie, *Reason*, Reason.com, September 29, 2004

139 *Overkill: The Rise of Paramilitary Police Raids*, Radley Balko, Cato Institute, 2006

140 "Supreme Court gives police victory in home searches of drug suspects," Associated Press, December 2, 2003; "Botched Raids Not Rare," Radley Balko, *Reason*, Reason.com, December 6, 2006

141 *Saying Yes: In Defense of Drug Use*, p. 20

142 *Reefer Madness: Sex, Drugs and Cheap Labor in the American Black Market*, p. 225

143 "'Colorable' = Red Eyes, 'Reasonable' = Red Eyes + Bad Attitude," Jacob Sullum, *Reason*, Reason.com, September 20, 2006

144 "Are Pee Tests a Drain on Student Morale?" Jacob Sullum, *Reason*, Reason.com, October 31, 2007

145 "NYC Has the Most Marijuana Arrests in the World (But Don't Worry, White People, It Won't Be You)," Ezekiel Edwards, AlterNet.org, October 4, 2007

146 "'Writing About Things on the Internet is a Crime,'" Jacob Sullum, *Reason*, Reason.com, August 23, 2007; "British memoirist is denied U.S. entry," Motoko Rich, *New York Times*, March 20, 2008

147 "Zero Tolerance for Artificial Alertness," Jacob Sullum, *Reason*, Reason.com, December 5, 2007

148 "Briton jailed for four years in Dubai after customs find cannabis weighing less than a grain of sugar under his shoe," *Evening Standard*, February 9, 2008

149 "High court sticks to ruling on dogs' sniffing for drugs," Associated Press, April 4, 2005

150 "Sewage Tested for Signs of Cocaine," Bill Turque, *Washington Post*, March 27, 2006

151 "State justices OK practice to find drugs," Derrick Nunnally, *Milwaukee Journal-Sentinel*, May 18, 2006

152 *Reefer Madness: Sex, Drugs and Cheap Labor in the American Black Market*, p. 52

153 "Lost Taxes and Other Costs of Marijuana Laws," Dr. Jon Gettman, DrugScience.org, October 2007

154 *Saying Yes: In Defense of Drug Use*, p. 277

155 Ibid., p. 277

Notes

156 "This Christmas, Remember a Champion of Joyful Eating," *Buffalo News*, December 21, 2004

157 *Saying Yes: In Defense of Drug Use*

158 "Hooded Progressivism," Jesse Walker, *Reason* magazine, Reason.com, December 2, 2005

159 "Think twice about what you hear," JustThinkTwice.com, sponsored by the U.S. Drug Enforcement Administration, 2005

160 "Another soccer mom's take on the drug war," *Denver Post*, July 7, 2006

161 *Saying Yes: In Defense of Drug Use*, p. 44

162 "Underage Drinking Study: Wasteful and Biased," Citizens Against Government Waste, September 9, 2003; "The Anti-Drunk Driving Campaign: A Covert War Against Drinking," Charles Pena, American Beverage Institute, ABIOnline.com, 2003; "Time to rethink the battle against DUI," John Doyle, *Hill*, HillNews.com, February 16, 2005

163 "Bar Tabs Going Up As States Tax Alcohol," Associated Press, May 24, 2005; "Alcohol tax increase has retailers drowning sorrows," Allison Wollam, *Houston Business Journal*, May 13, 2005; "Higher state tax on beer?" Mike Zapler, the *San Jose Mercury News*, April 11, 2008

164 "State uncorks effort to stop wine seller," David Chanen, *Star Tribune* (Minneapolis / St. Paul, Minnesota), July 12, 2006

165 "Shut up and drink, Lilburn bar patrons told," Steve Visser, *Atlanta Journal-Constitution*, March 6, 2007

166 "The night they raided Chelsea," Bret Liebendorfer, *New York Press*, April 12, 2006; "Dance Police at The Saloon," George F. Will, *Washington Post*, March 20, 2008

167 "Hopsicles," Radley Balko, *Reason*, Reason.com, June 22, 2007

168 "After Car Crash, Liquor Laws and Airlines Are Debated," Dan Frosch, *New York Times*, February 19, 2007

169 "Senate passes bill to make keg parties a thing of the past," David White, *Birmingham News*, January 18, 2006; "West Virginia bans high-proof grain alcohol," Lawrence Messina, Associated Press, November 16, 2005

170 "Big Nanny Is Watching You," Philip Dawdy, *Seattle Weekly*, January 18, 2006

171 "Tainted Vodka Kills Dozens as Russians Turn to Bootleg Liquor," Peter Finn, *Washington Post Foreign Service*, November 2, 2006

172 "State to keep tabs on bars," Matt Phinney, *San Angelo Standard-Times*, September 16, 2005; "Prohibition Returns," David Harsanyi, *Reason*, November 2007

173 "Arrests Inside Bars Leave Bitter Hangover in Fairfax," Carol Morello, *Washington Post*, January 16, 2003, p. B04

174 "State to keep tabs on bars," Matt Phinney, *San Angelo Standard-Times*, September 16, 2005

175 "The War on Booze is nothing new," Dan Sweeny, *Modern Drunkard*, ModernDrunkard.com, 2006

176 Candy Lightner, quoted from "MADD Struggles to Remain Relevant," *Washington Times*, August 6, 2002

177 "The Anti-Drunk Driving Campaign: A Covert War Against Drinking," Charles Pena, American Beverage Institute, ABIOnline.com, 2003

178 Ibid.

179 "The James Fagan Employment Act," Radley Balko, *Reason*, Reason.com, March 17, 2008

180 "Prohibition Drip by Drip," Center for Consumer Freedom, ConsumerFreedom.com, June 14, 2004

181 "Single Glass of Wine Immerses D.C. Driver in Legal Battle," *Washington Post*, October 12, 2005

182 "The Anti-Drunk Driving Campaign: A Covert War Against Drinking," Charles Pena, American Beverage Institute, ABIOnline.com, 2003

183 "Prohibition Drip by Drip," Center for Consumer Freedom, ConsumerFreedom.com, June 14, 2004

184 "DUI deputy may have wrongly jailed dozens," Casey Cora, *St. Petersburg Times*, June 15, 2007

185 "In Their Own Words," American Beverage Institute, ABIOnline.org, 2004, p. 8

186 "MADD enters 25th year with change on its mind," Jayne O'Donnell, *USA Today*, September 29, 2005

187 "MADD's Position Statements: Other Positions," Mothers Against Drunk Driving, MADD.org

188 "Designated Driver May Go Bust," Veronique deTurenne, *Los Angeles Times*, May 19, 2003

189 "Teens to get alcohol test kits," Senta Scarborough, *The Arizona Republic*, May 12, 2003

190 Glynn Birch, letter to *Washington Post*, August 15, 2005, p. A14

191 *Saying Yes: In Defense of Drug Use*, p. 95

192 "Justices: DUI Suspects Can Run But Can't Hide," Associated Press, June 1, 2006

193 "Yet More Neoprohibition," Radley Balko, TheAgitator.com, July 15, 2004

194 "A broken system works in favor of cops busted for DUI," Eric Nalder and Lewis Kamb, *Seattle Post-Intelligencer*, August 6, 2007

195 "Special license plates shield officials from traffic tickets," Jennifer Muir, *OC Register*, April 4, 2008, quoted from "Petty Tyranny in California," Radley Balko, *Reason*, Reason.com, April 8, 2008

196 "Defense bill pays for Breathalyzers, Lewis and Clark celebrations," Roxana Tiron, *Hill*, January 4, 2006

197 "Alcohol harder to find as shop owners fear radicals' wrath," Associated Press, July 19, 2004; "Rough justice: 80 lashes for 'immoral' Iranian who abused alcohol and had sex," David Williams, *Daily Mail*, August 22, 2007

198 "Appeals court says requirement to attend AA unconstitutional," Bob Egelko, *San Francisco Chronicle*, September 8, 2007

199 "Law Lets Police Take Car for 1st DWI; Mayor Signs Bill at MADD," Jeff Proctor, *Albuquerque Journal*, April 28, 2005

200 "Yet More Neoprohibition," Radley Balko, TheAgitator.com, July 15, 2004

201 "Pennsylvania Ponders Parody-Proof Paternalistic Proposal," Radley Balko, *Reason*, Reason.com, March 27, 2007

202 "In-car sobriety devices challenged," Associated Press, September 13, 2004

203 "We Card," Radley Balko, *Reason*, Reason.com, August 17, 2007

Notes

227

204 "Marines have earned adult rights," Fredrick J. Falls, *Mansfield News Journal*, November 3, 2007

205 Appearance on Fox News Channel, April 7, 2008, quoted from "MADD Founder Hates Troops Almost As Much As She Hates Alcohol," Marty Beckerman, *Radar Online*, RadarOnline.com, April 10, 2008

206 "Breathalyzer Tests Now The Law At N.J. High School," WCBSTV.com, local CBS affiliate, January 4, 2008

207 "Age of Propaganda," David J. Hanson and Matt Walcoff, *Reason*, Reason.com, October 2004

208 The American Forum at American University, moderated by Dr. Jane Hall, February 8, 2005

209 "After 20 years, State drinking age is still 21," Laura Jerpi, University of Pittsburgh *Pitt News*, September 9, 2004

210 "Drinking Age Paradox," George Will, *Washington Post*, April 19, 2007

211 "The suit against Coors for a drunk driving accident," Anthony J. Sebok, CNN.com, April 22, 2004

212 *Saying Yes: In Defense of Drug Use*, p. 95

213 "Guilty by Association," *Chicago Tribune*, June 15, 2004; "5 Colby students face alcohol charges," Amy Calder, *Morning Sentinel*, MorningSentinel.MaineToday.com, March 8, 2005

214 "Guilty by Association," *Chicago Tribune*, June 15, 2004

215 "A Suffocating Temperance," Radley Balko, FoxNews.com, January 29, 2003

216 The Federal Office for Substance Prevention, quoted from "Booze Busting: The New Prohibition," James Bovard, Future of Freedom Foundation, FFF.org, December 1998

217 "Drinking and legislating," Radley Balko, *Tech Central Station*, TechCentralStation.com, March 24, 2005; "Drunken driving deaths up in 22 states," Associated Press, August 20, 2007

218 "How to Lose Your License Without Really Trying," Katherine Mangu-Ward, *Reason*, Reason.com, December 3, 2007

219 "A Toast to Mom and Dad," Stanton Peele, *Wall Street Journal*, WSJ.com, September 3, 2007

220 "Drug Abuse Resistance Education: The Effectiveness of DARE," David J. Hanson, PhD, AlcoholFacts.org, quoting "DARE's dying gasp," James Bovard, Future of Freedom Foundation, FFF.org, September 2000

221 "Spanish youths in mass drink binge," Reuters, March 17, 2006

222 "Booze Busting: The New Prohibition," James Bovard, Future of Freedom Foundation, FFF.org, December 1998

223 "Student expelled 1 year for Advil," WorldNetDaily.com, December 5, 2003

224 "Boy charged with felony for carrying sugar," Kristina Wang, *Chicago Sun-Times*, February 11, 2006

225 "Parsley-pot ruse gets kids suspended," *Daytona Beach News-Journal Online*, November 29, 2005

226 "Girl suspended over 'Jell-O shots,'" Associated Press, December 7, 2004

227 "Kids Visit Margaritaville," TheSmokingGun.com, September 29, 2004

228 "Toddler Served Margarita in a Sippy Cup," Associated Press, June 15, 2007

229 "Want to live longer? Toss back a few cocktails," Reuters, December 12, 2006

230 "Daily Drink Helps Keep Brain Sharp, Data Suggest," *Washington Post*, January 20, 2005

231 "Moderate drinkers show lower obesity risk," Amy Norton, Reuters Health, December 5, 2005

232 "Alcohol cuts risk of developing rheumatoid arthritis," Agence France-Presse, July 5, 2008

233 "The Anti-Drunk Driving Campaign: A Covert War Against Drinking," Charles Pena, American Beverage Institute, ABIOnline.com, 2003

234 "That drooping feeling: Heavy smokers 40 percent likelier to be impotent," Agence France Presse, March 22, 2006

235 "Mystery compound in beer fights cancer," Andy Coghlan, *New Scientist*, NewScientist.com, January 19, 2005; "Beer, with Benefits," Matt Allyn and Matt Bean, *Men's Health*, MSN. com, 2008

236 "The health pros and cons of drinking," Linda Formachelli, CNN.com, December 4, 2007; "Don't Forget: Drink a Beer—Or Two—Daily!" Nikhil Swaminathan, *Scientific American*, SciAm.com, September 26, 2007

237 "Fruity cocktails count as health food, study finds," Reuters, April 20, 2007

238 "The Health Risks of Not Drinking," Jacob Sullum, *Reason*, Reason.com, November 7, 2007

239 "Alcohol use helps boost income: study," Agence France Presse, September 14, 2006

240 "The more successful you are, the more you drink, research finds," Martin Hickman, *Independent*, January 23, 2008

241 "World's oldest person sprightly until the end," Agence France Presse, August 14, 2007

242 *Selling Sin: The Marketing of Socially Unacceptable Products*, D. Kirk Davidson, Quorum Books, 1996, p. 145

243 "Neo-prohibitionists attack the First Amendment," Benjamin G. Wolff, Esq., *Healthy Drinking*, May/June 1995

244 *Communism, Fascism and Democracy: The Theoretical Foundations* edited by Carl Cohen, Random House, 1962, p. 420

245 "The spirits of 1776," Ian Williams, Salon.com, July 2, 2005

246 *What Would the Founders Do?* Richard Brookhiser, Basic Books, 2006, p. 42

247 Ibid., p. 42

248 *Saying Yes: In Defense of Drug Use*, p. 56, 58, 61, 63, 64

249 *Gentleman's Guide to Grooming and Style*, Bernhard Roetzel, Barnes & Noble Books, 2004, p. 235

250 "World anti-smoking pact in force," Reuters, February 27, 2005

251 *Smoke-Filled Rooms: A Postmortem on the Tobacco Deal*, W. Kip Viscusi, University of Chicago Press, 2002, p. 1; "When Will the CDC Admit That Cigarettes Are Killing Fewer Americans?" Jacob Sullum, *Reason*, Reason.com, July 19, 2007

252 *Smoke-Filled Rooms: A Postmortem on the Tobacco Deal*, p. 140

Notes

253 Ibid., p. 1; *Consuming Fears: The Politics of Product Risks*, Harvey Sapolsky, Basic Books, 1986, p. 19

254 *Smoke-Filled Rooms: A Postmortem on the Tobacco Deal*, p. 9–11

255 "No Such Thing As a Reasonable Smoker," Jacob Sullum, *Reason*, Reason.com, May 22, 2006

256 "Activists continue smoke-free push," Associated Press, January 20, 2007

257 "Nursing homes not building special rooms, forcing smokers outside," Phinjo Gombu, *Toronto Star*, February 2, 2007

258 "The Smoking-Drinking Problem," William Saletan, Slate.com, April 4, 2008

259 "Surgeon General Favors Tobacco Ban," Marc Kaufman, *Washington Post*, June 4, 2003

260 *Smoke-Filled Rooms: A Postmortem on the Tobacco Deal*, p. 13, 18

261 "Smoking Ban Takes Effect, Indoors and Out," John Broder, *New York Times*, March 19, 2006, "Clean Air Calabasas," Jacob Sullum, *Reason* magazine, March 8, 2006; "Oakland Restricts Smoking In Outdoor Areas," KNTV, local NBC affiliate, NBC11.com, October 17, 2007

262 "Cigarette surveillance program begins today," Tom Humphrey, *Knoxville News Sentinel*, September 27, 2007

263 "Bus-station smoker tussles with police, jailed," Torsten Ove, *Pittsburgh Post-Gazette*, January 18, 2007

264 "Smokeless Tobacco Ban in Effect for SF Parks," KCBS, local *CBS News* affiliate, March 29, 2005

265 "Cigarette Nazis on the march," Walter E. Williams, Creators Syndicate, December 10, 2001; "Smoking foes bring the fight to apartment buildings," Sanjay Bhatt, *Seattle Times*, January 16, 2007

266 "Smoke Out," Ed Koch, *New York Press*, July 13, 2007

267 "Online sales of cigarettes go up in smoke," Bod Tedeschi, *New York Times*, April 4, 2005

268 "Smoke-free college trend growing," Judy Fortin, CNN.com, November 12, 2007

269 "Smokers told to quit or surgery will be refused," Dan Newling, *Daily Mail*, June 4, 2007

270 *Smoke-Filled Rooms: A Postmortem on the Tobacco Deal*, p. 18; "Buy Cigarettes for the Kids," Jacob Sullum, *Reason*, Reason.com, July 25, 2007; "Options for Funding SCHIP Expansion: Cigarette Taxes Least Defensible Alternative," Gerald Prante, Tax Foundation, TaxFoundation.org, July 13, 2007

271 "Cigarmakers in a panic," James Thorner, *St. Petersburg Times*, July 17, 2007

272 "World anti-smoking pact in force," Reuters, February 27, 2005

273 "'£10 licence to smoke' proposed," BBC News, February 15, 2008

274 "Beijing adding 40,000 smoking inspectors," United Press International, April 25, 2008

275 Bill Godshall of SmokeFree.net, quoted from TheAgitator.com, Radley Balko, January 19, 2006; a University of Florida professor quoted from *Brainwashed: How Universities Indoctrinate America's Youth*, Ben Shapiro, WND Books, 2004, p. 26

276 "Secondhand smoke debate 'over,'" Liz Szabo, *USA Today*, June 27, 2006

277 "Nonsmokers can be cancer victims, too," Associated Press, August 10, 2005

278 "What You Need to Know on Smoking and Lung Cancer," *Time*, Time.com, August 10, 2005

279 "Regular showers may cause brain damage: US study," *Sydney Morning Herald*, July 3, 2005

280 *Smoke-Filled Rooms: A Postmortem on the Tobacco Deal*, p. 184

281 Ibid., p. 24

282 Ibid., p. 178; "Smoking rate among high schoolers remains constant," CNN.com, July 6, 2006

283 "U.S. smoking rate stalled at 21 percent, CDC says," Maggie Fox, Reuters, November 8, 2007

284 "Big Nanny Is Watching You," Philip Dawdy, *Seattle Weekly*, January 18, 2006

285 "That drooping feeling: Heavy smokers 40 percent likelier to be impotent," Agence France Presse, March 22, 2006

286 "No smoking—but killing teachers is fine, says new Taleban rulebook," Tim Albone, *Scotsman*, December 11, 2006

287 "Somalia: Islamist cops nab 22 in raid on smokers," Agence France Presse, November 14, 2006

288 *Bad Trip: How the War Against Drugs is Destroying America*, Joel Miller, Nelson Current, 2004

289 "The History of Tobacco Part I," Gene Borio, Historian.org, 1997

290 *Cigarettes: Anatomy of an Industry from Seed to Smoke*, Tara Parker-Pope, New Press, 2001, p. 7

291 Ibid., p. 15

292 Ibid., p. 17

293 "The Solution," SmokeFreeMovies.com, hosted by the University of California, San Francisco

294 "MPAA to consider smoking in ratings criteria," Carl DiOrio, *Hollywood Reporter*, May 11, 2007; "More Hollywood Studios Say 'No Smoking,'" Michael Cieply, *New York Times*, September 30, 2007

295 "Can the New James Bond Measure Up?" Janice Kaplan, *Parade*, October 1, 2006, quoted from Reason.com, October 4, 2006

296 "Beatles' cigarettes erased from box set cover," Canada.com, March 28, 2006; "Beatles Abbey Road cigarette airbrushed," BBC News, January 21, 2003; "Airbrushed from History," SmokersRights.org.uk, 2004; "Clinton Dedicates Memorial, Urges Americans to Emulate FDR," *Washington Post*, May 3, 1997

297 "Smoking cuts for classic cartoons after UK complaint," Mike Collett-White, Reuters, August 21, 2006

298 *Generation Risk: How to Protect Your Teenager from Smoking and Other Dangerous Behavior*, Corky Newton, M. Evans and Company, 2001, p. 24

299 "Study: Anti-smoking ads have opposite effect on teens," Andrea Jones, *Atlanta Journal-Constitution*, July 19, 2007

300 *Cigarettes: Anatomy of an Industry from Seed to Smoke*, p. 133

301 Ibid., p. 18–20

302 *The Hobbit*, J. R. R. Tolkien, 1937

303 *The Physiology of Taste*, Jean-Anthelme Brillat-Savarin, 1825

304 *Fast Food Nation: The Dark Side of the All-American Meal*, Eric Schlosser, Houghton Mifflin Company, 2002, p. 240

305 Ibid., p. 6

306 Ibid., p. 53

307 Ibid., p. 262

308 Ibid., p. 241-42

309 "Obesity is 'deadlier than smoking' and can knock 13 years off your life," Daniel Martin, *Daily Mail*, October 17, 2007

310 "California files french fry lawsuit," Reuters, August 27, 2005

311 "McDonald's targeted in obesity lawsuit," BBC News Friday, November 22, 2002

312 "Some thought for fast food," *Washington Post*, October 16, 2002

313 "Head of Cleveland Clinic Is Attacking Big Mac And in Hospital Lobby, McDonald's Fights Back," Ceci Connolly, *Washington Post*, December 15, 2004

314 "The War On Personal Responsibility," Center for Consumer Freedom, ConsumerFreedom. com, May 3, 2004

315 "Starbucks Cutting Trans Fats From Food," Associated Press, January 2, 2007; "KFC gets burned for using unhealthy fat," Reuters, June 14, 2006

316 "Dora the Exploiter," Jacob Sullum, *Reason*, Reason.com, January 25, 2006

317 "Lines Are Drawn for Big Suit Over Sodas," Melanie Warner, *New York Times*, December 7, 2005

318 "Pop Out," Jacob Sullum, *Reason*, Reason.com, May 10, 2006

319 "According To The Latest Study, You Can't Eat Or Drink Anything," Center for Consumer Freedom, ConsumerFreedom.com, February 11, 2005; "Do we really want food Nazis to rein in U.S.?" Walter Williams, *Nashville City Paper*, June 13, 2003

320 "CSPI: Snuff Out Tasty Food," Center for Consumer Freedom, ConsumerFreedom.com, November 18, 2004

321 "The War on Fat," Jacob Sullum, *Reason*, August/September 2004

322 "A Modest—and Slimming!—Proposal," John G. Sotos, *Washington Post*, April 7, 2006

323 "New York Calls In the Food Police," *New York Times*, December 10, 2006, cited from "The Freedom to Be Unhealthy Is the Opposite of True Freedom," Jacob Sullum, *Reason*, Reason. com, December 11, 2006

324 "Soda Tax the Wrong Way to Help Curb Obesity," Sara Cseresnyes and Andrew Chamberlain, *Denver Post*, July 21, 2006

325 "Rise of food fascism," Peter Ferrara, *Washington Times*, May 31, 2003

326 "'Fat tax' could save 3,200 lives each year," Peter Griffiths, Reuters, July 12, 2007

327 "Penny a pound," Jake Halpern, Slate.com, December 4, 2007

328 "Study: 3 percent follow health advice," Reuters, April 26, 2005

329 Koplan J.P., Liverman C.T., Kraak V.I., eds. *Preventing childhood obesity: health in the balance,*

National Academies Press, 2005. Quoted from "Food Marketing and Childhood Obesity—A Matter of Policy," Marion Nestle, Ph.D., *New England Journal of Medicine*, June 15, 2006

330 "Study: Food in McDonald's wrapper tastes better to kids," Associated Press, August 6, 2007

331 "The War on Fat," Jacob Sullum, *Reason*, August/September 2004

332 "Food Fight," Kelly Jane Torrance, *Reason*, Reason.com, December 23, 2003

333 "Lawmakers want junk food out of schools," Libby Quaid, Associated Press, April 7, 2006; "Schools go on health kick as federal law takes hold," Associated Press, July 13, 2006; "Lawmakers Consider School Food Limits," Kim Severson, *New York Times*, December 2, 2007

334 "News briefs from California's Central Coast," Associated Press, November 8, 2004

335 "Obesity down in sugar-free schools: Swedish study," Agence France-Presse, April 23, 2007

336 "Feds fruitless in getting kids off junk food," Martha Mendoza, Associated Press, July 5, 2007

337 "Study links juice, chubby children," Associated Press, February 7, 2005

338 "Student Suspended for Eating Staff Member's Cookie," Associated Press, June 5, 2006

339 "School clears kids in contraband candy caper," Associated Press, March 12, 2008

340 "Duxbury schools banish birthday cupcakes," *Boston Herald*, June 4, 2004

341 "Lawmaker Wants Teachers In Hawaii Weighed For Obesity," TheDenverChannel.com, an ABC News affiliate, March 28, 2005

342 "Junk Food Ban Costing L.A. Schools," Associated Press, December 3, 2004

343 "Candy creates confusion in Arkansas schools," Associated Press, November 8, 2004; "Small Minority of Protestors Can Cause Big Trouble," Bill O'Reilly, Fox News Channel, FoxNews. com, August 29, 2004

344 "Students turn a profit from candy sales," Rachel Byrd, *Victorville Daily Press*, March 20, 2008

345 "Obesity indicator on student report cards?" The Associated Press, January 19, 2005

346 "In Obesity Fight, Many Fear a Note From School," Jodi Kantor, *New York Times*, January 8, 2007

347 "School sends home obesity notices with students, parent upset," Nelson Garcia, KUSA-TV, local NBC affiliate, October 11, 2007

348 "Well-Intentioned Food Police May Create Havoc With Children's Diets," Harriet Brown, *New York Times*, May 30, 2006

349 "Disciplinarian Parents Have Fat Kids," Reuters, June 5, 2006

350 "Baby Workouts Touted to Ward Off Obesity," Kristen Gelineau, Associated Press, June 13, 2004

351 Ibid.

352 "Vegan couple sentenced to life over baby's death," Associated Press, May 9, 2007

353 "Has Cookie Monster given up sweets?" The Associated Press, April 7, 2005

354 "Total ban for junk food ads around kids' shows," Mark Sweney, *Guardian*, November 17, 2006; "TV ban on adverts for cheese, the latest 'junk food'," *Daily Mail*, January 2, 2007

355 "Rated D for Deliciousness," Jacob Sullum, *Reason*, Reason.com, June 22, 2007

356 "Hil frets chips will be put in kids' brains," Michael McAuliff, *New York Daily News*, July 21, 2006

357 "Don't Blame SpongeBob for Child Obesity," Radley Balko, Fox News Channel, FoxNews. com, March 2, 2005

358 "When Moms Work, Kids Get Fat," Tim Harford, Slate.com, September 30, 2006

359 "First, do no harm," Jonah Goldberg, *National Review*, NationalReview.com, August 29, 2004

360 "Please Do Not Feed the Humans," William Saletan, Slate.com, September 2, 2006

361 "Lawyers see obese U.S. ripe for fat lawsuits," Marguerite Higgins, *Washington Times*, September 20, 2004

362 "Man Resorts to Surgery to Adopt Child," Grant Slater, Associated Press, August 25, 2007

363 "Woman Arrested, Cuffed for Eating Candy," Associated Press, July 29, 2004

364 "Mississippi Pols Seek To Ban Fats," *The Smoking Gun*, TheSmokingGun.com, February 1, 2008

365 "Pros and Cons of a Zoning Diet: Fighting Obesity by Limiting Fast-Food Restaurants," Manny Fernandez, *New York Times*, September 24, 2006; "Limits proposed on fast-food restaurants," Tami Abdollah, *Los Angeles Times*, September 10, 2007

366 "Publicans fear Executive wants 'unhealthy' bar meals banned," Russell Jackson, *Scotsman*, May 5, 2006

367 "Why ice-cream vans face total meltdown," Rajeev Syal and David Sanderson, *Times of London*, May 8, 2006

368 "New Zealand bars British man's 'fat' wife," Paul Chapman, *Telegraph*, November 18, 2007

369 "Japan's Bulging Waistlines Trigger Flab Tests in Land of Sumo," Patrick Rial and Kotaro Tsunetomi, Bloomberg, Bloomberg.com, March 12, 2008

370 "The World Health Organization Global Strategy on Diet, Physical Activity and Health," quoted from the European Public Health Alliance, EPHA.org, May 25, 2004

371 "'Talking' CCTV scolds offenders," BBC News, April 4, 2007

372 "The Royal pasty that's unhealthier than a Big Mac," *Evening Standard*, ThisIsLondon.co.uk., March 19, 2007

373 "'NHS should not treat those with unhealthy lifestyles' say Tories," *Daily Mail*, April 9, 2007

374 "Being a celebrity is the 'best thing in the world' say children," *Daily Mail*, December 17, 2006

375 "Fat police lock up Chris," by Jacqui Thornton, *Sun*, February 22, 2005

376 "Overweight boy can stay with mother," Press Association, February 27, 2007

377 "BA steward suspended 'for eating left over muffin' on passenger's meal tray," *Evening Standard*, December 19, 2007

378 "Make all staff exercise for an hour, says top health adviser," Georgina Littlejohn, *Evening Standard*, October 23, 2007

379 "Curb Your Enthusiasms," Radley Balko, *Reason*, March 2006

380 Ibid.

381 "Why Did the Former Mrs. Ted Turner Bother with All That Aerobicizing?" Nick Gillespie, *Reason*, Reason.com, October 2, 2007

382 *Stolen Harvest: The Hijacking of the Global Food Supply*, Vandana Shiva, South End Press, 1999, p. 118

383 *Fast Food Nation: The Dark Side of the All-American Meal*, p. 243; "Would You Like a Bomb with Your Burger?" The Center for Consumer Freedom, ConsumerFreedom.com March 4, 2003

384 "FBI, ATF address domestic terrorism," Terry Frieden, CNN.com, May 19, 2005

385 "Would You Like a Bomb with Your Burger?" The Center for Consumer Freedom, ConsumerFreedom.com, March 4, 2003

386 "Is It O.K. to Be Pudgy?" Christine Gorman, *Time*, Time.com, May 2, 2005; "Study: A little extra weight not deadly," Associated Press, November 6, 2007

387 "Hospital Mortality Linked to BMI for Critically Ill Adults," press release from the Ohio State University Medical Center, May 4, 2006

388 "Plump males have better odds in crash, study says," John Fauber, *Milwaukee Journal Sentinel*, March 1, 2006

389 "U.S. Life Expectancy Hits All-Time High," Mike Strobe, Associated Press, December 8, 2005; *Consuming Fears: The Politics of Product Risks*, Harvey Sapolsky, Basic Books, 1986, p. 8

390 "Chocolate Linked to Lower Blood Pressure," Carla Johnson, Associated Press, February 28, 2006; "Chocoholics rejoice!" Reuters, November 14, 2006

391 "Study: Chocolate may boost brain power," Reuters, May 25, 2006

392 "A doughnut a day keeps stress at bay, scientist says," Tom Spears, *Ottawa Citizen*, November 16, 2005

393 "Coffee: The New Health Food?" Sid Kirchheimer, WebMD.com, January 26, 2004

394 "SF Considers a Tax on Caffeine," KCBS, KCBS.com, December 17, 2007

395 "Can a High-Fat Diet Beat Cancer?" Richard Friebe, *Time*, Time.com, September 17, 2007

396 "Pizza as health food? Food chemists say yes," Reuters, March 27, 2007

397 "Bad foods that are actually great for your waist," Camille Noe Pagan, CNN.com, January 2, 2008

398 "Obese men less likely to commit suicide, study finds," Denise Gellene, *Los Angeles Times*, March 13, 2007

399 "A Really Big Idea," Bret Begun, *Newsweek*, May 23, 2005, p. 48

400 "Perspectives," *Newsweek*, May 9, 2005, p. 25

401 "Thick lawyers and thickburgers," Ben Shapiro, Creators Syndicate, December 8, 2004

402 *Pharmacracy: Medicine and Politics in America*, Thomas Szasz, Praeger, 2001, p. 149

403 "Big Brother Prescribes," Ronald Bailey, *Reason*, Reason.com, July 14, 2006

404 *The Law*, Frederic Bastiat, 1850

Notes

III. THE PROMISED LAND

1   *Permission to Believe: Four Rational Approaches to God's Existence*, Lawrence Kelemen, Targum Press, 1990, p. 40

2   Ibid., p. 60, 62

3   "Major Religions of the World Ranked by Number of Adherents," Adherents.com, April 29, 2005; "Gallup: Poll Finds Americans' Belief in God Remains Strong," *Editor and Publisher*, December 13, 2005

4   *Brainwashed: How Universities Indoctrinate America's Youth*, Ben Shapiro, WND Books, 2004

5   "I've found God, says man who cracked the genome," Steven Swinford, *Times of London*, June 11, 2006

6   Cardinal Robert Bellarmine, "Letter to Foscarini," April 12, 1615

7   *Freethinkers: A History of American Secularism*, Susan Jacoby, Metropolitan Books, 2004, p. 131

8   "Creeping Sharia," Andrew Sullivan, AndrewSullivan.com, March 26, 2007

9   "Vatican calls verbal attack on Pope 'terrorism,'" Reuters, May 2, 2007

10 "Muslims nations: Defame Islam, get sued?" Rukmini Callimachi, Associated Press, March 14, 2008

11 *The Battle for God: A History of Fundamentalism*, Karen Armstrong, Ballantine Books, 2001, p. 7

12 Ibid., p. 16, 23

13 *Beyond Freedom and Dignity*, B.F. Skinner, Random House, 1971, p. 199

14 *Society and its Discontents*, Sigmund Freud, 1930

15 *Today's ISMS*, William Ebenstein, Prentice-Hall, 1967 edition, p. 5

16 *Communism, Fascism and Democracy: The Theoretical Foundations*, edited by Carl Cohen, Random House, 1962, p. 177

17 *The Sexual Revolution: Toward a Self-Governing Character Structure*, Wilhelm Reich, Noonday Press, p. 219 of the 1969 edition

18 "The Russian Effort to Abolish Marriage," *Atlantic Monthly*, July 1926, Volume 138, No. 1, p. 108–114

19 *The Sexual Revolution: Toward a Self-Governing Character Structure*, p. 168

20 Ibid., p. 171

21 *Red Scare or Red Menace? : American Communism and Anticommunism in the Cold War Era*, John E. Haynes, Ivan R. Dee, 1996, p. 6

22 *The Autobiography of Bertrand Russell*, Bertrand Russell, Routledge, originally serialized between 1967 and 1969

23 *Communism, Fascism and Democracy: The Theoretical Foundations*, p. 193–194

24 Ibid., p. 187, 215–216

25 *Today's ISMS*, p. 76, 78

26 Ibid., p. 47, 54

27 Ibid., p. 17

28 Ibid., p. 44

29 *American Populism*, George McKenna, Capricorn Books, 1974, p. 215; *Communism, Fascism and Democracy: The Theoretical Foundations*, p. 235

30 *Communism, Fascism and Democracy: The Theoretical Foundations*, p. 351, 363

31 *The True Believer: Thoughts on the Nature of Mass Movements*, Eric Hoffer, Perennial Classics, 1951, p. 86

32 "Poll: Creationism Trumps Evolution," CBS News, CBSNews.com, November 22, 2004

33 "Chimp and human DNA is 96% identical," Clive Cookson, *Financial Times*, August 31, 2005

34 "Gallup: Poll Finds Americans' Belief in God Remains Strong," *Editor and Publisher*, December 13, 2005, "Poll: Creationism Trumps Evolution," CBSNews.com, November 22, 2004, "From Jesus to Christ," *Newsweek*, March 28, 2005

35 1999 Gallup poll quoted from *Smoke-Filled Rooms: A Postmortem on the Tobacco Deal*, W. Kip Viscusi, University of Chicago Press, 2002, p. 143

36 Speech to U.S. House of Representatives, June 16, 1999

37 "What Matters in Kansas," William Saletan, Slate.com, May 11, 2005

38 "Thousands attend opening," Mike Rutledge, *Cincinnati Enquirer*, May 29, 2007

39 "The new Monkey Trial," Michelle Goldberg, Salon.com, Jan. 10, 2005

40 Ibid.

41 "Georgia Lawmaker: Jews Secretly Behind Evolution," Right Wing Watch, Americans United for Separation of Church and State, AU.org, February 15, 2007

42 "Bible Course Becomes a Test for Public Schools in Texas," Ralph Blumenthal and Barbara Novovitch, *New York Times*, August 1, 2005

43 "AMA: No Evidence that Abstinence Sex Ed Works," Peggy Peck, FoxNews.com, December 09, 2004; "Surprise—Teens Ignore Adults Who Tell Them to Not Have Sex," Ronald Bailey, *Reason*, Reason.com, April 14, 2007

44 "Is Sex Ed Working?" Kate Barrett, ABC News, ABCNews.com, March 24, 2008

45 "Some Abstinence Programs Mislead Teens, Report Says," Ceci Connolly, the *Washington Post*, December 2, 2004

46 "Blue Balls for the Red States," *Harper's*, February 2005

47 "The Education Censors," Tom Hilliard, MetroLand.net, March 24, 2005

48 "Battle over Texas sex-ed textbooks," Reuters, August 5, 2004

49 "Walking the walk on family values," William V. D'Antonio, the *Boston Globe*, October 31, 2004

50 "Abstinence [Retard]ie Busted!" Timothy Noah, Slate.com, April 28, 2007

51 *Persecution: How Liberals Are Waging War Against Christianity*, David Limbaugh, Perennial, 2004, p. 25; "Deal reached on praying toddler," Ellen Sorokin, *Washington Times*, June 12, 2002

52 "PC on earth for Santa: Boy Claus booted out of N.H. school dance," Kevin Rothstein, *Boston Herald*, December 24, 2004

53 "UK: GIRL SENT HOME FROM SCHOOL FOR WEARING A CRUCIFIX," *Drudge Report*, DrudgeReport.com, December 5, 2005

54 *Persecution: How Liberals Are Waging War Against Christianity*, p. 49

55 "District pulls plug on speech," Antonio Planas, *Las Vegas Review-Journal*, June 17, 2006; *Persecution: How Liberals Are Waging War Against Christianity*, p. 5

56 *Persecution: How Liberals Are Waging War Against Christianity*, p. 58

57 "Altered Pledge of Allegiance stuns students," Valerie Richardson, *Washington Times*, April 22, 2005

58 "The Church of the Non-Believers," Gary Wolf, *Wired*, November 2006

59 *Beyond Freedom and Dignity*, B.F. Skinner, Random House, 1971, p. 61, 62, 162, 173

60 *Freefall of the American University: How Our Colleges Are Corrupting the Minds and Morals of the Next Generation*, Jim Nelson Black, WND Books, 2004, p. 87

61 "Climate change, is democracy enough?" David Shearman, OnlineOpinion.com.au, January 17, 2008 quoted from "Liberal Fascism Watch," Andrew Sullivan, AndrewSullivan.com, February 12, 2008

62 Sheryl Crow, "Crow calls for limit on loo paper," BBC News, April 23, 2007

63 "CleanScapes Cleans Up," David Weigel, *Reason*, Reason.com, October 24, 2007; "Warning to homeowners as the green vision is unveiled," James Chapman, *Daily Mail*, March 14, 2007

64 "California wants to control home thermostats," Felicity Barringer, *International Herald Tribune*, January 11, 2008

65 "Eco-Extremist Wants World Population to Drop below 1 Billion," Dan Gainor, Business & Media Institute, BusinessAndMedia.org, May 6, 2007; "The Tragedy of the Commons," Garrett Hardin, *Science*, December 13, 1968

66 "Eco-Extremist Wants World Population to Drop below 1 Billion," Dan Gainor, Business & Media Institute, BusinessAndMedia.org, May 6, 2007

67 "Scientists threatened for 'climate denial,'" Tom Harper, *Telegraph*, March 11, 2007

68 "Neocons on a Cruise: What Conservatives Say When They Think We Aren't Listening," Johann Hari, *Independent*, July 17, 2007

69 "Convention ends with Satan and immigrants," Caleb Warnock, *Daily Herald* (Utah), April 29, 2007

70 *The Enemy At Home: The Cultural Left and Its Responsibility for 9/11*, Dinesh D'Souza, Doubleday, 2007

71 "The Myth of the 'God Gulf,'" Steven Waldman and John Green, BeliefNet.com, February 2004

72 Richard Scheinin, *San Jose Mercury News*, September 11, 1993; "Philanthropy Expert: Conservatives Are More Generous," Frank Brieaddy, BeliefNet.com, 2006

73 "Christians are more likely to experience divorce than are non-Christians," Barna Research Group, December 1999

74 *USA Today* / Gallup poll, February 2007, quoted from AndrewSullivan.com

75 "Study Ties Political Leanings to Hidden Biases," Shankar Vedantam, *Washington Post*, January 30, 2006

76 "The joys of parenthood," *The Economist*, Economist.com, March 27, 2008, quoted from "Extreme Happiness," AndrewSullivan.com, April 1, 2008

77 *The Political Brain: The Role of Emotion in Deciding the Fate of the Nation*, Drew Westen, PublicAffairs, 2007

78 "Poll: Bias 'alive and well' in press," Jennifer Harper, *Washington Times*, March 16, 2007

79 "FCC's hands tied on airwaves," Jim Puzzanghera, *Los Angeles Times*, April 14, 2007

80 "Supreme Court Upholds Oregon Suicide Law," Gina Holland, Associated Press, January 17, 2006

81 Presidential debate, St. Louis, Missouri, October 8, 2004; "House Dems may roll back anti-abortion provisions," Alexander Bolton, TheHill.com, June 5, 2007

82 "Tuning Out Free Speech," Jesse Walker, *American Conservative*, April 23, 2007; "Fair and Balanced Radio?" Radley Balko, *Reason*, Reason.com, July 11, 2007; "Democrats block amendment to prevent Fairness Doctrine," Frederic J. Frommer, Associated Press, July 13, 2007

83 *Communism, Fascism and Democracy: The Theoretical Foundations*, p. 485

disinformation·